Marx and Modern Fiction

Edward J. Ahearn

MARX AND
MODERN FICTION

Yale University Press
New Haven and London

Published with assistance from the Kingsley Trust Association Publication Fund established by the Scroll and Key Society of Yale College.

Designed by Nancy Ovedovitz and set in Baskerville type by Huron Valley Graphics, Inc. Printed in the United States of America by Braun-Brumfield, Inc., Ann Arbor, Michigan.

Library of Congress Cataloging-in-Publication Data

Ahearn, Edward J.
    Marx and modern fiction / Edward J. Ahearn.
    p.   cm.
    Bibliography: p.
    Includes index.
    ISBN 0-300-04356-2 (cloth)
    ISBN 0-300-05024-0 (pbk.)
    1. American fiction—History and criticism. 2. Social problems in literature. 3. Capitalism and literature. 4. Marx, Karl, 1818–1883—Views on literature. 5. Melville, Herman, 1819–1891. Moby-Dick. 6. English fiction—History and criticism. 7. French fiction—19th century—History and criticism. I. Title.
PS374.S7A37   1989
809.3'9355—dc 19   88–18709
                                                        CIP

The paper in this book meets the guidelines for permanence and durability of the Committee on Production Guidelines for Book Longevity of the Council on Library Resources.

10   9   8   7   6   5   4   3   2

For my parents and my children

Contents

Preface

*T*he premises of this book are several: that it is important to have read widely in Marx (a condition singularly lacking in American education) and that such reading is illuminating and expansive for literary studies. The second proposition would be espoused by few critics prominent on the American scene other than Fredric Jameson. A third premise is introduced by the author of *The Political Unconscious* himself, since in my view his admirable book, with its need to master and subjugate all conflicting theory, may somewhat obscure the direct usefulness of Marx for criticism of specific works. In the present study I intend instead to delineate a number of leading concepts and analyses in Marx's writing as a whole and then to show—through detailed interpretation of a range of novels—the richness of these arguments for literary study.

The assertion that Marx's work is not extensively or intimately known to Americans will not surprise many. Even well-educated people generally react with some amazement at the idea of a Marxist perspective on literature, with "Marx and *Moby-Dick!*" representing the greatest degree of wonder or outrage. Such reactions have something to do with the global conflict of capitalist and communist ideology, which is reflected in our educational practice. Although many historians know Marx's work, departments of economics may dismiss his views out of hand, while in political science programs he may figure somewhat marginally, in a course on radical theorists, or in a week's study in a survey course. There is perhaps a tendency also to use the *Manifesto* to define, hence encapsulate, his and Engels's thought. Even in literature and related programs of a historical bent, study may be centered on comments scattered throughout the production of these two writers, as collected in Lee Baxandall and Stefan Morawski's useful *Marx and Engels on Literature and Art: A Selection of Writings* (St. Louis: Telos Press, 1973), rather than on thorough investigation of Marx's major works (he evidently being the more important thinker of the two). It is also my experience that many good scholars and teachers of literature who have worked their way through the intricacies of Derrida, Lacan, or Althusser have paid rather little attention to, have read rather little in, Marx.

This is a great loss in general intellectual terms; we have much to gain from appreciating Marx's thought, in its range, interdisciplinary coherence, almost demonic incisiveness, ethical passion, and explanatory power. More specifically, I am concerned in this book to show the insights his thinking affords, both along thematic lines and also for subtle interpretations of form, in a representative spectrum of works.

These include writing by Austen, Balzac, Melville, Flaubert, James, Joyce, and Faulkner. Among these novels the realist line is well represented, but so are modernism and, in the case of works by Balzac, Melville, and Faulkner, a subversive romance or demonic tradition as well. Hence, I will bring Marx's system of thought to bear on some of the authors, some of the great works of modern European and American fiction that are most familiar to the educated American public, while not neglecting writings that tend to deflect that main line of our literature. The works also span from the aftermath of the French Revolution to the years after World War I, illustrating the relevance of Marx for the literature of our century as well as his, and the significance of his insistence on the links between cultural creations and history.

I hope that in this work persuasive readings will be produced through the agency of Marx's ideas, insights reflected in the juxtapositions of works—*Pride and Prejudice* with *Madame Bovary*, *The Golden Bowl* with *Ulysses*, *Le Père Goriot* with *Absalom, Absalom!*

These groupings are justified by the novels in question but correspond as well to arguments put forward by Marx. They aim at
preserving the specificity of each work while comparatively illuminating them in a new perspective. Moreover, although the
chapters are arranged roughly chronologically, I treat Melville's
Moby-Dick last—as a synthesizing work drawing together much
that has been studied in the preceding chapters in a context that
is both American and international.

I do not intend this book to be a basic introduction to the
development of Marx's thought, or to his particular terminol-
ogy, or to scholarship about him. I refer the reader to David
McLellan's *The Thought of Karl Marx: An Introduction* (New York:
Harper Torchbacks, 1974), to Robert C. Tucker's *Marx-Engels
Reader*, 2d ed. (New York: Norton, 1978), and to the bibliogra-
phies they provide. Similarly, while I invoke when appropriate
notable Marxist critics (for example, Georg Lukács), I treat systematically neither the large field of Marxist criticism nor recent
debates on the nature of ideology and the relation of literature
to it. Those interested should consult the work of Jameson, not
only *The Political Unconscious: Narrative as a Socially Symbolic Act*
(Ithaca: Cornell University Press, 1981) but also *Marxism and
Form: Twentieth-Century Dialectical Theories of Literature* (Princeton: Princeton University Press, 1971), and especially the subtle
arguments of Raymond Williams in *Marxism and Literature* (Oxford: Oxford University Press, 1977).[1]

My own observations about Marx are grouped in the three
sections of chapter 1. In the first I argue that Marx's depiction
of the growth of European capitalism and its impact on the
non-European world is the appropriate context in which to
read modern Western fiction. I examine not only the "content"
of this history but also methodological problems and Marx's
solutions to them as relevant for works of literature. In the
second section I present a related series of concepts and critiques, from religion and the family to commodities and money,
that account for much of the unsettling and controversial insightfulness of Marx's thought and have links to salient features
of modern fiction. I conclude with some reflections on the status and value of works of literature in the perspective of Marx's

ideas. I am convinced of the fundamental continuity of Marx's thinking on key issues throughout his production.[2] Moreover, despite some formulations about "ideology" that have been criticized even by Marxists, his thinking in my view need not lead to reductive treatments of literature; nor is he a determinist. Rather, his views on ideology—the myriad forms of expression that mold and may obfuscate our consciousness—open up complex and rich areas of literary interpretation.

For ease of access to many important passages by Marx (and some by Engels) I will refer to the Tucker anthology through parenthetical page numbers; all such references unaccompanied by an initial letter are to this volume. In order to identify particular works I will abbreviate as follows, always in relation to Tucker:

Civil War—The Civil War in France
Class Struggles—The Class Struggles in France, 1848–1850
18th Brum—The Eighteenth Brumaire of Louis Bonaparte
EPM—Economic and Philosophic Manuscripts, or Paris manuscripts
GI—The German Ideology: Part 1 (with Engels)
JQ—"On the Jewish Question"
Manifesto—Manifesto of the Communist Party (with Engels)
TF—"Theses on Feuerbach"
Engels's *Origin of the Family, Private Property, and the State* is also quoted from Tucker.
Of greatest importance are:
Cap I—Capital, volume 1
Cap III—Capital, volume 3
G—Grundrisse, or *Foundations of the Critique of Political Economy*
Passages from these that do not appear in Tucker or where the translation is preferable will be quoted from the Marx Library (New York: Random House) editions: *Grundrisse,* trans. Martin Nicolaus (1973); *Capital,* vol. 1, trans. Ben Fowkes (1977); and *Capital,* vol. 3, trans. David Fernbach (1981). For these three volumes it will always be made clear whether Tucker or the Marx Library is the source.
Translations of Marx are satisfactory, and I will reserve my

few comments for footnotes. For translations of French novels, as with the English language texts, I have chosen readily available editions, among the most likely used by students or general readers. When it seems important to offer an alternative translation of a given passage, I do so explicitly, while retaining the page reference to the English language edition. Finally, while a book of this scope cannot make exhaustive reference to the immense body of scholarship on each of the novelists studied, I nonetheless incorporate in my notes recent approaches, particularly those having greatest bearing on the line of argument pursued here.

Acknowledgments

I am grateful to Ross Chambers, Albert Cook, William Crossgrove, Naomi Schor, Duncan Smith, Arnold Weinstein, and especially Ellen Graham, for encouraging my work on this book or reading some or all of it in manuscript. Rimli Bhattacharya, Ellen Douglass, Robin Mitchell, and Stephen Donatelli have been extraordinarily helpful with bibliographical research, Anne Jourlait provided a typewriter at a critical juncture, and Laura Jones Dooley edited the manuscript with a light touch. Heidi Schulz indexed the book. This study originated in an interdisciplinary course for which I had an incentive grant from Brown University. My ideas have developed in interaction with Brown students and with participants in summer seminars sponsored by the National Endowment for the Humanities. But my greatest debt, for personal support and intellectual exchange, is to my wife, Michèle Respaut.

Marx and Modern Fiction

One
THE ANATOMY
OF CIVIL
SOCIETY

*K*arl Marx's depiction of the origin of European capitalism, which in the first volume of *Capital* he says is "written in the annals of mankind in letters of blood and fire" (433), and of the Western world's exploitation of the rest of the globe, provides the appropriate historical context for modern Western fiction, with surprisingly precise echoes in the literary works to be studied here. It is a horrendous story, and in it the past "weighs like a nightmare on the brain of the living" (595) as much as in the thoughts of the youthful protagonists of historically acute twentieth-century fiction by Joyce and Faulkner.

That celebrated sentence at the opening of *The Eighteenth Brumaire of Louis Bonaparte* reminds us of Marx's equally lucid consciousness of the burden of history, unproductive repetitions of the past, deluded consciousness, the difficulty of overcoming ideology and arriving at a true appreciation of history. In *The German Ideology* and *The Poverty of Philosophy* his goal is to overcome idealist historical schemes and the distortions of "morality, religion, metaphysics, all the rest of ideology," in favor of "true," economics-based history (154–55). According to the later preface to *A Contribution to the Critique of Political Economy*, such history, centered in the broad field of political economy, can be written with "the precision of natural science"—again in contrast to the "legal, political, religious, aesthetic or philosophic—in short, ideological forms in which men become conscious" of economic conflict (5). Not to speak of his concept of science, Marx's dismissal of virtually all forms of cultural production as deceptive, his assumption that the realities of history can be unveiled without dealing with "what men say, imagine, conceive, nor [with] men as narrated, thought of, imagined, conceived," has been criticized, most acutely perhaps in Raymond Williams's *Marxism and Literature,* as in general undialectical and in particular leading to reductive literary criticism. This, however, does not invalidate the argument that cultural productions, including great works of literature, may convey elements of ideology—although the debate becomes more interesting when one adds the idea that these works may also be "great" in exposing such elements. This is obviously the case with Flaubert and Joyce and in substantial measure, I suggest, with the others treated here.

The passage in *The German Ideology,* moreover, breaks off after expressing the awareness that the "real depiction"[1] of historical material involves not only observation but problems of arrangement, sequence, and levels, difficulties the removal of which is governed by premises that Marx says "it is quite impossible to state here." The removal of the difficulties is, however, substantially accomplished in "The Method of Political Economy" section of the *Grundrisse* (236–46). In a now famous argument, Marx shows how the earliest economists assumed that by starting with the population they were dealing with the "real and the concrete" but discovered that the population was an abstraction unless considered in the light of fundamental categories (class, labor, capital, exchange, division of labor, money, and so on) that eventually came to light. Only after developing such conceptual categories and returning to the study of the population does political economy, in a move that Marx now calls the scientifically correct method, attain the concrete. The concrete so revealed is defined as "a rich totality of many determinations and relations," "concentration of many determinations, hence unity of the diverse."

Georg Lukács is not the only one to have noted the nearly Aristotelian character of this definition, which dovetails with notions of historical typicality in fiction and with traditional views of the work of art as a complex of forces and elements that transcends the particular and attains a totalizing significance.[2] At

the same time, since later in "Method" Marx calls the object of
study—bourgeois society—"only a contradictory form of development," there is a strong basis in his writing for the tendency of
recent Marxist criticism, nourished by structuralist and deconstructionist arguments, to perceive highly unified works of art as
nonetheless penetrated by discontinuity, conflict, contradiction.[3]
Finally, whereas in the preface to *A Contribution to the Critique of
Political Economy* the architectural metaphor of base and superstructure seems to attribute a lesser degree of reality to cultural
productions in relation to economic processes, in "Method" no
such differentiation is introduced. Rather, Marx affirms that
"the method of rising from the abstract to the concrete is only
the way in which thought appropriates the concrete, reproduces
it as the concrete in the mind." And he adds that in our minds
the concrete is produced by the "working-up of observation and
conception into concepts."

The working-up of observation into concepts, the effort to
reproduce the concrete mentally, all of this described as an effort of appropriation, of making our own—these notions apply
of course as much to literature as to political economy. They
correspond closely, for example, to Flaubert's discussion in his
letters of the process, intention, typicality, form, and meaning of
Madame Bovary.[4] This is so evident as a general proposition that
Marx makes the connection: "The totality as it appears in the
head, as a totality of thoughts, is a product of a thinking head,
which appropriates the world in the only way it can, a way different from the artistic, religious, practical and mental appropriation of this world." Doubtless Marx is committed to the central
validity of the wide-ranging discipline of political economy, but
no "theory of levels" intrudes: there are a variety of ways to
appropriate reality, all different but apparently all existing on
the same "level." Moreover, "Method" is closely followed by the
fragmentary passage that many (though not all) have found un-
satisfactory in explaining the continuing aesthetic appeal of
Greek literature. The same passage presents imagination, myth,
literature, and technology as means of mastering reality (although not all would agree with Marx's assertion that with the
advent of technology myth is no longer possible); further, Marx

takes pains here to emphasize the disproportion between Greek society and Greek art, the irreducibility of artistic forms to economic structures (245–46).

"Method" combines awareness of the specificity of artistic forms with a theoretical finesse concerning the relation between concept and concrete detail in economic history and social analysis. Theoretical rigor together with empirical research account for the compelling nature of Marx's writing. This is the case primarily in the first volume of *Capital,* whose opening theoretical chapters are followed by the "masterly historical account of the genesis of capitalism which illustrates better than any other writing Marx's approach and method."[5] But it is also true of the third volume of *Capital* and of numerous articles, manuscripts, and books on colonies and former colonies, developments in midcentury France, and so on.

As this list suggests, and as Marx emphasized, the history he wrote is that of the modern Western world, and he resisted efforts to generalize by imposing it as a model for future developments in other regions of the globe. Nonetheless, due to international exploitation by what Herman Melville's Ishmael calls the "all-grasping western world," it is also world history. As Marx argues in *The German Ideology* and the *Manifesto,* the creation of the world market not only enormously augments alienation, it also for the first time creates "world-historical" consciousness, the possibility of "comprehending theoretically the historical movement as a whole" (161–63, 477–81). It even creates world literature, studied in some quarters under the rubric of comparative literature, an enterprise resisting the division of labor in literary and other fields in favor of judicious interdisciplinary juxtapositions.

Hence Marx illustrates the world-historical dimension of economic development by the example of the invention of a machine in England "which deprives countless workers of bread in India and China, and overturns the whole form of existence of these empires" (172). Pursuing connections of this kind in an international perspective between literary works and history as Marx depicts it opens up the apparent self-containedness of these works and expands their significance, giving us an enhanced awareness of their perhaps not fully appreciated world-

historical perspectives. After all, that same machine, when introduced into France, together with other forces sucked many into
the ranks of the proletariat, as the fate of Emma Bovary's daughter illustrates. Its voracious appetite changed the "patriarchal"
black slave system brutally imagined by a Vautrin into the even
more brutal capitalistically organized system of the pre–Civil
War South. And that war brought ruin to countless textile workers in the British Isles as well as to Southern planters of Thomas
Sutpen's stripe.

In evoking the history from which modern Western literature can really never be isolated, several of Marx's concepts
need to be kept in mind. The first is alienation, deriving from
Hegel but related to Marx's more realistically dialectical view of
human interactions with the external world. According to this
view human activity of all kinds, including cultural productions,
involves externalization or projection of human energy. This
can occur strictly within the realm of imagination, as in Marx's
view of mythology evoked earlier; in religion such projection
for Marx (as, say, for the Blake of *The Marriage of Heaven and
Hell*) involves the creation of an imaginary supreme being, a
form of estranged energy before which human beings prostrate
themselves. Projection-alienation is also used to explain labor,
technology (Marx's symbol of human psychology), the state,
and complex societal and economic systems. Hence, the evolu-
tion of international capitalism has produced a situation in
which economic relations appear to human beings as "overwhelming natural laws, governing them irrespective of their
will, in the form that the world market and its conjectures, the
movement of market prices, the cycles of industry and trade
and the alternation of prosperity and crisis prevails on them as
blind necessity."[6] Marx is at pains to insist that this alienation
dominates all, including capitalists and owners.

Second, the concept of division of labor, initially visible in the
family and attaining myriad productive and estranged guises in
modern society, has its historically most fundamental role in the
opposition between country and city, which is said to sum up
"the whole economic history of society" (158, 393). Marx and
Engels are not the only nineteenth-century writers to realize that

the country-city antagonism has taken on unprecedented proportions in the industrial era—witness the city poetry of Blake,
Wordsworth, and Baudelaire, among others.[7] The crowding and
alienation Engels describes in *The Condition of the Working Class in
England in 1844* has a parallel in the evils encountered by the
speaker in Blake's "London," just as the globally uprooting reach
of the European capitals is suggested by the sickly black woman
evoked in Baudelaire's Paris poem "Le Cygne." These considerations are relevant for such a non-urban book as *Moby-Dick*. How
much more so does the city-country opposition appear in writing
by Balzac and Flaubert—but also, as we shall see, by Austen and
even Faulkner. Despite Bloom's reveries and Molly's exaltation
of nature, and despite Adam Verver's renting of the estate at
Fawns, twentieth-century novels like *Ulysses* and *The Golden Bowl*
are utterly urban, conforming to Marx's argument that by the
mid-nineteenth century nature unmodified by man had virtually
disappeared and that the countryside was already both marginalized and regulated by the city-based economy: "The town
already is in actual fact the concentration of the population, of
the instruments of production, of capital, of pleasures, of needs,
while the country demonstrates just the opposite fact, isolation
and separation" (*GI*, 176).

Class related to sources of revenue is a closely linked notion.
Although the paragraph from which the sentence above is
quoted mentions the existence of two basic classes, owners and
workers, and although *The German Ideology* and the *Manifesto*
stress the conflict between country and city, in volume 3 of *Capital* (951*ff.*), a somewhat more complex picture emerges. There
three classes—capitalists, landowners, and workers—are related
to their sources of revenue—profit, ground rent, and wages.
Further, the *Grundrisse* follows David Ricardo in tracing the evo-
lution of feudal lord into modern landowner, stressing the relations of capital, wage labor, and ground rent, and asserting that
if the history of landed property were written, it would be "the
history of the formation of modern capital" (252–53, 275–78).
Such considerations are relevant for the study of a novel such as
Pride and Prejudice, which only appears to depict a traditional
landed society untouched by the urban and capitalist order. The

analysis in volume 3 of *Capital* and the *Grundrisse,* moreover, is of the English example, which involved expropriation of agricultural workers and centralization of land.[8] In France industry was slower to develop, and the finance aristrocracy (bankers, speculators) dominated until the upheaval of 1848. Parcelization of land, the persistence of the peasant class, the exploitation of it and elements of the lower middle class through taxation and through "secondary forms" of capitalist expropriation, features studied by Marx in his analyses of events in midcentury France, are strikingly evident in *Madame Bovary.* Marx's ideas on country and city, class and revenue, vividly illuminate processes of economic and social history as depicted by two writers who are sometimes thought to be quite ahistorical.

The fourth concept to be noted is that of mode of production. The preface to *A Contribution to the Critique of Political Economy* schematically enumerates "Asiatic, ancient, feudal, and modern bourgeois modes of production" (5), by which it will be seen that the term, alternately "organization of production" (241), designates the most fundamental conditions of production and all forms of intercourse corresponding to them. In the preface as well as *The German Ideology* (195–96) Marx presents the course of history as the sequence of more or less violent collisions of new modes of production with the property and other relations of earlier ones. The preface expresses distrust of human beings' consciousness of such transformations, but the passage in *The German Ideology* explains how in the absence of violent revolution traditional power may persist despite changed economic circumstances. This may give rise to the opposite from what is argued in the preface—that is, consciousness of underlying change on the part of some individuals without yet an actual reversal of socioeconomic power. Along similar lines, "Method" argues that the most complex organization of production, capitalism, may allow insights into "vanished social formations . . . whose partly still unconquered remnants are carried along within it," in "stunted form, or even travestied"—for example, "communal property" (241). Characters like Lady Catherine and Collins in *Pride and Prejudice,* Sutpen's childhood in *Absalom, Absalom!* and the interaction of personages from the various classes in Balzac's *Goriot* and

Flaubert's *Bovary* are all illuminated by these considerations. But then their creators appear as possessing superior insight (a greater or lesser degree of world-historical consciousness) concerning the immense complexities of transformations of modes of production in the lives of individuals.

All of these concepts play a role in Marx's delineation of the development of capitalism and of its ravages in Europe and the non-European world. Pursuing the economists' concept of the "so-called primitive accumulation" at the origin of the system, he concludes:

> The discovery of gold and silver in America, the extirpation, enslavement and entombment in mines of the indigenous population of that continent, the beginnings of the conquest and plunder of India, and the conversion of Africa into a preserve for the commercial hunting of blackskins, are all things which characterize the dawn of the era of capitalist production. These idyllic proceedings are the chief moments of primitive accumulation. Hard on their heels follows the commercial war of the European nations, which has the globe as its battlefield. It begins with the revolt of the Netherlands from Spain, assumes gigantic dimensions in England's Anti-Jacobin War, and is still going on in the shape of the Opium Wars against China, etc.
>
> The different moments of primitive accumulation can be assigned in particular to Spain, Portugal, Holland, France and England, in more or less chronological order. These different moments are systematically combined together at the end of the seventeenth century in England; the combination embraces the colonies, the national debt, the modern tax system, and the system of protection. These methods depend in part on brute force, for instance the colonial system. But they all employ the power of the state, the concentrated and organized force of society, to hasten, as in a hothouse, the process of transformation of the feudal mode of production into the capitalist mode, and to shorten the transition. Force is the midwife of every old society which is pregnant with a new one. It is itself an economic power. (*Cap I*, 915–16; also Tucker, 435–36)

This is representative Marx. Scorn for apologists of the system ("idyllic proceedings . . . of primitive accumulation") and insistence on the monstrosity of what the Christian world was willing to perpetrate on others ("commercial hunting of blackskins," statistics on bounties for Indians in Puritan Massachusetts [917–18]) do not prevent a cool assessment of the inevitability of economic developments: "Force is the midwife of every old society which is pregnant with a new one." Even more significant is the unified view of an extraordinarily complex, still ongoing historical process. In a letter of 1846 (141) Marx had written of "the terrible wars which are being prepared between the different classes within each nation and between different nations," and here in *Capital* he brings "this vast, prolonged and complicated movement" up to the Opium Wars. We should have to add the even more monstrous wars that have occurred since and reflect to what extent this global violence is at the center of, or on the horizon of, or absent from, the fiction studied here. Completely invisible in *The Golden Bowl*, but certainly on the borders of *Pride and Prejudice*, *Le Père Goriot*, *Madame Bovary*, and *Ulysses;* at the heart of *Absalom, Absalom!* in terms of the Civil War (but that novel opens to the wars of the twentieth century). On the edges, again, of *Moby-Dick*, a book, however, that insistently recalls the global history of extermination, colonization, slavery, and exploitation which Marx sketches.

The passage in volume 1 of *Capital* is also compelling in linking colonization and war to the flow of precious metals from the New World, taxes, public debt, and international banking, all effective levers for "the concentration of capital." The argument produces some powerful formulations, even some of a Blakean, visionary intensity, about the expropriation of the "constituents of the lower middle class" through systematic overtaxation and about the concealing effect of the international credit system: "A great deal of capital, which appears today in the United States without any birth-certificate, was yesterday, in England, the capitalized blood of children" (*Cap I*, 920–21).

This sentence illustrates the continuity of Marx's thought on central issues. It repeats his argument in the Paris manuscripts about the creation of profit literally at the cost of workers' lives, a theme documented overwhelmingly, not least regarding child labor, in the first volume of *Capital*. That this profit then travels internationally in another form is not surprising, since Marx all along has understood the global nature of the capitalist mode of production.

These links are most insistent throughout his work—and not incidentally of considerable relevance for our novels—in his treatment of the textile industry. For when Marx seeks to account historically for the existence (in addition to the primitive accumulation) of the other ingredient in the capitalist system, huge numbers of workers who are "free" in the ironic sense of possessing nothing but their labor power, he recounts the violent process by which feudal agricultural workers were driven from the land and onto the labor market. This centuries-long phenomenon occurs in England, the classic case, as well as in Ireland and Scotland, in the interest of landowners and the textile business and includes the transformation of spinning and weaving, originally secondary domestic crafts, into wage-labor, more and more concentrated, eventually in the industrial cities of the nineteenth century. But this development is inevitably linked to the supply of raw materials, and Marx shows how the increase in English textile production later augmented cotton growing in the American South, the African slave trade, and slave breeding in the border states, whereas the growth of the English woolen industry eventuated in the decimation of agricultural populations in Ireland and Scotland.[9] Hence Marx's conclusion: "While the cotton industry introduced child-slavery into England, in the United States it gave the impulse for the transformation of the earlier, more or less patriarchal slavery into a system of commercial exploitation. In fact the veiled slavery of the wage-labourers in Europe needed the unqualified slavery of the New World as its pedestal" (*Cap I*, 925).

In a section interestingly titled "The Greed for Surplus-Labour: Manufacturer and Boyar," the latter phase of Southern slavery is said to have been based on the calculation that slaves would be killed off through overwork within seven years (Tucker, 364–65). Marx characteristically links that calculation not only to perhaps even more vicious destruction of slaves in the West Indies but to comparable decimation of workers in Europe, where the "industrial reserve army" was constantly nourished by orphans, pauper children, and other unfortunates (Tucker, 374–75, 427–30). He argues that American slavery is therefore industrial, that without its partnership with European wage-labor its "social conditions . . . would immediately turn into pre-civilized forms" (G, 224). And as I have suggested he studies the American Civil War in terms not only of unemployment of textile workers in the British Isles but also of agitation in the United States to shorten the industrial workday only after slavery was abolished and the general consequences of the Civil War for American society: "a colossal national debt . . . a heavy tax-burden, the creation of a finance aristocracy of the vilest type . . . the granting of immense tracts of public land to speculative companies. . . . In short . . . a very rapid centralization of capital" (Cap I, 940; see also Cap I, 390–414, Cap III, 215–34).

From that period emerges such a figure as Henry James's Adam Verver, mildest but most acquisitive of American capitalists, in a novel rife with accumulations and abuses of money, art, and people. And before that period, despite the light surface of Pride and Prejudice and other Austen books (which nonetheless reveal social conflict with hints of the history sketched here), are figures like Vautrin, whose patriarchal slave dream is ironically accomplished by Sutpen, a child of Scotch and English immigrants who grows up precisely in precivilized conditions and who tries to make his fortune in the French West Indies before succeeding in Mississippi. We will see later too that other characters in our French works in addition to Berthe Bovary, the pauper orphan who joins the ranks of the industrial reserve army at the end of Flaubert's novel, are illustrative figures of Western economic and social history—among them Rastignac, Goriot, and Nucingen, Rodolphe Boulanger de la Huchette, Homais, and Emma Bovary herself. Further, Ulysses clearly emerges from the historical context of Ireland's ravishment by England, so pointedly described by Marx and Engels. The challenge with that work is to understand how so much in it that seems exclusively "aesthetic" is also deeply historical. And Moby-Dick, mid-nineteenth-century American and international masterpiece, in its relevance for today's as well as yesterday's events, reminds us not only that these literary works are in large part expressions of the global, protracted, and immensely violent history delineated by Marx but also that this history is continuing and that we are irremediably involved in it.

This sombre history is accompanied in Marx by a series of themes that are equally sobering and equally useful for the study of literature. These include analyses and critiques of religion, democratic values, the family, labor, possession, need, objects and the senses, commodities, and money. The range of issues and their often controversial nature are matched by the provocative insightfulness with which they are treated.

As suggested earlier, Marx (together with other "young Hegelians") began with the critique of religion as the necessary first step in the movement toward liberation, at one point expressed (in terms that will remind readers of *Ulysses* of Stephen at the end of *Circe*) as the "struggle against [one's] *own internal priest, against [one's] own priestly nature.*"[10] Although Marx asserted as early as the Paris manuscripts that socialism no longer required the mediation of atheism (92–93), we have seen that he never missed an opportunity to skewer the greed and hypocrisy of the religious, in consonance with arguments sketched in the "Theses on Feuerbach" and developed in "On the Jewish Question." In the fourth thesis on Feuerbach he argues that the phenomenon of "religious self-alienation" (that is, religion itself) derives from "cleavages and self-contradictions with [the] secular basis," which therefore must also be criticized (144). And in "On the Jewish Question" (26–52) he sermonizes another of the young Hegelians to the effect that the abolition of state religion in no way abolishes the spirit of religion. He proves the point by showing how in North America the privatization of religion has enormously increased religiosity, leading to an "infinite fragmentation of religion." Although some formulas in this essay smack of anti-Semitism, Marx's main point in pursuing the image of the Jew as someone whose religion demands avarice is to show that this stereotype is a kind of smokescreen behind which those of the dominant (here Protestant) religion themselves practice the pursuit of money at the expense of others. In this sense, "the Jew is the practical Christian." And Marx illustrates this assertion by a vehement presentation of the pursuit of money in North America, where the *"preaching of the Gospel* itself, Christian preaching, has become an article of commerce." This is close to the treatment less than a decade later of Quaker religion and the profit motive in *Moby-Dick* and points to the issue in even more disturbing form in the United States of the 1980s. Although I will not highlight the theme in the chapters that follow, it is worth at the outset reflecting on the role of religion in our novels—virtually nil in *The Golden Bowl,* ludicrously so in the Collins of *Pride and Prejudice,* frequently criticized or presented as contributing to unhappiness in *Le Père Goriot, Madame Bovary, Ulysses,* and *Absalom, Absalom!.*

As the fourth thesis on Feuerbach suggests, the critique of religion quickly leads to the critique of the political order (and of the family, as we shall see shortly). "Theses" 6, 9, and 10, as well as passages on Jean-Jacques Rousseau and *Robinson Crusoe* in "On the Jewish Question" and at the opening of the *Grundrisse* (222–23), attack the notion that the "natural" essence of humanity is to exist in isolation in the conflictual world of "civil society"[11]—in favor of a vaguely glimpsed notion of collective social life which Marx retains throughout his writings (and which itself might be thought to contain an essentially religious note of conversion). And although in "On the Jewish Question" Marx recognizes the political emancipation of French and American democratic government as "great progress," he criticizes the rights that these political forms grant as liberties of "man regarded as an isolated monad, withdrawn into himself," dubiously constrained by the principle of not infringing on the rights of others—a recipe for egotism, for the *"bellum omnium contra omnes."*

In such an analysis the political state becomes an illusory guarantor of rights, and that most sacred of rights, freedom, is questioned: "In imagination, individuals seem freer under the dominance of the bourgeoisie than before, because their conditions of life seem accidental; in reality, of course, they are less free, because they are more subjected to the violence of things" (*GI,* 199, also 34, 160–61). Granted the criticism of Marx's search for a more collective mode of social life expressed above and the realiza-

tion that democratic societies are enormously freer than totalitar-
ian states, it is still possible to wonder whether the considerable
American underclass feels much protected by the Constitution,
whose bicentennial was so politically celebrated in 1987? Or if the
unemployed auto worker who loses his house because he cannot
make mortgage payments, the man who is driven off his family
farm, or the banker or farm official he murders (all hardly isolated events of the 1980s in the United States) have been free or
have simply until then been shielded from "the violence of
things"? It is hardly to draw back from such "real life" events that I
refer to the devastating relevance of these arguments by Marx for
the literary works studied here—the grasping characters in *Pride
and Prejudice, Goriot, Madame Bovary,* and *The Golden Bowl;* the
monstrous egotism of a Sutpen or an Ahab; the few (arguable)
examples of happiness, in the relations of Darcy and Elizabeth,
Rastignac and Delphine; the homosexual counterexperiences
proposed demonically by Vautrin (with echoes in Ahab and
Sutpen), sensuously and fraternally by Ishmael.

This brings us to Marx's (and Engels's) critique of family and
marriage. In the fourth of the theses the critique of religion
immediately leads to the imperative of analyzing and revolution-
izing the family, formulated more drastically in *The German Ideology* as the abolition of the family, or as the *Manifesto* has it, of the
hypocritical mirage of the bourgeois family (157, 487–88). *The
German Ideology* notes the slavery latent in the division of sexual
and other functions in the family (151, 159), a theme that is
interestingly expanded in a note by Marx included in Engels's
Origin of the Family, Private Property, and the State: "The modern
family contains in embryo not only slavery (*servitus*) but serfdom
also, since from the very beginning it is connected with agricultural services. It contains within itself in *miniature* all the antago-
nisms which later develop on a wide scale within society and its
state" (737).

This suggests (if it does not develop) a more organic connection between problems of the family and the issue of landed
property raised earlier than might otherwise have been sus-
pected. Furthermore, following Marx's but more importantly
Lewis H. Morgan's lead, in this book Engels argues that sexual

love is a recent phenomenon, that marriage historically has had little to do with sex and nothing with love. Integrally accompanied by hetaerism, concubinage, and prostitution, the institution assured male sexual pleasure, property, wealth, and succession, while minimizing all of the above for women. Marx and Engels argue that bourgeois society exacerbates this situation, described in the *Manifesto* as reducing "the family relation to a mere money relation" and as treating women as "mere instrument[s] of production." The combination of marital infidelity, sexual control over proletarian women, and public prostitution constitutes the bourgeois sexual order as a "system of wives in common," a system of "prostitution both public and private" (488, also 476). As we shall see, these views converge strongly with what is depicted in the novels treated in this study.

Marx and Engels say little about homosexuality. Marx indeed celebrates the heterosexual, in the Paris manuscripts presenting the *"relation of man to woman"* as emblematic of relations between human beings and between mankind and the external world. He argues that from the sexual relationship "one can therefore judge man's whole level of development" and that, since even socialist utopias perpetuate *"woman* as the spoil and handmaid of communal lust," modern human society has attained a state of "infinite degradation" (82–83). To these points we may add the ideas of Luce Irigaray, the feminist psychoanalyst and theoretician who draws on Marx and Engels to produce an argument about heterosexuality and homosexuality, male and female, that again corresponds closely to what is depicted in our works of fiction.[12]

Briefly, Irigaray argues the following: Marxism reveals the problem of women's subservience, as use- and exchange-value, among men. A social order in which women's sexual pleasure and sexual anatomy are obscured, except as pornographic pleasure for men, in which men control exchange of women, goods, currency, and signs, and in which heterosexual roles are assignments for production (of goods or people)—such an order is homosexual: male homosexuality is the law that (clandestinely) regulates the sociocultural order; all economic management is homosexual. But this truth may be expressed only in disguised form; otherwise the entire organization of society would be threatened. Nonetheless, Irigaray holds out the "utopian" possibility of generous, nonexploitative, non-"patriarchal" human relations. By her account, the novel not only serves as the mirror of Engels's amusing version of the two forms of bourgeois marriage, Catholic and Protestant, French and German, emphasizing either infidelity or the "wedded life of leaden boredom" (741–42). In figures like Vautrin and Sutpen, Ahab and Ishmael, fiction also can reveal in more or less attractive or repellant form the male sexuality that selfishly and sometimes monstrously seems at work in, or in ambiguous reaction against, the socioeconomic order. This tentative formulation, drawing on Irigaray's controversial but suggestive argument, should acquire further meaning in our analysis of literary works, especially *Moby-Dick*.

The other themes listed at the outset of this section—labor, possession, need, objects and the senses, commodities, and money—can all be approached through the production-alienation concept described earlier. Marx's writing on labor and alienated labor illustrates once more the continuity of his ideas on a major topic from the Paris manuscripts to the first volume of *Capital,* though the former is more exalted in tone, the latter somewhat more restrained. The Paris manuscripts describe nature as mankind's *"inorganic* body," in interaction with which human beings produce their lives, so that man "contemplates himself in a world that he has created" (75–76). This view, again connected with Marx's desire for a more collective and social experience of human life ("The object of labour is . . . the *objectification of man's species life"*), is opposed to the estranged nature of (wage-) labor in the bourgeois system, in which the worker's energy is objectified in, *congealed* in alien objects, the product of his work. The view of the "labour process" in the first volume of *Capital* is the same—a metabolism between human beings and nature through which we "appropriate the materials of nature in a form adapted to" our needs, thus modifying both the external world and our own nature (*Cap I,* 283–84; Tucker, 344–45).

As this passage notes, an "immense interval of time" passes

between the first instinctive forms of labor and "the state of things in which a man brings his labour-power to market for sale as a commodity," working in often inhuman conditions in order to produce objects that can be sold for the owner's profit ("exchange-values"). Characteristically, this "valorization process" is illustrated from the textile industry. Passing from unrest to being, from motion to objectivity, the worker's energy contributes to the production of a new object: "At the end of one hour, the spinning motion is represented in a certain quantity of yarn; in other words, a definite quantity of labour, namely that of one hour, has been objectified in the cotton" (*Cap I*, 296; Tucker, 354). The yarn is a commodity or exchange-value that will be transformed into other commodities (clothing, and so on), which however will be saleable only if they satisfy some need or use (only if they are also "use-values"). Labor and commodities are therefore linked to questions of need, desire, gratification, possession, and of course money.

If Marx has with considerable justification been thought to contribute little to our understanding of human emotion, desire, passion, the Paris manuscripts do not live up to that image. In addition to their intensity concerning the sexual relation, the manuscripts include extremely interesting comments on the senses in relation to nature, art, and human gratification (87–91). Marx asserts that the need to *own* things has diminished our ability to appreciate through the senses, and thus "appropriate," objects in the external world: "Private property has made us so stupid and one-sided that an object is only *ours* when we have it—when it exists for us as capital, or when it is directly possessed, eaten, drunk, worn, inhabited, etc." The system of private property and wealth in this sense is an "estrangement of *all* these senses," and to it Marx opposes "the *rich human being* and rich *human* need." This describes the person whose "*orientation to the object* . . . appropriation of that object," is free of "crude practical need," free also of the need to own, sensitive to "beauty of form," directly satisfied as sensuous and aesthetic apprehension, experiencing fully "human gratifications." In this sense, the "*forming* of the five senses is a labour of the entire history of the world down to the present."

The trouble is that after the basic needs, such as food, shelter and clothing, which, as *The German Ideology* points out, must daily be fulfilled in order to sustain life, there is the historical fact of the creation of new needs (156). The Paris manuscripts show how this phenomenon is massively multiplied in a commodity-centered economy, in which "every person speculates on creating a *new* need in another," each "new mode of *gratification*" threatening "economic ruin." Here the "increase in the quantity of objects is accompanied by an extension of the realm of the alien powers to which man is subjected, and every new product represents a new *potency* of mutual swindling" (93). Not to speak of the scandalous contrast between the multiple needs of the wealthy and the impoverished needs of the poor (for slum-dwellers not including clean air or sanitation, for example), the system threatens many in between, the classic literary example being Emma Bovary at the hands of Lheureux. But, as we recognize in a related discussion in the *Grundrisse* ("The need which consumption feels for the object is created by the perception of it. The object of art—like every other product—creates a public which is sensitive to art and enjoys beauty" [230]), Flaubert's art is itself caught in the system of commodification that Marx denounces, a theme explored differently in *The Golden Bowl*.

Marx's insights on objects, needs, and gratifications are thus of considerable interest for students of literature and the other arts—here for all of the works considered, not only the two just mentioned.[13] That he writes so passionately about economic matters seems appropriate, since, due to the system of commodification, it is in and through the realm of the economic that desire is gratified. Confusions and conflicts in the libidinal and the economic constitute a frequent theme in the chapters that follow.

But we should also keep in mind as part of these contradictions the mysterious, magical, fetishistic quality of commodities as Marx describes these apparently innocuous objects—say a hat one owns—in the first chapter of *Capital*, volume 1 (163–77; Tucker, 319–29). As opposed to items produced in other real or imagined modes of production, commodities have, in addition to the qualities that may satisfy us as use-values, a whole other dimension as generators of profit, as exchange-values. Moreover, in contrast to other systems in which exchange, regardless of its fairness or unfairness, is directly personal, when we purchase a commodity we never contact its producer(s), who may exist on the other side of the globe. The exchange is mediated only by the passing of money and by the commodity itself. Hence the conclusion that in the overall system the myriad exchanges of commodities constitute "a social relation" not between the producers but "between the products of their labour"—"material relations between persons and social relations between things." The fact that we are not even conscious of this when we purchase an item is perhaps the strangest feature of the arrangement.

Once again, *Madame Bovary* closely corresponds to Marx's arguments on commodities, beginning in the opening scene with the famous description of Charles Bovary's hat—a mean but fantastic object which, interestingly in terms of our discussion above, has an obtrusive if forlorn sexual quality. But rather than continue with Charles's much discussed headgear, let me quote from a hat of my own, which I was once led to do during a class on Marx's analysis of commodities. Sewn inside the cap I wore for protection that rainy winter day (fundamental need) is a label with a fairly crude image of a cottage and countryside, the motto "Donegal Handwoven," and the following message:

> This tweed was handwoven from pure new wool in my small cottage in county Donegal, Ireland.
> Like my forefathers, I have put something of my own character into this cloth, ruggedness to wear well, softness for comfort, colours from our countryside.
> Joy and health to you who wear this.

The message is "signed" by "W. McNelis, Weaver"—that is, the name appears in the form of a written signature, different from the characters and color of the message and the word *weaver*.

Here is a commodity trying to overcome (or conceal) its condition of commodity, an object trying to create a social relationship, apparently striving to have its purchaser hear the voice of its producer. This involves a rolling back of history, a return to the traditional cottage industry (and therefore preindustrial mode of life) practiced by the forefathers (reinforced by words like *handwoven, pure, new, small*). The message is entirely devoted to the hat's use-value, which is humanized; the cap is said to embody the qualities supposedly characteristic of the Irish and their country: ruggedness, durability, softness, comfort, the beauty of nature. The very use-value of the hat (to be worn) is transformed into a wish for the wearer's well-being. How much more intimately personal could the exchange (sale and purchase) of an item be?

The cap has served me well as a use-value. It is attractive, soft, warm, and durable, although rain has shrunk it and it no longer fits very well; its current usefulness is the one to which I am now submitting it, as well as its personal associations for me. Indeed, it was purchased by my French mother-in-law in a shop specializing in Irish clothes in Providence, Rhode Island, in full knowledge that I am of Irish-American descent.

But then of course the ironies, historical and other, multiply. First, recall Marx's depiction of the massive suffering caused by the development of the textile industry. As the first volume of *Capital* puts it, Ireland had reduced its population by nearly half in the famine and emigration of the mid-nineteenth century and "is at this moment undergoing the process of still further reducing the number of its inhabitants to a level which will correspond exactly with the requirements of its landlords and the English woolen manufacturers" (572). At the beginning of that historical process, in the Paris manuscripts Marx had illustrated the impoverished needs of the workers by the figure of the Irishman, who "no longer knows any need now but the need to *eat,* and indeed only the need to eat *potatoes*—and *scabby potatoes* at that" (94–95). Second, the circumstances of nationality and geographic location involved in the purchase of my hat mark it as an instance of the international market, and indeed the luxury segment of that market—Lord knows what my mother-in-law paid for the cap in that expensive store. Third, the personal communication from W. McNelis is a facsimile only—the whole label, including the "signature," is machine printed. Is there a W. McNelis? Finally, "McNelis" claims only to have woven the wool for the hat. Who (where? using what machine?) cut the wool, sewed the parts, inserted visor and lining, attached the label with its attractive and deceptive message? Under what conditions do they work, to what extent are they submitted to the alienation of labor that Marx describes? Having in an almost literal way interacted socially with the object that is my hat, I am as removed from its producer(s) as Marx showed was the case with all commodities.

If the fetishism of commodities needs to be revealed, how much more so that of money and of money as capital? Marx's writing on the subject from the Paris manuscripts to "The Chapter on Money" and "The Chapter on Capital" in the *Grundrisse* to the first two volumes of *Capital* is fascinating and voluminous, too massive to be covered extensively here. A number of features are interesting, however. One is the attraction of precious metals, whose beauty is accompanied by heavy specific gravity and absolute resistance to oxidation and which therefore historically become ideal means of circulation and accumulation (display of excess, wealth). But the process by which the precious metals become money is mysterious:

> What appears to happen is not that a particular commodity becomes money because all other commodities express their value in it [which is the actual case], but, on the contrary, that all other commodities universally express their values in a particular commodity because it is money. The movement through which this process has been mediated vanishes in its own result, leaving no trace behind. . . . This physical object, gold or silver in its crude state, becomes, immediately on its emergence from the bowels of the earth, the direct incarnation of all human labour. Hence the magic of money. (*Cap I*, 187)

Here the mysteriousness and arbitrariness of the money system are stressed rather than the qualities of the precious metals that initially gave them value. This instability is all the more notable in the case of coins that contain diminished quantities of precious metal, or none at all, and finally in the case of paper money (*Cap I*, 221–27). Yet, despite the ideality of the system, wherein iron can be sold for gold (money), not any money equivalent can really be used as money, as is proved by the imaginary example of the owner of some iron who tries to use it to purchase other commodities: "Hard cash lurks within the ideal measure of value" (Cap I, 197–98).

The discrepancy between ideal value and hard cash is not merely theoretical but is closely related to issues of value in human terms. The Grundrisse shows how in the money system isolated individuals exist in an alienated social bond that expresses itself through control over, or submission to, exchange-values. Thus the "individual carries his social power, as well as his bond with society, in his pocket"; in such a system "personal capacity" depends on "objective wealth," with little relation to individuality (156–57, 222). This recalls the more direct assertion of similar themes in the Paris manuscripts, where Marx laments that, no matter how lacking one may be in personal qualities, one can obtain all through money—beautiful women, talented workers, "art, learning, the treasures of the past"—to the point even that "the less you are, the more you have." Formulated more bluntly: "Money is the pimp between man's need and the object, between his life and his means of life" (96, 102–4). The relevance of such themes for characters like Darcy in Pride and Prejudice, Goriot, Rastignac, and Delphine in Goriot, Flaubert's Emma Bovary and Lheureux, and the characters in The Golden Bowl will be clear when we turn to discuss those works.

Marx's extended theoretical analyses of the contradiction of money often turn out to have such pointedly human meaning. One example is his interest in the separation in time between sale and payment (G, 148, 200), creating the case (Emma Bovary's, we will see) of the "indebted purchaser": "If he does not pay, his goods will be sold compulsorily. The value-form of the commodity, money, has now become the self-sufficient purpose of the sale, owing to a social necessity springing from the conditions of the process of circulation itself" (Cap I, 234). This sounds dense and abstract but is really extremely concrete, as perhaps only a fiction can make us perceive. Emma Bovary takes possession of goods for personal satisfaction, but in Lheureux she is up against someone wholly devoted to the economic system, which at the time of the seizure of her possessions indeed unfolds with "a social necessity springing from the conditions of the process of circulation itself."

Or again, Marx is interested in the differences between accumulating precious metals, or other commodities, or money itself. In the first, accumulation reveals wealth directly, and no other capacities of the owner are necessarily involved. In the second, this is no longer the case: "To accumulate grain requires special stores. . . . to accumulate slaves or land requires relations of domination and accumulation." But, third, in a later historical economic mode, "money as the *general* representative of wealth absolves me of this." Yet money "in its final, completed character now appears in all directions as a contradiction, a contradiction which dissolves itself," not least of all because, though apparently secure, money "can be separated from me by any accident" (*G*, 231–34). We may note the link between Marx's examples and the activities of characters like Goriot and Sutpen—accumulating grain, slaves—and the qualities that in *Goriot* and *Absalom* they are therefore shown to possess. As Marx suggests, however, neither figure is immune to forces beyond his control. As we will see in chapter 4, both attain standing through money, but both are ruined, Sutpen by an entire revolution in modes of production, the industrial replacing the "patriarchal." Goriot, an early practitioner of the capitalist mode, is progressively drained of his wealth, to the point of twisting into ingots and selling the precious metals that at the outset guarantee his stature. As much as Emma Bovary represents the fatal danger of the commodity, Goriot represents the mortal destructiveness of the money system.

That Goriot was once a capitalist and that in the novel this fact is obscured and must be revealed corresponds to another, central element in Marx's argument—namely, that capitalist profit is based on massive contradiction and deception—mysteries that Marx sets out to unveil by his analyses of commodities, money, and the creation of profit through exploitation of labor. In the chapters that follow we will pursue the question of capitalist profit—of how money is made, of how capitalist ventures are hidden, of what *narrative* devices are employed to obscure or pierce such secrets. Doubtless there are interesting works that more frontally treat the issue of the capitalist and how he makes his money. In the figures of Darcy (and Gardiner), Lheureux, Verver, and Sutpen the elusiveness of the question is perhaps more representative, more revealing. To the fascination with precious metals, the instability of value, the corruption of the personal by the mediating "pimp" of money, and the mortal contradictions of the money system is added the mystery of capital.

Readers used to conventional approaches might suspect me of being guilty of the error ascribed to Marx by Peter Demetz, who accuses him of naively treating the characters in Eugène Sue's *Mysteries of Paris* as if they were real people.[14] I do not take the creations of my writers to be real in this limited sense, but I do take these fictions to be every bit as much reproductions, representations, workings up, appropriations of human reality as those of political economy or other social sciences. After hearing an actual political speech that contained the very words he had previously written for a speech at the fair scene in *Bovary*, Flaubert exclaimed: "When literature arrives at the precision of an exact science, it's staggering."[15] I would not dispute Flaubert's claim, rather extend it to the other texts studied here, and to many more. Literary works by our most powerful authors are often concrete representations of world historical developments in Marx's sense of those terms.

The idea of world historical consciousness also illuminates the problem of art and ideology mentioned early on, particularly concerning a group of writers many of whom are known for their conservative stances on class and other issues (including at least Austen, Balzac, Flaubert, James, and Faulkner). Engels's handling of this problem (Balzac's novels reveal societal and historical realities far more inclusive than his consciously professed monarchism)[16] might be completed by Jameson's concept of the political unconscious, derived from Freud and Lévi-Strauss in a Marxist perspective. Jameson uses a Balzac story to suggest that his personal unconscious contains or expresses the unconscious and contradictory social desires of an entire historical period, a notion which will prove useful for our analysis of *Pride and Prejudice* and *Madame Bovary*. But I tend to see consciousness rather than its opposite as the likely source of acute historical insight in fiction.

It is true that Marx's and Engels's distrust of cultural productions derives from their argument that the "ideas of the ruling class are in every epoch the ruling ideas. . . . The class which has the means of material production at its disposal, has control at the same time over the means of mental production, so that thereby, generally speaking, the ideas of those who lack the means of mental production are subject to it" (*GI*, 172). They reject out of hand the counterarguments of the bourgeois whom they so vigorously address in the *Manifesto:* "But don't wrangle with us so long as you apply . . . the standard of your bourgeois notions of freedom, culture, law, etc. Your very ideas are but the outgrowth of the conditions of your bourgeois production and bourgeois property" (487). I do not find "outgrowth" reductive; *The German Ideology* is convincing, for example, on the link between the period of aristocratic dominance and the concepts of honor, loyalty, and so on, on one hand, and the connection between the rise of the bourgeoisie and notions of freedom and equality on the other (173).

But Flaubert's Homais precisely represents the latter phenomenon, as has been widely recognized, and Lady Catherine of *Pride and Prejudice* the former, as we shall see. Austen and Flaubert must in some important way illustrate the importance of the qualification "generally speaking" in the above passage from *The German Ideology.* Thus, though I shall be led to speak of ambiguities of stance in these two novels, of ideological mixed messages in *Goriot* and *Absalom, Absalom!,* of the dangers of the attraction to the aesthetic in James and Joyce, and of both ideology and exposure of same in *Moby-Dick,* all of this shows Marx's inquiry into the ideological dimension of cultural productions as leading to interpretations of literature that are more rather than less complex. We might conclude on this issue that such works are in varying degrees the productions of writers who, like the "bourgeois ideologists" of the *Manifesto,* "have raised themselves to the level of comprehending the historical movement as a whole" (481).

Seeing the historical movement as a whole, as opposed to being mesmerized by a portion of its visible phenomena, is a major part of the intention (and the effectiveness) of Marx's multidisciplinary writing. In the preface to the Paris manuscripts he notes the difficulty of combining material on various subjects with methodological clarity and thus promises to "issue the critique of law, ethics, politics, etc., in a series of distinct, independent pamphlets, and at the end try in a special work to present them again as a connected whole showing the interrelationship of the separate parts" (67). Even in the manuscripts themselves he aims to synthesize within the domain of political economy: "Now, therefore, we have to grasp the essential connection between private property, avarice, and the separation of labour, capital and landed property; between exchange and competition, value and the devaluation of men, monopoly and competition, etc.; the connection between this whole estrangement and the *money-system*" (71).

It is an oft noted irony that these manuscripts, like much else Marx wrote, including the *Grundrisse,* with its methodologically crucial argument about concreteness and concept, were never published by him. Hence, as suggested earlier, McLellan argues that the "table of contents" with which "The Method of Political Economy" section of the *Grundrisse* ends is more inclusive in proposed scope than the totality of Marx's published writings:

> The order [for the study of capitalist society] obviously has to be (1) the general, abstract determinants which obtain in more or less all forms of society. . . . (2) the categories which make up the inner structure of bourgeois society and on which the fundamental classes rest. Capital, wage labour, landed property. Their interrelation. Town and country. The three great social classes. Exchange between them. Circulation. Credit system (private). (3) Concentration of bourgeois society in the form of the state. Viewed in relation to itself. The "unproductive" classes. Taxes. State debt. Public credit. The population. The colonies. Emigration. (4) The international relation of production. International division of labour. International exchange. Export and import. Rate of exchange. (5) The world market and crises (244).

Enough material from Marx has been given thusfar to show that this list is relevant to our novels and that it condenses manifold information into "inner structure" (together with comprehensive scope). This recalls the assertion in the published preface to *A Contribution to the Critique of Political Economy* that political economy provides the key to the "anatomy of civil society" (4). The anatomical metaphor perhaps raises fewer hackles than the structural analogy of base and superstructure in the same preface. Both, however, point to the concrete/category problem at issue in all intellectual inquiry and much literary creation. *Anatomy* as a literary term calls attention to this issue also in that it designates works that are encyclopedic both in content and in mixing forms. Hence in his correspondence Flaubert praises Rabelais and others who created encyclopedias of their eras. Despite its high degree of formal unity, *Madame Bovary* is arguably such a work. Carlyle's *Sartor Resartus* and a book that it influenced, *Moby-Dick,* are notable anatomies, as is *Ulysses.* The bewildering combinations of literary and other forms in *Ulysses* create an effect not unlike Ishmael's "careful disorderliness" and Marx's synthesizing yet endlessly fragmentary productions; all are works so comprehensive, so inclusive, that final unity is lacking. This line of argument can be related to the theory of the romantic novel, that total art form undermined by self-conscious irony, conceptions variously endorsed by Engels and the early Lukács, conceptions valorizing complexity and multiplicity of literary form.[17]

The major theorist of romantic irony and the romantic novel, Friedrich Schlegel, is a transcendental thinker whose vocabulary of absolute self and world soul is (somewhat mournfully) absent from Lukács's *Theory of the Novel* and clearly at odds with the thought of Marx and Engels. But irony and ironic literary forms as resistances to the oppression of material and historical forces, as safeguards of inner freedom, visible in a work like *Ulysses,* are not without an echo in Marx's thinking. I suggested this at the outset, regarding Marx's Hegel-derived irony about world historical facts and personages occurring twice, the second time as farce. He goes on to assert that "Men make their own history, but they do not make it just as they please; they do not make it under circumstances chosen by themselves, but under circumstances directly found, given and transmitted from the past. The tradition of all the dead generations weighs like a nightmare on the brain of the living" (*18th Brum.,* 595).

This is a bleak version of what Marx had written in more neutral terms in *The Poverty of Philosophy.* While viewing society as "the product of men's reciprocal action," he argues there that human beings are not free to choose the forms of their socioeconomic lives—because those have been acquired, produced by previous generations.[18] Here we can see that, though showing how we are subjected to the socioeconomic order into which we are born, Marx is no determinist. The concept of alienation rather than determinism is again pertinent. Another proof of the point is his belief in the possibility of collective transformation of society through revolution, as in the famous eleventh thesis on Feuerbach. In describing this "revolutionising practice" as the "coincidence of the changing of circumstances and of human activity," in the third thesis Marx rejects the determinism of (an insufficiently dialectical) classical materialism: "The materialist doctrine that men are products of circumstances and upbringing, and that, therefore, changed men are products of other circumstances and changed upbringing, forgets that it is men who change circumstances and that it is essential to educate the educator himself" (144–45).

The jump from changing circumstances to educating the educator is a bit rapid but implies that a change in consciousness, and inevitably a change in consciousness among those who form the minds of others, is necessary for social transformation to occur. Significantly, the passage in the *Grundrisse* about Greek art mentioned earlier occurs just after the concluding table of contents of "Method," as part of a jotting down of "points to be mentioned here and not to be forgotten." Among these points, in addition to a brief mention of education, one finds: "*Accusations about the materialism of this conception*"; "*The uneven development of material production relative to e.g. artistic development*"; "*This conception appears as necessary development. But legitimation of chance. How.* (Of freedom also, among other things.) (Influence of means of communication. World history has not always existed; history as world history a result.)" (244–45).

No one would argue that these notes constitute fully worked out positions. But it is obvious that Marx wants to answer objections to his materialism and that he opposes reductive views of the relation between art and the economic realm. The "how" in the next item may imply either that he does or does not know

how to account for chance and freedom within historical developments, which, according to the first volume of *Capital*, unfold
with "iron necessity" (296–97). Interestingly, the clues to unravel-
ing this problem have to do with education in a large sense—the
means of communication, the creation of a consciousness of
world history. Education in its most profound meaning, and I
would include through the literature that Marx does not want to
eliminate from consideration, is one key to glimpsing or aug-
menting freedom.

That transforming society and enlarging freedom cannot for
Marx be accomplished through mental, even broadly cultural,
"acts" is clear from the attack on all forms of idealism from the
theses and *German Ideology* on, as well as from the assertion in
Capital, volume 3, that the "realm of freedom actually begins
only where labour which is determined by necessity and mundane considerations ceases" (441). Characteristically, Marx argues there that the capitalist system, although guilty of the evils
which he attacks, nonetheless prepares the possibility of greater
freedom, attainable for all only when the "associated producers"
rationally regulate "their interchange with Nature" (another recurrent and much debated theme, as we have seen). Then, with
the shortening of the working day as its basic prerequisite, "the
true realm of freedom . . . can blossom forth," though always
with "the realm of necessity as its basis."

As such writers as Herbert Marcuse in *Eros and Civilization*
have shown, the capitalist system has been extremely successful
in subverting the realm of freedom created by the reduction in
labor time. As "leisure time" it has become an arena for the
creation and manipulation of gratifications (in entertainment,
attire, travel, tourism, and so on), in keeping with Marx's arguments about production, needs and consumption. But the authentic realm of freedom must still exist, must be sought for all,
and must inevitably feature the intellectual and the aesthetic. In
The German Ideology Marx imagines it in a communist society in
which production has been rationally organized, eliminating the
"fixation of social activity" that goes with specific jobs. Then an
individual would be able to hunt, fish, raise cattle, engage in
intellectual criticism, as and when he or she wished (160).

This is whimsical, utopian perhaps, but seriously intended, and needs to be completed by the positive references to the aesthetic in the Paris manuscripts—to aspects of nature as objects of art, to human production in accordance with "the laws of beauty" (75–76), to the sense of music. In a passage foreshadowing the one on necessity and freedom, the manuscripts contrast crude need with aesthetic and intellectual sensitivity: "The care-burdened man in need has no sense for the finest play; the dealer in minerals sees only the mercantile value but not the beauty and the unique nature of the mineral: he has no mineralogical sense" (89). This is typical in showing economic activity as threatening full human satisfaction and also in not dichotomizing aesthetic and scientific realms (beauty, mineralogical sense). Note too that the phrase "finest play" may evoke Kant's analysis of the experience of the beautiful, as seems more clearly the case in a surprising element of the description of alienated labor in the first volume of *Capital*: "The less [the worker] is attracted by the nature of the work and the way in which it has to be accomplished, and the less, therefore, he enjoys it as the free play of his own physical and mental powers, the closer his attention is forced to be" (*Cap I*, 284).

This is close to phrasing in *The Critique of Judgment*[19] (though of course adding the physical dimension of labor) and indicates the extent to which the gratifications that Kant assigned to the aesthetic are envisioned by Marx for all forms of human activity and production in their ideally unalienated state. It is an aspect of our estranged situation that for us the aesthetic is largely limited to artistic productions (*not* the case for Kant) and that they are viewed as losing their specialized quality if "extra-aesthetic" issues are introduced in relation to them. It is not at all "un-Marxist" to prize the aesthetic dimensions of novels by Austen and Flaubert, Balzac and Faulkner, James, Joyce, Melville, and others. But it *is* unfaithful to his thought (and intellectually crippling) not to realize that these "satisfactions" are related to insights into the horrendous realities that his work (and to a large extent these novels also) afford.

Two
RADICAL JANE
AND THE
OTHER EMMA

Austen and Flaubert may seem so different that it is
salutary to view them together in Marx's terms.
Pride and Prejudice and *Madame Bovary* frame the period of the
onset of the bourgeois order to the point that they seem to follow
directly one upon the other, Austen's book concluding with an
anticipation of the end of the Napoleonic Wars (when Wickham
and Lydia are sent home), Flaubert's opening with a reference to
1812 (when Charles Bovary's corrupt father is forced to retire
from the imperial army).[1] Published in 1813, *Pride and Prejudice*
(on superficial reading) seems to depict a world as yet untouched
by the urban industrial system, whereas *Madame Bovary* (1856–
57), although situated *en province,* clearly supposes that system.
In this respect, Marx's thought helps correct a misconception
about both works—that they are not very historically pointed.
On the contrary, in various ways together they suggest the transformations of modes of production and hence human relations
that Marx delineated: the gradual diminishment of the power of
landed wealth, despite the continuing importance of the aristocracy; the development of massive cities, industrial production,
and commodities and the creation of needs for them; the accumulation of wealth in the form of capital; new relations among
the classes and increasing alienation among individuals, including vicious economic struggle and the unhappiness of women in
what Marx and Engels sneeringly called "bourgeois marriage."

Not only are these thematic convergences, as well as the significant differences in Austen's and Flaubert's handling of marriage, sexuality, money, class, country, and city, and so on, historically resonant. Marx's ideas also help us to relate, hence understand in more coherent fashion, features of the writing of
these novelists that have been noted, although sometimes as isolated or idiosyncratic. These include the informing obsession
with marriage as the increasingly problematic locus of a woman's
happiness and the related conflict of romance and realism and
distrust of the language of passion, particularly in connection
with the special kinds of irony that both writers notably, and
sometimes viciously, deploy. Flaubert the misanthropist is a familiar stereotype, but many readers of Austen may have wondered aloud if she was a nasty person. More important than such
personalized reactions is the growing awareness of the subversive quality of Austen's writing, produced by "the notorious instability of her novelistic irony."[2] This sounds like Jonathan Culler
on Flaubert, and one almost awaits an *Austen: The Uses of Uncertainty,* with the difference that recent Austen criticism, as has
long been the case for Flaubert, relates such narrative ambiguity
to the complex class situation in which she lived her life and
which her novels evoke.

Class identity and aspiration, and the effort to surmount them
in the interest of superior insight, can also be explored in Austen's and Flaubert's practice of counterpointing subjective and
omniscient voices. Moreover, irony needs to be related to the
question of plots and endings as essentially comic or pessimistic.
The marriages at the end of *Pride and Prejudice* and the bleak
conclusion of *Madame Bovary* have to be seen together, not so
much as expressing individual authorial psychology but as mobilizing or deflating, at the onset and end of a historical period of
intense class conflict, the impulses of what Jameson has aptly
called the political unconscious.

> And now nothing remains for me but to assure you in the most
> animated language of the violence of my affection. To fortune
> I am perfectly indifferent, and shall make no demand of that
> nature on your father, since I am well aware that it could not
> be complied with; and that one thousand pounds in the 4 per

cents. which will not be yours till after your mother's decease, is
all that you may ever be entitled to. (75)

Despite its comic touch (here evident in Collins's absurd proposal to Elizabeth) and satisfying outcome, *Pride and Prejudice* is
scandalous in its presentation of marriage as the key to survival—
survival in crude financial terms, in terms of the quality of life, in
terms finally of life itself. Collins's hypocritical indifference to
fortune, characteristic of so many in the book, recalls the opening
sentences' presentation of marriage in relation to possession, fortune, property. His research on how much Elizabeth will inherit
parallels the insistence throughout on specifying how much everyone is worth. Bingley has four or five thousand pounds a year,
Darcy ten thousand, and their sisters have inherited twenty thousand and thirty thousand, respectively. In contrast, Mrs. Bennet
has inherited but four thousand, and her husband's yearly income, in addition to the problem of the entail, is only two
thousand—which explains the pressing economic aspect of the
Bennet sisters' marriage search. As Collins points out to Elizabeth
when she refuses him, she may never get a better offer. Such logic
underlies Mrs. Bennet's comic pursuit of sons-in-law, Charlotte's
"disinterested desire of an establishment" (85), and Fitzwilliams's
complaint: "Younger sons cannot marry where they like" (127).
Carried to an extreme, it contemplates property as more important than the lives of others—witness Bennet's joke about Collins's
possession of his estate after his death, Collins's "mortifying" appreciation of his future property (45), Lady Lucas's calculating
"with more interest than . . . ever . . . before, how many years
longer Mr. Bennet was likely to live" (86)—where the much remarked financial vocabulary reinforces the inhumanity of the
thought.[3] Finally, Collins's egregiously mechanical reference to
libidinal emotion and expression indicates the threat to the erotic
that is posed by the economic.

The Wickham-Lydia affair is the unhappiest instance of the
difficult conjunction of love, marriage, and money, exposing not
only their defects but also those of Mr. Bennet, who is criticized
for not having provided for Lydia: "Had he done his duty . . .
Lydia need not have been indebted to her uncle, for whatever of

honour or credit could now be purchased for her. The satisfaction of prevailing on one of the most worthless young men in Great Britain to be her husband, might then have rested in its proper place" (211). This judgment fittingly adopts the accents almost of Bennet's own irony, as when he remarks that Wickham is a "pleasant fellow, and would jilt [Elizabeth] creditably," adding later, "He simpers, and smirks, and makes love to us all. . . . I defy even Sir William Lucas himself, to produce a more valuable son-in-law"(96, 226). Even as Bennet is criticized for financial irresponsibility, the contamination of the sexual by the monetary is again stressed in the vocabulary of debt, credit, purchase, worth, particularly in the sarcastic reference to Wickham's "value" in "making love"—the only use of the phrase that I find in the book. (Moreover, although Bennet supposedly is not sharp on money matters, even he is not beyond profiting from the generosity of Gardiner and Darcy in buying Lydia's marriage—"It will save me a world of trouble and economy" [260].)

As for Lydia and Wickham themselves, they are more troubling if we allow ourselves to experience a certain compassion for them as casualties of the marriage-money system, which the novel, despite its criticism of them, does not preclude. Lydia's compulsion to marry is shared by all at the end, even by Elizabeth: "And they *must* marry! Yet he is *such* a man!" (208). Such a man indeed: Wickham pursues in illegitimate ways what most everyone else is after. In view of parallels and contrasts among Collins, Wickham, and Darcy (Collins succeeds in areas for which Wickham was first destined, Collins was mistreated by his father whereas Wickham was favored by Darcy's father), moreover, we may feel that Darcy and Wickham are a bit too close for comfort and may trace in the latter's bitterness more than a hint of class *ressentiment*. Lydia's pathetic letter provides ammunition for such an interpretation: "It is a great comfort to have you so rich, and when you have nothing else to do, I hope you will think of us" (267).

Against this radical delineation of economic struggle and the difficulties of sexual love, it is the major thrust of the novel to delay, then bring about, the "good" marriages. All are assured about the personal suitability of Bingley and Jane, who also promises to be financially responsible: "Imprudence or thought-lessness in money matters, would be unpardonable in *me*" (239). And the much more important marriage, that of the heroine, is slowly worked out through the plot, until Elizabeth recognizes that Darcy is "exactly the man, who, in disposition and talents, would most suit her" (214).

This suitability is conditioned by Darcy's great wealth, as those critics have recognized who stress that she is not being com-pletely "unserious" in dating her change of heart from her first seeing "his beautiful grounds at Pemberley" (258). In that scene she is *immediately* moved by an attraction to possession: " 'And of this place,' thought she, 'I might have been mistress! With these rooms I might now have been familiarly acquainted! Instead of viewing them as a stranger, I might have rejoiced in them as my own' " (167). This is uncomfortably reminiscent of the book's opening lines and even of Collins's avidity: "The hall, the dining-room, and all its furniture were examined and praised; and his commendation of every thing would have touched Mrs. Bennet's heart, but for the mortifying supposition of his viewing it all as his own future property" (45).

But Elizabeth is a sympathetic character who tries—on the whole if not always successfully—to combine financial realism, genuine affection, and respect for persons. Attracted to Wick-ham, who however is wooing Miss King's ten thousand pounds, she wonders, "Where does discretion end, and avarice begin" (106), and ruefully admits that "handsome young men must have something to live on, as well as the plain" (104). But when Lydia later makes a denigrating remark about Miss King, Eliza-beth has the surprising self-discovery that "the coarseness of the *sentiment* was little other than her own breast had formerly harboured and fancied liberal!" (151). Concerning Fitzwilliam, moreover, she is less self-aware and thoughtful. To his remark about younger sons quoted earlier, she makes the "lively," and justified, but somewhat cruel response: "And pray, what is the usual price of an Earl's younger son? Unless the elder brother is very sickly, I suppose you would not ask above fifty thousand pounds" (127). And once Darcy makes his first proposal and writes his letter, Fitzwilliam quickly fades as a source of interest:

"Colonel Fitzwilliam had made it clear that he had no intentions at all" (130); "Elizabeth could but just *affect* concern in missing him; she really rejoiced at it. Colonel Fitzwilliam was no longer an object. She could think only of her letter" (144–45).

We may read in this youthful thoughtlessness, but also evidence of the tendency to give persons consideration only to the extent that they can be viewed as financially suitable marriage partners. Earlier we learned that in her mother's mind Elizabeth rated only a husband of the Collins sort: "Elizabeth was the least dear to her of all her children; and though the man and the match were quite good enough for *her,* the worth of each was eclipsed by Mr. Bingley and Netherfield" (73). In Elizabeth's self-absorbed marital shorthand, something of the same treatment is given to Fitzwilliam, who has "no intentions," who besides Darcy is "no longer an object," and who indeed from this point on is "eclipsed" from the novel.

Marriage and property, objects to own, objects of desire: at every point *Pride and Prejudice* reveals a problematic relation between ownership and love. Austen's frequently remarked distrust of romantic infatuation and its effusive mode of expression is visible in the satire of Collins, the criticism of Lydia and her father, and particularly in the lesson for Elizabeth of the danger of her attraction to Wickham. Mrs. Gardiner calls her use of the phrase "violently in love" hackneyed (97), and she herself adopts an ironic tone in relating to her aunt the realization that she had not felt a "pure and elevating passion" for Wickham (104). Moreover, in feeling as well as expression, Elizabeth is reflective rather than passionate in her responses not only to Wickham and Fitzwilliam but especially to Darcy. This is not to say that she lacks desire. Rather, as already intimated, the strong emotion of sexual love, revealed through blushing and related physical and emotional reactions and rarely if ever verbalized, is mediated— for her and for the reader—by property, specifically Darcy's.

Her cool response to Darcy is noted, and justified. Recognizing his "ardent love," she in contrast is aware of respect, gratitude, and power over him (181, 189). Under the blow of Lydia's flight, she realizes that she "could have loved him," and this is legitimated by a supposition that relates narrator and reader: "If gratitude and esteem are good foundations of affection, Elizabeth's change of sentiment will be neither improbable nor faulty." A further supposition, to the effect that a love-at-first-sight scenario might be more "interesting," is expressed ironically—the narrator seems to be chastening our romantic tendencies (190–91). Even near the end, Elizabeth "rather *knew* that she was happy, than *felt* herself to be so" (257).

But powerful emotion is not lacking. In the first proposal Darcy says his feelings "will not be repressed," adding, "You must allow me to tell you how ardently I admire and love you" (130). Austen does not allow him to tell any more in his own words; the rest comes to us through Elizabeth's reaction, indignation, which he rapidly comes to share. But when he seeks her out again, the responses that earlier expressed anger now have a different meaning: "The colour which had been driven from her face, returned for half a minute with an additional glow, and a smile of delight added lustre to her eyes" (229). Signs of emotion in eye and cheek, combined with reticence of expression, also characterize the second proposal:

> Elizabeth feeling all the more than common awkwardness and anxiety of his situation, now forced herself to speak; and immediately, though not very fluently, gave him to understand, that her sentiments had undergone so material a change, since the period to which he alluded, as to make her receive with gratitude and pleasure, his present assurances. The happiness which this reply produced, was such as he had probably never felt before; and he expressed himself on the occasion as sensibly and as warmly as a man violently in love can be supposed to do. Had Elizabeth been able to encounter his eye, she might have seen how well the expression of heart-felt delight, diffused over his face, became him; but, though she could not look, she could listen, and he told her of feeling, which, in proving of what importance she was to him, made his affection every moment more valuable (252).

The speech of neither is quoted, as again the narrator mobilizes our imagination, with a "probably" and an invitation to "suppose" what a man "violently in love" might say. Elizabeth's reactions continue to be expressed in terms of gratitude, pleasure and value, but of Darcy the narrator uses the phrase that earlier her aunt called hackneyed. The index of the real "violence" of his love is there, though, in the "expression of heartfelt delight, diffused over his face."

The passionate eye, color diffused over the face, like Elizabeth's eyes and complexion, which first attracted Darcy—these are the signals in the novel's discrete code of bodily energy. Elizabeth's inability to raise her eyes is equally expressive. She listens nonetheless to the language of love; while hers in not "fluent," his is both "sensible" and "warm." But as noted, neither is given directly—verbal revelations of love are even rarer than bodily ones. The latter, degraded in Lydia's vulgar energy, are "displayed" innocently only in the Gardiner children on the return of their parents: "The joyful surprise that lighted up their faces, and displayed itself over their whole bodies, in a variety of capers and frisks, was the first pleasing earnest of their welcome" (195). And the former, verbal communication of desire and gratification, is given fullest expression in Elizabeth's reaction—not to Darcy's person but to his estate.

From early on Elizabeth has been attracted to Pemberley as the model of the great country house (25), as opposed to the dwellings of others: the vulgar furnishings of the Philipses, the crowded house at Hunsford, the Bennet property so impertinently evaluated by Lady Catherine, even Rosings, by which Elizabeth is "but slightly affected" despite Collins's expectation of "raptures" (111). The raptures will be reserved for Pemberley.

By the time of her visit, Pemberley has been invested with feelings of desire and loss. It is after Darcy's letter and the frustration of Elizabeth's attraction to Wickham, and after her remark about men which Mrs. Gardiner says "savours strongly of disappointment," that the trip, first planned as a tour of the Lakes District, is proposed. Elizabeth responds with a satirical but compensating burst of ecstatic language, foreseeing "delight," "felicity," "life and vigour," "transport." She laughingly displaces such emotion from the men who have disappointed her to sublime nature: "What are men to rocks and mountains?" And she mocks the conventions of nature description, intending to remember clearly what she sees so that her "effusions" will be bearable (107). There is then a further process of expectation, frustration, and substitution, as the trip on which Elizabeth "had set her heart" is shortened. In Derbyshire rather than at the Lakes, her "alarms" over encountering Darcy are "removed," and she feels she can indulge the "curiosity" of seeing his house in his absence (164–66).

Her parodic project for an orderly but excited evocation of sublime nature becomes, in the narrative handling of her visit, a systematic and rapturous description of Darcy's estate (166–77). Meticulous organization is apparent in the progression of the travelers (and reader): the arrival in the park, which is traversed from "one of its lowest points" to an "eminence, where . . . the eye was instantly caught by Pemberley house"; then the descent to the house, whose rooms and floors are visited in systematic fashion. The subsequent tour with the gardener (Elizabeth has all along been with the Gardiners) is preceded by the appearance of Darcy, whom they meet twice (as there are two portraits and more than one gardener). To be sure, the visit has presaged Darcy's arrival, and the meeting between him and the Gardiners serves powerfully to draw him and Elizabeth together.

Like Elizabeth's idea for a description of the lakes, the Pemberley chapter is also an "effusion," accumulating expressions of emotional response. This is natural in the meetings with Darcy, which produce flushes and silences, reactions of "surprise," "wonder," and so on; it is also natural before Darcy's arrival, as Elizabeth blushes about the first portrait, pays "keenest" attention to Mrs. Reynolds, and goes "in quest" of the second portrait. But her heightened state, her emotions of anticipation and gratification, are stressed from the beginning and are first directed toward Pemberley: "Elizabeth, as they drove along, watched for the first appearance of Pemberley Woods with some perturbation; and when at length they turned in at the lodge, her spirits were in a high flutter"; "Elizabeth's mind was too full for conversation, but she saw and admired every remarkable spot and point of view"; "Elizabeth was delighted"; "Elizabeth . . . went to a window to enjoy its prospect. . . . she looked on the whole scene . . . with delight."

The vocabulary of pleasurable response is matched by de-

scriptive praise, a panegyric to Darcy's estate, which is characterized by magnitude and quality. The park is "very large," with a
"great variety of ground" and "a beautiful wood, stretching
over a wide extent." Elizabeth admires the "remarkable" views
as they ascend "for half a mile." From within, "every disposition
of the ground was good"; rooms and furnishing are "large,
well-proportioned . . . handsomely fitted up," "lofty," filled
with "real elegance." The grounds as seen later are "beautiful,"
"nobler," "finer," with "many charming views of the valley, the
opposite hills, with the long range of woods overspreading
many." To the visitors' question about touring the whole, the
gardener answers triumphantly that it is "ten miles round."

Nowhere else in the novel is there such a passage of laudatory
description;[4] for Elizabeth, and for the reader, Pemberley is a
magnificent object of attraction. The word *object*, earlier designat-
ing a man of marriageable potential, now refers to things, not
artifacts but aspects of nature visible from Darcy's house: "The
hill, crowned with wood, from which they had descended . . .
was a beautiful object"; "As they passed into other rooms, these
objects were taking different positions; but from every window
there were beauties to be seen."

As the double meaning of *object* suggests, the scenery may be
charged with desire. During the tour of the grounds, near the
narrowing path, Elizabeth "longed to explore its windings."
Shortly before, she could think only of where Darcy was and
"longed to know what . . . was passing in his mind." Even
before his arrival, Darcy's house is described in this way: "It was
a large, handsome, stone building, standing well on rising
ground, and backed by a ridge of high woody hills, and in
front, a stream of some natural importance was swelled into
greater, but without any artificial appearance." The last note
leads to appreciation of the relation of nature and art in Darcy's
estate, to the admiration of all, and to the attraction to ownership mentioned earlier: "They were all of them warm in their
admiration; and at that moment she felt, that to be mistress of
Pemberley might be something!"

Much in the sentences quoted evokes Pemberley in a straightforward manner. But the libidinal dimension, while light, is

unmistakable—the longing to explore narrow windings, the delight in standing and rising, in the high back and swelling front. In the last passage cited, the sexual overtones lead rapidly to Elizabeth's desire for ownership. (Note that Darcy is more than once referred to as Pemberley's owner or proprietor, especially in his abrupt appearance: with Gardiner "conjecturing as to the date of the building, the owner of it himself suddenly came forward".) A quite "warm" libidinal notion thus eventuates in a very warm desire for possession.

Fredric Jameson has brilliantly shown how the description of the house and grounds of an unattractive old maid in a Balzac story is charged with an almost sexual intensity and builds an argument about the desire to possess property through marriage as representing the "political unconscious" of postrevolutionary France, an unrealizable urge to roll back history and overcome class conflict. Neither Darcy nor Elizabeth is unattractive, and Austen's novel is a more uncensored expression, at a slightly earlier time and in a different national context, of the urge to class reconciliation. The Pemberley chapter, the turning point that leads to Elizabeth's marriage, is crucial in this regard, since it is by far the most ardent piece of writing in the book, the passage in which language most intensely "makes love" with its "object." This remark is relevant for the protagonist but also for Austen's readership (then and now) in its response to the narrative tissue of the work. The chapter is an unprecedented *textual* investment of desire, an expression in a discreetly libidinal register of the fascination of magnificent property, wealth, and power.

The class dimensions of Elizabeth's marriage have attracted attention by critics who have come to see Austen's fiction as "the very evidence of social history."[5] Of punctual historical detail there is indeed little. Rather, the indication at the end that Lydia and Wickham remain unsettled "even when the restoration of peace dismissed them to a home" (267) has a deeper sociohistorical significance. Although shadowed by undesirable elements, the marriage of Elizabeth and Darcy is seen (or wished) to coincide with the peaceful resolution of a period of international turbulence that had shaken the social world of Austen's England. That world includes aristocracy (Lady Catherine, Darcy), gentry (Bennet), a "pseudogentry" of clergy, lawyers, and business-men (Lucas, the Philipses, Collins, and—unsuccessfully—Wick-ham), and an urban-based commercial class (the Gardiners). Mobility within this framework is remarkable and accounts for many of the work's strains and satisfactions—Bennet's and Lydia's inferior marriages, the social ascension capped by Bing-ley's purchase of an estate at the end, the Gardiners' association with Darcy, the elder Bennet sisters' marriage into vastly supe-rior status. Satire of pseudogentry and rigid aristocracy in the figures of Lucas, Mrs. Bennet, and Lady Catherine is clear. But Darcy overcomes such limitations. That he is early on attracted to Elizabeth, defending himself only through "the inferiority of her connections" (35), indicates the extent to which the narra-tive *retard* derives from the dynamics of class. Further, since Lady Catherine's project of uniting two noble families fails, and since the daughters of these families are presented as sickly or unnaturally shy, whereas Darcy benefits from the lively Eliza-beth, it is hard not to see their marriage as a historical allegory with overtones of class stagnation, mobility, and reconciliation. By her arrogance Lady Catherine precipitates Darcy's second proposal, and her "infinite use" in that regard is noted (263). But even more "useful" are the Gardiners, who in the last lines of the book deserve Elizabeth's and Darcy's gratitude for bring-ing them together.

The splendid marriage of an attractive young woman of the middle classes to the scion of a rich, ancient, and powerful family thus occurs through the agency (negative) of an inflexible aristoc-racy and (positive) of a new commercial class, urbane in all the senses of the word. The role of the Gardiners, their identifica-tion with the economic activity of the city, and the meanings suggested by their name as well as that of Lady Catherine unbal-ance somewhat the comfortable setting of the great country es-tate that Elizabeth inhabits at novel's end. This adds to our sense of discrepancies and fissures that the book strives to contain.[6]

Though centered in the country and the lives of the landed classes, *Pride and Prejudice* insistently signals the importance of London. A suggestive nomenclature of distance, proximity, and value is stressed in the country-urban theme—Netherfield, Longbourn, Hunsford, Rosings, Pemberley, Grosvenor Street, Cheapside, Gracecourt Street. The geography underlines discussion of country and city: Miss Bingley's criticism of Elizabeth's "country town" ways (24) and her wish to bring in a London doctor for Jane (shades of Flaubert); Lady Catherine on London's cultural and educational attractions; Darcy's complaint about the country's "confined and unvarying society" (29), his claim that the fifty miles between Hunsford and Lucas Lodge is "a *very* easy distance." Elizabeth responds that this judgment reflects his wealth (it also reflects the importance in the period of improved transport throughout the country and between country and city). Darcy accuses her of provincialism, then reveals his admiration: "*You* cannot have a right to such very strong local attachment. *You* cannot always have been at Longbourn" (123–24). And we have read that Elizabeth and Jane "had frequently been staying . . . in town" with their aunt (97).

The role of London and the Gardiners in making Elizabeth and Jane finer than their sisters (hence worthy of superior marriages) fits with another aspect—that the three marriages of the Bennet sisters are strongly associated with movement to or through "town." Before Mrs. Bennet and her daughters lay eyes on Bingley, he is "obliged to be in town"—"gone to London" to get a party for the ball, among whom is Darcy (5–6). Afterwards his projected short trip becomes instead a departure by his whole party "on their way to town" (81), a fact confirmed by two letters about the London season from Miss Bingley. Jane goes to London but does not meet Bingley, even as Elizabeth's discussions with her aunt there do not resolve her confusion over marriage and money. Darcy's letter after his first proposal recapitulates all concerning Bingley, including the plan to get him away to London. Bingley finally proposes while Darcy stays away in the city (having confessed his role to Bingley "on the evening before . . . going to London" [256]).

Wickham too arrives "from town," with Denny, "concerning whose return from London Lydia came to inquire" (50). He disappoints Elizabeth by not attending Bingley's ball, pretexting business in London. Later, the fact that he and Lydia have gone to London is the first indication that they do not plan marriage.

We then learn of Bennet's search for them there, his return to Longbourn (at the same time that Mrs. Gardiner returns to the capital), Gardiner's efforts and finally Darcy's success in locating them and imposing marriage, which occasions a flurry of movement between Pemberley and London: "When all this was resolved on, he returned again to his friends, who were still staying at Pemberley; but it was agreed that he should be in London once more when the wedding took place, and all money matters were then to receive the last finish"—before he was to "leave town again" (222–23).

Here Darcy's trips between country estate and London accentuate the money-marriage (and now -city) nexus. And so many iterations of the significance of going to or leaving London! But such is also the case for the central marriage, influenced by the Gardiners and Lady Catherine, in both cases with pointed reference to London. Why is Elizabeth's trip shortened? Because her uncle is "prevented by business from setting out till a fortnight later in July, and must be in London again within a month" (164). And after the confrontation with Elizabeth, Lady Catherine returns home through London, causing Elizabeth to worry that Darcy "would return no more. Lady Catherine might see him in her way through town; and his engagement . . . of coming again to Netherfield must give way" (248). But she soon learns that she owes her happiness to the provocation of Lady Catherine, "who *did* call on him in her return through London" (253)!

What all of this shows is a structure that cannot be accidental: though largely "about" the landed classes, the novel keeps calling our attention to London, where other forces—undescribed but evidently determining, even in the countryside—are at work.[7] This is a literary equivalent to Marx's arguments about country and city and to the concept of the historical opposition, persistence, and coexistence of competing modes of production. In Marx's terms, the urban capitalist mode of production, despite the persistence of earlier forms, is already achieving a position of dominance, but such characters as Lady Catherine and Mr. Bennet do not know that—although, in some profound way, their creator does. We can appreciate this further by examining the

Gardiners, Lady Catherine, and Darcy in terms of the city-country dialectic and related social and economic elements.

Lady Catherine's adherence to aristocratic forms is flagrant, and most extreme in her argument with Elizabeth. Her assumption that the assertion of noble prerogatives will win the argument is countered by Elizabeth's self-assurance in being "a gentleman's daughter," which provides a readerly satisfaction based in class identity and antagonism and which reduces Lady Catherine to repeating the code words for noble values in an almost incantatory way: "You have no regard, then, for the honour and credit of my nephew!"; "You refuse to obey the claims of duty, honour, and gratitude" (245–47). But the mere expression of such values is inefficacious, we might say, in changed historical circumstances.

Yet at Rosings Lady Catherine operates in a resolutely feudal way. Elizabeth observes that

> though this great lady was not in the commission of the peace for the county, she was a most active magistrate in her own parish, the minutest concerns of which were carried to her by Mr. Collins; and whenever any of the cottagers were disposed to be quarrelsome, discontented or too poor, she sallied forth into the village to settle their differences, silence their complaints, and scold them into harmony and plenty. (117)

In addition to Elizabeth's insightfulness (how different, we shall see, from Emma Bovary), we note the interactions among aristocracy, subordinate clergy, and cottagers and the unmasking of the economic nature of the relations of superiority and inferiority in the discordant series "quarrelsome, discontented . . . poor" and "settle . . . differences, silence . . . complaints, . . . scold . . . into harmony and plenty."

In the context of our earlier discussion of the implications of certain names, we should consider Lady Catherine's, which like Darcy's, suggests ancient French lineage. To be named de Bourg(h) while asserting claims to aristocracy, however, is to be caught in a historical paradox, since the word in medieval French designated a fortified town, whose inhabitants, possessors of a special status, existed in contradistinction to the landed nobility. The adjective deriving from the word is of course *bour-geois*. Lady Catherine is not only an anachronism; her name, associated with the origins of the modern European city and of the bourgeoisie, belies the purity of class hierarchies to which she is devoted. Perhaps this fits with her house, described as a "handsome modern building" (109), and with her ultimate reconciliation to Darcy's marriage despite the "pollution" of Pemberley by Elizabeth's city relatives (268).[8]

If Lady Catherine is a negative and contradictory figure, the Gardiners, unambiguously associated with the city, are presented in celebratory fashion. Their role is important and is developed with systematic care. We learn at first only that Mrs. Bennet has "a brother settled in London in a respectable line of trade" (18); Mrs. Hurst reveals that he lives in Cheapside (Miss Bingley appropriately exclaiming, "That is capital" [24]); later Mrs. Bennet mentions his name (30). In volume 2, we meet him and his wife and learn of their estimable qualities and their influence on Elizabeth and Jane. In the final volume their role becomes major. They contribute much to the union of Darcy and Elizabeth, and in the Wickham-Lydia affair Gardiner shows himself to be generous and at ease in the city—as opposed to Mr. Bennet. Again in opposition to Bennet, the Gardiners' family life is highlighted, particularly through the happiness of their children. If Elizabeth's marriage to the family-oriented Darcy is meant to repair some of the damage done by the Bennets' deficiencies, the Gardiners contribute much to this rehabilitation.

These positive qualities are implicit in the first description of the Gardiners early in volume 2:

> Mr. Gardiner was a sensible, gentlemanlike man, greatly superior to his sister as well by nature as education. The Netherfield ladies would have had difficulty in believing that a man who lived by trade, and within view of his own warehouses, could have been so well bred and agreeable. Mrs. Gardiner, who was several years younger than Mrs. Bennet and Mrs. Philips, was an amiable, intelligent, elegant woman. (96–97)

The Gardiners' superiority in nature and education is not unconnected with their name, which tells us briefly about them what

Darcy's estate reveals in a magnified way about him. Of course modifications of the natural include not only gardens and estates but cities, where they are often monstrous. Published two decades after Blake's "London," the novel depicts none of that, just as the glowing picture of the city businessman is hardly predictive for later fiction. Here however the message is clear: the Netherfield ladies, and Darcy, and the reader, are to recognize that urban commercial activity is not incompatible with "well bred" intelligence and elegance.

But this recognition is also postponed. Despite the visits to town in volume 2, no contact is made there with Bingley or Darcy, because, as Mrs. Gardiner explains, city geography also inscribes social differences: "We live in so different a part of town, all our connections are so different" (98). How satisfying, then, in class terms, is the concluding paragraph of the novel: "With the Gardiners, they were always on the most intimate terms. Darcy, as well as Elizabeth, really loved them; and they were both ever sensible of the warmest gratitude towards the persons who, by bringing her into Derbyshire, had been the means of uniting them" (268). This circle of intimacy, warmth, love, gratitude, and unity projects a societal wish fulfillment of large proportions, a political (not sub- but) superconscious, since all is so clearly delineated.

But the union between Elizabeth and Darcy is the important one. Darcy and what he has—ten thousand per annum, a great uncle who is a judge and an uncle who is a lord, patronage in the church, a house in town, a magnificent family library, as well as Pemberley—are the supreme objects of desire. Again Collins is close to the mark in the worldly judgment that Darcy has "every thing the heart of mortal can most desire,—splendid property, noble kindred, and extensive patronage" (250). Darcy's wealth and its source (only property?), his noble family, and what results from these, his power (in Collins's ecclesiastical terms, patronage), all need to be examined.

Darcy's influence over others is great; he is so wealthy that he exercises a fascination, whether that fascination is experienced as positive or negative. His control over Bingley may not appear malignant, since it contributes so much to the plot and since

Elizabeth is able to tease him about it at the end. No harm done either when he gets permission to marry Elizabeth before her father is assured that she loves him: "He is the kind of man . . . to whom I should never dare refuse any thing, which he condescended to ask" (260). His obstinacy (Mrs. Gardiner's word) in settling the Wickham affair makes Elizabeth proud of him (222, 224); ironically it also illustrates what Wickham has complained about all along—Darcy's power to impose his desires. With an ax to grind, too, Fitzwilliam presents a similar if more balanced view: "I am at his disposal. He arranges the business just as he pleases"; "He likes to have his own way very well. . . . But so we all do. It is only that he has better means of having it than many others, because he is rich, and many others are poor" (126). Finally, the fascination Darcy exercises is evident in the scenes in which others attempt to interpret his silent face, culminating in Elizabeth's contemplation of his portrait: "As a brother, a landlord, a master, she considered how many people's happiness were in his guardianship!—How much of pleasure or pain it was in his power to bestow!—How much of good or evil must be done by him!" (170–71).

Elizabeth is overwhelmed here by the sheer extent of Darcy's power, which according to Mrs. Reynolds and what the Gardiners later discover is indeed used as generous "guardianship" and which derives from inherited landed wealth. Note that she had earlier heard from Wickham an identical, but negatively colored, description of Darcy's uses of his wealth as based in pride:

> It has often led him to be liberal and generous,—to give his money freely, to display hospitality, to assist his tenants, and relieve the poor. Family pride, and *filial* pride, for he is very proud of what his father was, have done this. Not to appear to disgrace his family, to degenerate from the popular qualities, or lose the influence of the Pemberley House, is a powerful motive. He has also *brotherly* pride, which with *some* brotherly affection, makes him a very kind and careful guardian of his sister. (57)

Wickham's dishonesty is clear; so also is the contrast between Darcy and Lady Catherine and the softening of his arrogance by the end. But Wickham's analysis is not incorrect. Darcy's generosity is possible only because he has immense wealth, whereas others do not; his generosity, moreover, is a means of perpetuating that relationship of superiority and subservience. Darcy excercises magnanimously the power that Elizabeth unmasks in the case of his aunt, though not in that of her future husband. Wickham, a love temptation for Elizabeth, may also be seen—in a novel whose conclusion projects the union of the dominant classes—as an oppositional voice, discredited but not altogether silenced.

Austen hints that Darcy's wealth may not be exclusively of the landed kind. Lucas immediately sniffs out that he has a house in town, where his sister lives; Elizabeth later meets her London companion (17, 57, 182). Darcy himself spends more time there than anyone else but his sister and the Gardiners, for example the ten days during which Bingley proposes to Jane (236). In handling the Wickham-Lydia matter he functions more effectively there even than Gardiner. Perhaps some of those business letters that Miss Bingley would find "odious" to write concern interests "in town" (32)?

This conjecture may gather support from an important passage that to my knowledge has not drawn commentary, the late revelation by Lady Catherine about Darcy's (and her daughter's) lineage: "My daughter and my nephew are formed for each other. They are descended on the maternal side, from the same noble line; and, on the father's, from respectable, honourable, and ancient, though untitled families. Their fortune on both sides is splendid. They are destined for each other by the voice of every member of their respective houses" (245). Lady Catherine's vocabulary of aristocracy is still in evidence. The verbiage cannot hide the fact that neither Darcy nor her daughter comes from absolutely noble lineage; aristocracy in the novel as in history turns out to be a pseudoconcept. There have been in her generation two marriages with "untitled families," with another kind of wealth, presumably commercial in origin. The lateness of the revelation, just before the union of Darcy and Elizabeth, is suggestive; it is as if, before a new fusion of social elements can occur, an earlier one must be admitted. Admitted—but not foregrounded, in contrast to the narrator's early detailing of Bingley's economic and social background. Bingley's father did not marry into nobility and did not purchase an estate, but we are not told if Pemberley has been in Lady Catherine's family for generations or if Darcy's father purchased it. Either way, the traditional mode of life that reigns there has been infused with wealth deriving from another economic mode. And Darcy himself may easily be thought of as the "protocapitalist,"[9] whose business in the city is not narrated but whose power exercises a discreetly sexual fascination, at a time when the countryside is only beginning to be marginalized and the new economic forces seem to contribute smoothly to the maintenance of the marvelous "aristocratic" world of Pemberley.

In spite of its radical exposure of the often seamy financial dimension of marriage and its revelation of the fissures of the socioeconomic order, *Pride and Prejudice* accomplishes the union of the most powerful classes and does so through the primary agency of a well-educated and insightful heroine. A novel that begins rather than concludes with marriages and ends instead with suicide, poverty, and the destruction of a family, *Madame Bovary*[10] bears the traces of alienating transformations in political, but especially economic and social, history. Industry, transport, capitalism, urbanization, and economic and social conflict have an augmented, and surprisingly pertinent, role in the book's depressing story. Emma Bovary is a woman of the lower rural middle class, still close to her peasant roots, miseducated and lacking in intellectual penetration, aspiring to aristocratic status, one for whom the elements of desire, marriage, and possession take on an exacerbated and destructive force.

Unlike that single element in *Pride and Prejudice*, the military, whose presence reminds us that the private story cannot be separated from the historical scene, *Madame Bovary* quite frequently uses succinct historical detail. This apt grasp of history does not characterize Emma, whose education has given her a confused sense of the past, where she imagines nobility and romantically unfortunate women, unrelated ("sans aucun rapport entre eux" [32])—something like the ruins of the demolished chateau behind d'Andervilliers's modern residence, the portraits of his ancestors, or the still living but senile duc de Laverdière, whom Emma also romanticizes: "He had lived at court and gone to bed with queens!" (42). But within the overall narrative recent history is aptly if sparingly evoked—not only the date 1812 mentioned at the outset (3) and occasional references to specific occurrences, epidemics, and uprisings but also indirect notations—some of the fare at the marquis's ball (Spanish and Rhine wines, Trafalgar pudding, a menu for the Napoleonic Wars), or Homais's Arab products, Emma's harem incense, and Lheureux's Algerian scarves, reminders of the invasion of Algeria, begun in 1830. Importantly—as is apparent in the speeches at the fair and in d'Andervilliers's political ambitions (in power under the restoration, now having waited long enough after the leftward turn of 1830 to stand for election [39])—the book is set in the antirevolutionary atmosphere of the middle and late years of the July Monarchy. The Bovarys do not arrive in Yonville until after 1835 (61); given the passage of years, it is an unlooked for irony that Homais obtains the Legion of Honor by renouncing his hypocritical republicanism—not long before another revolutionary upheaval (300, 303).[11]

But the life of the character Flaubert thought typical of scores of provincial Frenchwomen is more intimately affected by larger features of economic history that are only on the margins of Austen's fiction. First textiles: it is no accident that as a medical student Charles sees the workers, the skeins of cotton, and the dyes that pollute the river (7), that years later at the opera he and Emma are surrounded by cotton merchants (192, 196), that Homais bores us with talk of the importance of a new spinning mill or that Lieuvain (what a name—"vain place") does so concerning flax at the fair—that agricultural event that nonetheless is also dedicated to industry, commerce, and the fine arts (87, 126)! We may be bored by but cannot ignore the impact of the development of textiles on the Bovarys. Charles's father wastes his wife's dowry in textiles before doing so in farming (4), and on the last page the degradation of the Bovary family takes the horrible form of the reduction of their child to the level of a worker in a cotton mill.

Expansion of industry, implying the depletion of the countryside for urban concentration, necessitating improved transport to the cities—these historical forces also correspond to some of the most obsessive impulses of the novel and its protagonist. The negative description of Yonville (60–63), where the ignorant Charles thinks his wife may be happy, exemplifies the isolation and mediocrity of provincial France. In spite of the construction of a minor road used only occasionally by commercial traffic, Yonville has remained stationary due to its lack of roads—a lack that has a direct and terrible effect on Emma: her illness is finally precipitated when the faithless Rodolphe drives past her house. As the narrator explains, "Rodolphe had decided to go to Rouen. Since the Yonville road is the only one between La Huchette and Buchy, he was forced to pass through the village" (179).

The other person most instrumental in Emma's unhappiness is more closely involved with road transport in the country-city context. Lheureux drives Tellier out of the hotel business (two more ironically apt names—*heureux* means "happy"), with the goal of starting a new coach service in the Rouen region, thereby attempting to ruin Mme. Lefrançois's Hirondelle service and monopolizing "the entire Yonville trade," a dream he has partially realized by the end (116–17, 183, 301). His financial destruction of the Bovarys, moreover, involves a process in which modest provincial wealth is transformed at great suffering into low-level capitalist accumulation. As we shall see, the passages on his concentration of funds for capital investment are explicit and include the revelation that he and his partner, Vinçart, gain possession of a rural house belonging to Charles's family. Marx's analysis of an aspect of economic history in mid-nineteenth-century France, the expropriation of small landed property by moneylenders, bankers, notaries, and tax officials (the functions of Lheureux, Vinçart, Guillaumin, Binet) is an astonishing parallel.

The cleavages that make Emma and Charles vulnerable to sexual discord and financial manipulation also include contrary preferences regarding country and city. Each has been educated—in differently deformed ways—in Rouen. As a medical student Charles misses the country and is not tempted to travel to Paris; he had earlier been the object of scorn by the biased Rouen narrator because of his countrified dress and manner (1–3, 8, 35). Emma's city education certainly is a source of unhappiness in the boring countryside—she imagines her former schoolmates living in the excitement of cities (38) and thinks back to her romantic reading "in the silence of the dormitory, broken only by the faraway sound of some belated cab rolling along the boulevards" (33). That late cab on the boulevards foretells another. If Emma's love for Rodolphe is expressed in her dream of travel to exotic countries and cities as well as in practical preparations for real travel (169–70), the affair with Léon begins at the opera in Rouen, is consummated in the famous cab ride through every imaginable neighborhood there (210–12), and is perpetuated by her weekly and then more frequent trips there.

In spite of her fantasies about Paris, Emma never sets foot in the capital. This fact, together with more insistent notation of a hierarchy of values associated with the city (in medical care, fashion, foods, and so on), shows the extent to which, in contrast to *Pride and Prejudice,* the city-country dichotomy has become extreme. Travel to and experience in the provincial capital condition and structure both Emma's passion and her financial ruin. Remember that Lheureux's first approach to Emma is based on his weekly trips to the best stores in Rouen (89); the incriminating riding crop is bought there, and Lheureux's control over Emma grows when he surprises her there on Léon's arm (163, 234). Her suicide occurs the day after her last trip to Rouen in search of funds.

But Emma's experience of passion is also noticeably structured by the city-travel complex. This is already visible in the description of the hotel on the outskirts of Rouen where the Bovarys stop before the opera. Like those found outside all provincial towns, the inn retains the odors of a village and has a café on the street side and a garden on the country side (190). From this liminal setting Emma passes during her three-day idyll with Léon to a romantic, Venice-like experience of the city (ironically, for earlier the narrator had called Rouen a "sordid little Venice" [7, 220–22]). Thereafter, in the chapter on Emma's Thursday infidelities the narrator systematically describes her journey to and arrival in Rouen.

From afar she sees the entire city as in a painting—its ships, factories, foundries, churches, boulevards, neighborhoods—a totalizing perspective common in nineteenth-century literature, which obviously has modeled Emma's perception of the urban. Characteristically, she reacts to the accumulation of population in libidinal terms: "There was something intoxicating in the sight of that vast concentration of life, and her heart swelled as though the hundred and twenty thousand souls palpitating there had all sent her a breath of the passions she attributed to them. Her love expanded in that space" (227). This leads to a transfiguration of the old Norman city into an immense capital, a Babylon. More romantic exaltation, followed by Emma's recurrent pattern—pleasure and possession, inevitable departure, depression. The city-country division becomes the central locus for the expression of Emma's romance-reality problem. Her destiny is marked by the alienation of country and city that Marx and Engels dissected but that she experiences through the ideological filter of romantic literature.[12]

In contrast to *Pride and Prejudice*, then, the country-city relationship is experienced as exasperated desire, in a narrative centered not in the aristocracy and upper middle class, which transit easily between province and capital, but in the rural lower middle classes, which on the whole do not. In this respect the dynamics of class are as central to Flaubert's novel as to Austen's. In his severely pessimistic perspective, neither marriage nor its pseudo-aristocratic alternative, adultery, produces the personal and social gratifications engineered in *Pride and Prejudice*. Flaubert resembles Austen both in precision of financial detail and in irony concerning the same, but in *Madame Bovary* class aspiration and desire are the driving forces of tragedy.

The lower classes, the impoverished, are not much seen but are not wholly absent: the wet-nurse whose sordid misery only annoys Emma (79–81), the rural and urban poor who so preoccupy Bournisien that he is deaf to Emma's needs (95–99), the uncomprehending peasant Catherine Leroux at the fair, the blind beggar, finally Berthe. Her fate helps to explain the harried concern for money in the background of the main characters, typified by Charles's mother's warning about squandering fortunes and landing in the poorhouse (237). Her marriage, to a man who had profited from his personal charm "to pick up a dowry of sixty thousand francs being offered to him in the person of a hosier's daughter who had fallen in love with his appearance [*tournure*]" (3), illustrates the proposition. So does Charles's first marriage, to "a Dieppe bailiff's widow, who was forty-five and worth twelve hundred livres a year" (9, my translation). In both cases modest provincial wealth—in contract, Rodolphe is supposed to have fifteen thousand livres a year (110)—is not secure: Charles's mother's money is wasted by his father, as we noted, and his wife's is stolen by her notary. But perhaps these marriage partners get what they deserve, given their displacement of personal by monetary and other external features, snidely noted by the narrator. The remark has relevance for Charles's second marriage, too, despite his sexual attraction to Emma and his love for her, and despite the initial impression of her father's prosperity (11–12). Rouault is not impressed with Charles's personal qualities but is losing money and wants Emma taken off his hands without too much haggling over the dowry (20).

A shepherd's granddaughter with a fancy education (according to Charles's jealous first wife [15]), Emma exemplifies the difficulties of a woman from a rural background who aspires to aristocratic wealth and style. In *Pride and Prejudice* Elizabeth is somewhat deficient in the "accomplishments" praised by Lady Catherine and possessed by the London-educated Bingley sisters, since her musical talent is mediocre and her training in visual arts nil. But she possesses that "more substantial" feature specified by Darcy, "the improvement of her mind by extensive reading" (26), in addition to the London influence of her aunt. By contrast, Emma's convent education, though set in Rouen, hardly exposes her to urban experience. Her accomplishments, *petit bourgeois* imitations of the aristocratic ones, serve her marriage only intermittently and sometimes further her adulteries (especially her "piano lessons" in Rouen with Léon). And her readings in romantic literature and cheap fiction in the convent constitute not an "improvement of her mind" but an immense mystification of political and social history, a novelistic version of

Marx's analysis of the creation of deluded consciousness by ideological means.[13]

In particular, the keepsake books smuggled into the convent create an appetite for aristocratic luxury—images of English ladies, servants, carriages, elegant greyhounds, to which is added an oriental exoticism that threatens to engulf the reader but is quickly seen as absurd: "And you too were there, sultans with long pipes . . . and especially you, wan lurid landscapes of dithyrambic regions, which often show us simultaneously palm trees, pines, tigers to the right, a lion on the left" (33, my translation). Emma's greyhound, Djali, significantly lost during the move to Yonville, is one index of the literal way in which she tries to live out such fantasies, she who occasionally reverts to her country roots but generally tries to act like a duchess, calling her husband and mother-in-law peasants, who charms Charles and Léon by her refinement and appears as a Parisienne to Rodolphe (113). With such style and aspirations, how can she be satisfied by her mediocre husband, rural wedding, depressing house in Tostes, secondhand *boc* that when refurbished almost resembles a tilbury (the kind of vehicle Rodolphe owns)?

In each of the novel's three parts, a passionate experience with a man—fleetingly with the viscount at La Vaubyessard, then with Rodolphe and Léon—expresses, in progressively less exalted form, Emma's class aspiration as well as her closely related desires for love and sexual gratification. Although d'Andervilliers's chateau is of modern construction, he is no male Lady Catherine, rather an up-to-date Darcy, distributing firewood in winter, calling for better roads in the district, preparing his candidacy (39–40). Emma's experience at La Vaubyessard (40–48) corresponds not to such political activity but to her idea of aristocratic life—exquisite furnishings, food, clothing, people who travel in Italy, race horses in England, and by their secret notes engage in illicit romance. At points the use of *vous* and *on* seems to draw us again into Emma's enchantment. Even though these words do not appear in the description of the richest men, it is hard to tell if their brutal fascination belongs to Emma's consciousness alone or is also projected between narrator and reader: "In their indifferent eyes there was the placidity that comes from the daily gratification of the passions; and their manners did not hide the special brutality deriving from half-easy triumphs, that test strength and satisfy vanity—the handling of thoroughbred horses and the company of lost women" (44, my translation).

But (unlike Austen's Pemberley chapter), here the narrator's perspective is normally distinct from and much superior to Emma's, particularly in noting the class dimensions of her experience. D'Andervilliers invites her because she is attractive and doesn't greet him like a peasant, "so at the château it was decided that the young couple could be invited without going beyond the limits of gracious condescension or causing anyone any embarrassment" (39). So much, from the start, for Emma's longings to participate in the aristocratic life: from the perspective of the chateau she is fixed not as a peasant but as below the sphere of noble "condescension." At the ball the sight of peasants gives her an acute remembrance of her childhood on the farm, which she wipes out by concentrating on the delicious immediacy of the moment—the maraschino ice, the gilt spoon between her teeth. How effectively does Flaubert's writing allow class dynamics and Emma's obliteration of same to appear in a moment of sensous and luxurious pleasure. But the effort to "prolong the illusion of that luxurious life which she would soon have to abandon" (46) gives way to inevitable departure, the return to her mediocre surroundings, the sense of a gap in her life. Then begins Emma's characteristic experience of time as empty and repetitive, counting the weeks that pass, until a year goes by and the anticipated reinvitation does not come. How different this is from the "gentry time" of town and hunting seasons that organizes the action in *Pride and Prejudice,* allowing Bingley and Darcy to return and make their proposals (helped, we have seen, by the city business time of Gardiner).

After the move to Yonville, the affairs with Rodolphe and Léon appear in part as degraded enactments of the aristocratic fantasy. Emma's relationship with Léon is delayed, giving attention to Rouen and to the mediocre circumstances of their hotel assignations and allowing the famous sardonic judgment: "Every notary bears within himself the remains [*débris*] of a poet" (251). This is borne out when Charles receives the wedding announcement of "Monsieur Léon Dubois . . . notary at Yvetot" (295–96). To Emma Léon incarnated a romantically poetic version of an aristocratic ideal, but at the end he chooses conventional middle-class solutions for family and work in a provincial setting.

The first of her lovers, robust and elegant, powerfully sexual and wealthy, Rodolphe is the closest Emma will come to the richest among d'Andervilliers's guests, those adept at dominating horses and women. (The narrator remarks on the numerous women he has had, and he of course first possesses Emma during their horseback ride.) But only the vulgar would mistake his style of dress and manipulation of romantic clichés for real rebellion against middle-class mores (119*ff*.), and it is not indifferent that his "bourgeois common sense" is opposed to Emma's exaltation (147). Reminding us of Austen's tactics, his name, Rodolphe Boulanger de la Huchette, somewhat ludicrously inscribes a social contradiction. In spite of the narrator's disclaimer (110), the "de" inevitably suggests pretensions to nobility, whereas Rodolphe sounds German and romantic and fits well with the language of passion, dreams, magnetism, and preexistence that he uses on Emma at the fair. But the rest of his name includes a double allusion to that most unaristocratic of foods, bread, *boulanger* meaning "baker," and *huche*, "bread trough" or "bread bin." Significantly, the narrative in the fair chapter counterpoints his seduction of Emma not only with prizes for pigs and fertilizers but also with Lieuvain's absurd disquisition on the role of the baker in producing food "for the poor as well as the rich" (125). Lieuvain's and Rodolphe's discourses occur literally on different levels, but both are lies, masking in different ways social and economic separation and antagonism—Lieuvain's in political terms, Rodolphe's in the erotic register mystified by romanticism. He is a fittingly ironic object for Emma's desire, a rich but ungenerous bourgeois replacement, given away by a fake name, for her impossible dream of aristocratic life.

Even considering the Pemberley chapter, *Pride and Prejudice* is chaste in its evocation of material objects and sexuality, whereas *Madame Bovary* is notorious for its thematics of passion and its abundance of description. Differences in temperament and national culture may go far to explain this contrast, but there is certainly a broader historical explanation. In *Madame Bovary* desire is both liberated and alienated, not least in its association with the myriad objects that throng the pages of a book already heavily marked by the culture of commodities.

Sexual acts or parts are not of course explicitly described in *Madame Bovary* (although one element, the names of prize winners at the fair, comes close: "Race porcine, prix *ex aequo:* à MM. Lehérissé et Cullembourg; soixante francs!").[14] Rather the novel may seem provocative in suggesting sexual activity that is not described, as when Rodolphe, bored with Emma, seeks "other pleasures" (*jouissances*) and turns her into "something compliant and corrupt" (165), and later in the cab ride. Emma's youthful sensuousness is nicely evoked in the opening chapters—the scenes in which she pricks her finger, provokes Charles by tonguing her glass, and blushes as their bodies make contact. Much indicates that this erotic potential is frustrated by Charles, and the scene at the end of the first part, in which she pricks her finger on her wedding bouquet, then burns it, producing imagery of a mythic and threatening intensity (burning bush, black butterflies), is doubly pregnant, announcing that Emma is expecting (although Berthe is hardly a love child) and indicating the degree of her sexual anger. What ensues—her exaltation first with Rodolphe and then Léon, the betrayal by each of them, her discovery in adultery of "all the dullness of marriage" (251) and of the incapacity of language to communicate passion (165)—all of this is clear and oft discussed, as is the modeling of her passion by her reading.

Desire is also mediated by and in the world of manufactured objects. As we have seen, in *Pride and Prejudice* few external objects are described, and none in detail. Those that are evoked involve property. Collins is ever present to translate them into money equivalents, but Elizabeth can safely ignore Mrs. Reynold's similar statements—everything tells her, and us, that the property at Pemberley represents great wealth and superb taste. In *Madame Bovary* the many man-made objects—as Claude Duchet has shown, the concept hardly applies any more to persons or scenery—also express socioeconomic themes: Charles's country clothes, Rouault's farm, the dress of those who attend Emma's wedding, the ostentation at La Vaubyessard, the unattractive village of Yonville. Even the objects evoked at the end of the dense paragraph describing the unattractive house where Emma begins her married life have meaning: "a big dilapidated room. . . . filled with old, rusty iron, empty barrels, broken agricultural implements and a number of other dusty objects whose uses were impossible to guess" (27). The contrast between this kind of writing and the uncluttered space of *Pride and Prejudice* does not derive from some stylistic obsession in Flaubert. We are here in a world where the rural and agricultural are waning in importance, a world overflowing with manufactured things so numerous as to defy comprehension.[15]

In this perspective even such a strange assemblage as Charles's famous hat (2) is significant, perhaps even emblematic. For Duchet it is the quintessential manufactured object, recalling such instances of kitsch as Emma's bouquet and wedding cake. Besides, as Tony Tanner has seen, its heteroclite shapelessness accords with the disconnected upbringing and education that Charles receives, not to speak of its forlorn and ridiculous sexual quality (various too thin "cordons," "sacs," and "glands" hang from it).

Moving from this negative example, we see that the libidinal dimension of things that we glimpsed in the Pemberley chapter, objects desired with an ardor that is all but sexual in intensity, is greatly magnified but debased in *Madame Bovary,* in keeping with a far more pervasive confusion of the personal and the economic. Marx's thinking on the alienating force of commodities—innumerable objects mediating deformed personal relations, the creation of ever increasing desires for such objects, "object-bondage" to the point that what one is is conceived as what one owns—is (contemporaneous and) consonant.

Binet's numerous useless napkin rings look like both an absurd protest against a world filled with such objects and a rather ludicrous replication of it. This may provide an interesting reflection on art for art tendencies in the nineteenth century: Binet is described as having "the jealousy of an artist and the egotism of a bourgeois" (65), and in Emma's visit to him at the end (264) he is shown making a wooden copy of an ivory, formed of complex geometric shapes, indescribable, and having no useful function. The link with Charles's hat, but also, in parodic form, with Flaubert's interest in the pure work of art, unsubmitted to the order of the useful and the commercial, must be noted. So also must the description of Binet's pleasure in his work and its product as nearly orgasmic and the supposition by Emma's nosy neighbors that she is talking about money and/or sex with the notably cold tax collector, who indeed reacts in horrified fashion.

This scene with Binet is strategically withheld until Emma's last day of life, for it is indeed she who most invests objects with desire, as it is she who most confuses economic realities with affective experience. Thus in the emptiness after La Vaubyessard she merges in "her longing [*désir*] . . . the pleasures of luxury with the joys of the heart, elegant customs with refined feelings" (51), and after Léon's departure she experiences "carnal desires, her longing for money and the melancholy of her . . . passion" as a single terrible suffering (94). In search of money at the end, she gives Lheureux the impression that she is trying to seduce him, perhaps makes such an effort with Binet, angrily rejects Guillaumin's clumsy sexual advances, then goes to Rodolphe in what the narrator judges an unconscious prostitution (267). After his refusal her madness consists in the utter confusion of love and money: "She no longer remembered the cause of her horrible state: the question of money. She was now suffering only through her love" (271).

But Emma has been indulging in and being victimized by such mistakes all along, in the form of the numerous articles purchased from Lheureux, who perfectly fits Marx's argument about the capitalist's stimulation of desires as needs. These items accompany, mediate, and displace Emma's quest for gratification with her lovers. Lheureux calls them her "fantaisies," "curiosités féminines," and "caprices" (108, 163, 219). Eventually she cannot do without his services, and with every new loan a "horizon of realizable whims [*fantaisies*]" opens up before her (224, 236)—that is, more of these objects to purchase. Here passionate love for another person has been replaced by the acquisition of supposedly luxurious articles. This may engender an illusory sense of ownership—in their weekly assignations she and

Léon feel that they own the familiar objects in the hotel room, just as Léon has the satisfaction of finally possessing a real mistress (228–29). As suggested in chapter 1, the extreme of such confusion of the personal and the "objective" occurs when one identifies with one's possessions, which is Emma's fate at the time of the seizure; as the bailiff and witnesses examine her things, "her whole existence, down to its most intimate details, was laid open like a dissected corpse" (255). Her life, embodied in her possessions, becomes a cadaver before she herself does.

In the face of this loss of all her *things* Emma goes desperately to the men who will refuse her. Somewhat as in the scene with Binet, in the last encounters with Guillaumin and Rodolphe their luxurious possessions, previously undescribed, exacerbate her need. Her arrival at La Huchette and the property itself are evoked in greater detail than on her first matinal visit (141, 267–68). And when Rodolphe rejects her pleas she is infuriated at the sight of the many costly objects he owns, the sale of some of which could solve her financial problems. Just before, when entering Guillaumin's house, she was less angry and more deluded. At the opening of the second part the notary's house is called the most beautiful in the area (61–62), but Emma goes there only on the last day of her life. The brief description of the English elegance of Guillaumin's dining room and the costly ostentation of his dress (261–62) have a great impact on her and on us. Pathetically, she thinks the kind of thought that has characterized and destroyed her life: "This is the kind of dining room I ought to have [*Voilà une salle à manger . . . comme il m'en faudrait une*]". The contrast between Elizabeth, at the opening of volume 3 of *Pride and Prejudice*, and Emma, at the end of part 3 of Flaubert's novel, attains its most painful form.

The different position of the visits to houses and estates is indeed revelatory. In both books the appeal of property comes first, but for Elizabeth it is followed by marriage to the owner. The most revealing contrast is not simply between Pemberley and La Vaubyessard but between Pemberley and the passionate investment that Emma, deprived of La Vaubyessard, makes in that privileged article found near there, the cigar case. The case draws together many strands of our analysis, concerning desire and things, class and economics, country and city, the role of education, reading, feminine "accomplishments" and insight, narrator and protagonist:

> She would look at it, open it and sniff its lining, which was impregnated with an odor of verbena and tobacco. Whose was it? . . . The viscount's. A present from his mistress, perhaps. It had been embroidered [*On avait brodé cela*] on a charming little rosewood frame, kept hidden from everyone else, which had occupied many long hours, and over which the curls of some pensive young lady [*la travailleuse pensive*] had swayed gently as she worked. A breath of love had passed through the mesh of the canvas; each stroke of the needle had fixed a hope or a memory there, and all those intertwined silken threads were the continuation [*continuité*] of a single silent passion. And then the viscount had taken it with him one morning. What had they talked about while it lay on broad mantelpieces, between vases of flowers and Pompadour clocks? She was in Tostes. He was now in Paris [*à Paris, maintenant, là-bas!*]. Paris! What was Paris like? What a titanic [*démesuré*] name! She repeated it to herself softly, for the pleasure of hearing it; it resounded in her ears like the great bell of a cathedral; it blazed forth before her eyes everywhere, even on [*jusque sur*] the labels of her pomade jars. (49)

The case is a prime example of how a single artifact, in contradistinction to the entirety of an estate, can crystallize desire. Indeed it is inconceivable that in *Pride and Prejudice* any individual fabricated object, as opposed to, say, Darcy's portrait, should be evoked so closely or have such evocative power. Its sensuous presence, its appeal to imagination and emotion, are clear. Even more important, Emma conceives of it as fabricated almost literally out of love. In this passionate labor theory of value ("many long hours," "the pensive worker"), the case appears as an anticommodity, a wholly personal product, in its physical constitution exteriorizing not alienated socioeconomic relations but the perfect union of love, which seems to have passed through it, been fixed in it, finally become identified with it.

All of this is profoundly deceptive; paradoxically, the case's imaginative power derives from delusions and alienations in

Emma. For her it is a quintessentially aristocratic object, made of silk and bearing arms like a carriage door (47), hence participating in that class and money code of vehicles mentioned earlier. But it also carries class connotations as being the product of one of the feminine accomplishments, aristocratic in Emma's eyes, attacked as falsely pretentious by Charles's jealous first wife, the ironically named Héloïse, who calls Emma not only "une demoiselle de ville" but "une brodeuse," which refers to embroidery but also suggests having "a glib tongue" (15). We have seen too that Emma's clumsiness with a needle is more expressive of sexual need and rebellion than of middle-class domesticity—no wonder she imagines the embroidered case as representing both passion and nobility. But, most importantly, the case turns out *not* to be unique, since she later buys one "just like it" for Rodolphe (164, my translation). Its fabrication likely has less to do with the young noblewomen she imagines than with the textile industry, which is glimpsed at points and which, precisely as a result of Emma's unrealizable desires, swallows her daughter at the end.

Similar contradictions emerge regarding country and city, the case giving rise in the following pages (49–59) to Emma's most intense fantasy about Paris. She imagines the case together with Pompadour clocks (the style Homais later chooses to give himself class [298]), but when she thinks of the viscount in Paris it is in connection with the labels on her makeup jars, distributed from the capital for purchase by provincial *petites bourgeoises* such as she. She herself is oblivious to such economic notes, as later when she hears the farmers begin their trip to Paris, thinking "They'll be there tomorrow!" without reflecting that they are making an exhausting night journey for commercial ends.

The remainder of the chapter (importantly the last in part 1) shows us Emma's flawed conception of Paris as opening again to the basic problems of her life. The narration is at pains to emphasize the incompleteness of her vision of the city. Even after considerable reading, she is interested only in ambassadors, duchesses, writers, and actresses, romantically conceived: "As for the rest . . . it was lost to her; it had no specific location and scarcely seemed to exist at all." As in the chapter on her education, various publications play a role in the creation of this inaccurate view. Her guides to Paris include street maps, women's magazines on fashion, society, and the arts, and novelists—Sue, Balzac, Sand. She reads Sue for descriptions of furnishings, the others in search of "imaginary gratifications of her desires." Doubtless each of these different writers has better uses; nonetheless Flaubert's novel is again insistent on the role that literature, along with utilitarian and commercial publications, may play for the unintelligent reader in the creation, Marx would say the *production,* of deluded consciousness, emotionally estranged, economically ignorant. To the point that when Emma's "own" voice surfaces through the indirect mode of narration, it seems a parroting of literature, an echoing of Balzacian and Hugolian clichés: "What was this Paris like? What a measureless name!"; "Paris, vaster than the ocean."

Typically, too, the power of the cigar case to evoke Paris wanes, and Emma's conflicts, confusions, and contradictions return—city and "boring countryside," luxury and love, the provincial and the exotic, the passionate and the domestic—the last represented most tellingly, we have seen, in the case of the pregnant wife who burns her wedding bouquet. Duchet notes that since the bouquet is one of the novel's mass-produced items, Emma's act has not only sexual but also socioeconomic significance. In the clear space of *Pride and Prejudice,* country and city, class and money, "objects" of desire and possession have a magical adequacy for Elizabeth's happiness. In the world of *Madame Bovary,* the desires and delusions of Flaubert's protagonist are mobilized by the cigar case, as mystifying a fetish as any commodity Marx ever analyzed.

The example of Emma's voice as a Hugolian cliché reminds us that the themes treated above are furthered in both novels by narrative tactics that are complex and of great interest. *Pride and Prejudice* and *Madame Bovary* use—though finally in opposing ways—a superior, ironic, at most points "objective" or "omniscient" voice, which is nonetheless variously characterized by indeterminacies of stance and meaning and which is set in unresolved relation with a more personal and limited perspective.

The narrative in both books involves the wide-ranging information that seems impossible in real life but is essential to traditional storytelling. Austen's narrator unequivocally conveys facts about the past lives, personal qualities, economic concerns, and love interests of the characters. Sometimes information is delayed for greater effect (for example, concerning the Gardiners) or to complicate the action (Elizabeth's misjudgment of Wickham). As the last indicates, the narrator's superior knowledge is crucial to advance the central love story: while observing Bingley's attention to Jane early in the story, for example, Elizabeth "was far from suspecting that she was herself becoming an object of some interest in the eyes of" Darcy (15).

The difference between the limited vision of Flaubert's characters and the range of his narrative perspective is more marked. Despite the subjective opening voice (of which more shortly), elsewhere the narrative seems at will to be capable of omniscience. There are many explanations of what individual characters do not know, frequent definitive formulations, ranging from Léon's pusillanimity to the portrait of the singer Lagardy, necessary background information, for example, concerning Charles's family. The expansive scope of the narrative can be illustrated by a detail—after Emma's burial it is indicated that both Rodolphe and Léon, who did not attend the funeral, are sleeping peacefully (294)—or by a symphonic sequence—the fair chapter.

Superiority in narrative perspective allows for negative judgments on characters' deficiencies, which can take the form of direct criticism (frequent in *Pride and Prejudice*), broad comedy (Collins, Mrs. Bennet), scorn (Mrs. Bennet again, Léon, Homais), many strains of irony. Irony in Flaubert is often devastating but is also sometimes insidious when it is expressed through his now famous indirect style. Charles's reaction after Héloïse's death and Emma's romanticization of the duc de Laverdière appear all the more inappropriate for being expressed in the third person through the narrative voice that has previously explained Héloïse's shock at the theft of her money and shown the duke drooling into his plate.

The effect of such indirect presentation can range from revelation of a character's mediocrity to withering criticism and can involve third-person reporting of speech as well as thoughts. Hence Charles's whining first wife: "She would begin to tell him of her woes: he was neglecting her, he was in love with another woman! She should have listened when people warned her she'd be unhappy! And then she would end by asking him for some kind of tonic to make her feel better, and a little more love" (9). Hence also Homais, who delivers his pretentious religious opinions in his own voice (67) but whose pompous defense of Racine's art despite the "fanaticism" of *Athalie* is given in third-person form (77–78) and whose hypocrisy is reemphasized at the end through a hilarious melange of his speech and writing and the narrator's critical commentary:

> He was the happiest of fathers, the most fortunate of men.
>
> But no! [*Erreur!*] He was gnawed by a secret ambition: he wanted the cross of the Legion of Honor. He had ample qualifications:
>
> 1° Conspicuously distinguished himself, during the cholera epidemic, by boundless devotion to duty; 2° published, and at my own expense, various works useful to the public, such as . . . (and he referred to his treatise entitled *Cider: Its Fabrication and Its Effects;* in addition, observations on the wooly aphis that he had sent to the Academy; his volume of statistics, and even his pharmacist's thesis); not to mention my membership in several learned societies (he belonged to one).
>
> "Finally," he exclaimed, executing a pirouette, "the mere fact of my conspicuous service in fire-fighting!"
>
> Then he began to incline toward the government. He secretly rendered great services to the Prefect during elections. In short, he sold himself, prostituted himself. (300, my translation)

No misinterpretation is possible here—the negative presentation of Homais is clear and all the more disturbing that he is no fool and about to be awarded the Legion of Honor. Nonetheless the passage is disconcerting in its form, in its outrageous mixing of persons, speech, and writing, the discourse of narrator and character, which in more subtle instances has been found so disturbing in the novel.

Indeed, despite the "omniscience" noted above, Flaubert's use of the indirect mode is so pervasive and subtle, particularly in presenting his protagonist, that critics have correctly identified that mode as a major source of ambiguity, of narrative indeterminacy. At various points we have suggested how the device is used to draw the reader ambiguously into Emma's experience—her romantic reading and her evening at La Vaubyessard but also her longings for the ideal man (35), her continuing boredom and yearnings with Léon (245), and so on. In these and other passages it is often hard to separate Emma's consciousness from the narrative voice, difficult to decide whether the narrator expresses criticism or sympathy, or both, about her. In the face of such ambiguity, Dominic LaCapra concludes that the novel is ideologically subversive in troubling the supposed clarity of accepted norms of ethical evaluation and of narrative communication.[16]

Recent criticism is acutely aware of similar ambiguities in Austen, although perhaps overstating the case somewhat for *Pride and Prejudice*. Compared to Flaubert, Austen's use of the indirect mode in this novel is relatively infrequent and relatively unambiguous. Yet these critics are right to assert that her writing is less univocal than has often been thought. Take for example Lady Lucas's "report" on Bingley to the Bennet ladies:

> Her report was highly favourable. Sir William had been delighted with him. He was quite young, wonderfully handsome, extremely agreeable, and to crown the whole, he meant to be at the next assembly with a large party. Nothing could be more delightful! To be fond of dancing was a certain step towards falling in love; and very lively hopes of Mr. Bingley's heart were entertained. (5)

The basic meaning is clear: Lady Lucas reports on an attractive young man to the delight of Mrs. Bennet and her daughters. But there is more. We are at the beginning, and receive our first information on Bingley from someone who has met him—who however is not Lady Lucas, since she transmits the "second-hand intelligence" of her husband's impressions. We do not yet know that Sir William is a fool, or that Bingley is a man of inconsequent qualities, or that he will turn out to be relatively unimportant, the match with him being overshadowed by Darcy and Elizabeth's marriage.

Within the quoted passage itself the indirect mode makes for small but not insignificant ambiguities. The narrator's discourse seems to be located in the first sentence and last clause; in between, the speech of Lady Lucas is reported indirectly. But "Nothing could be more delightful!" could appear in quotes, since it sounds like the direct expression of a happy reaction. Who "says" it? Lady Lucas or one or more of the Bennets? The "lively hopes" are not "located" either but apparently express a general reaction of all the ladies. Finally, the statement linking dancing and falling in love is more interesting than as the allusion to rituals of mating in Austen's England that traditional criticism has (correctly) seen. Is it "said" by someone or "thought" by one or all? Does the narrator present it in her or his own voice? If so, does it have the ironic quality of the "universal" truth enunciated in the book's famous opening sentences? Like those sentences, in the context of the whole work the *dicton* about dancing takes on more complex resonances. Darcy and Elizabeth will marry, despite his early refusal to dance. (Later when attracted to her he does ask her to dance, and it is she who refuses.) Thus the *dicton* seems at first to reflect a certain female silliness, then to be contradicted and later to be fulfilled. Similarly, as has been pointed out, it is difficult to harmonize the irony of the opening sentences with the conclusion, which happily realizes them.

The happy ending is related to the narrator's partiality for Elizabeth. Unlike Emma Bovary, Elizabeth is capable of self-analysis and growth in understanding; though criticized, she is not the victim of the cutting irony applied to others (and neither are the Gardiners or Darcy). Although the narrative is normally distinct from her consciousness, it is nonetheless capable of rendering her thoughts and emotions indirectly, particularly regarding Darcy: "How it could occur a second time therefore was very odd!" (frequent "chance" meetings with him); "That he should have been in love with her for so many months!" (after the first proposal); "How could she deny that credit to his assertions, in one instance, which she had been obliged to give in the other?" (on rereading his letter); "It would be dreadful!" (to encounter

him at Pemberley); "And his behaviour, so strikingly altered,—
what could it mean?" (after encountering him there [125, 134,
144, 166, 172]). Thus juxtaposed, these passages create an amusing, smilingly ironic effect—as the heroine edges toward conscious acceptance of a love that she unavowedly desires.

At the same time, the narrator marks the progress of Elizabeth's insight, earlier calling her "less clear-sighted perhaps,"
later stressing her "more extensive information" (104, 229). At
points, indeed, her knowledge is nearly coextensive with that of
the narrator, for example, in a passage in which Miss Bingley's
reference to Wickham brings pain to Darcy and his sister, apprehension to Elizabeth, and some confusion to the reader:

> Not a syllable had ever reached [Miss Bingley] of Miss Darcy's
> meditated elopement. To no creature had it been revealed,
> where secrecy was possible, except to Elizabeth; and from all
> Bingley's connections her brother was particularly anxious to
> conceal it, from that very wish which Elizabeth had long ago
> attributed to him, of their becoming hereafter her own. He
> had certainly formed such a plan, and without meaning that it
> should affect his endeavour to separate him from Miss Bennet,
> it is probable that it might add something to his lively concern
> for the welfare of his friend. (184)

Elizabeth and the narrator here have knowledge of which Miss
Bingley is ignorant. The intricacy of the writing, moreover, makes
this a rare instance in which it is difficult to separate Elizabeth's
views from those of the narrator. We can puzzle out the pro-
nouns, realizing that "her own" refers to Georgiana, which implies a plan by Darcy to marry Miss Bingley. Elizabeth's attribu-
tion of this goal to him is noted and reiterated: "He had certainly
formed such a plan." Is this Elizabeth's view, or the narrator's? If
the latter, it seems contradicted by evidence throughout that
Darcy cares little for Miss Bingley's charms. Yet the sentence
seems to end in the register of the narrator by switching from the
pluperfect to a present probability: "it is probable." However we
may try to resolve these difficulties, the passage is a small but
revealing example of the indeterminacies of meaning that can be
produced when the discourse of narrator and protagonist draw
together.

As noted earlier, ideologically oriented criticism has related such ambiguities to the complexities of Austen's class situation as imaged in her texts. In spite of the book's lucid dissection of class, money, and marriage, there is the investment of value in Elizabeth, the Gardiners, and finally Darcy, the critique of rigid aristocracy and pseudogentry alike, the libidinal presentation of Pemberley, the reconciliations of the conclusion. In the light of these discrepancies, it is important to remark another, and quite fundamental, discontinuity—namely, the stunning fact that the "omniscient" narrator suddenly at the end turns out to be, or is metamorphosed into, merely an individual: "Happy for all her maternal feelings was the day on which Mrs. Bennet got rid of her two most deserving daughters. With what delighted pride she afterwards visited Mrs. Bingley and talked of Mrs. Darcy may be guessed. I wish I could say, for the sake of her family, that . . ." (265–66). Here the comic potential of Mrs. Bennet persists. So does the appeal to the reader that we remarked at several key moments. Most importantly, for the only time, the narrator speaks to us as another person, of superior insight no doubt, but limited to the perspective of the desiring and narrating "I"—"I wish I could say. . . ." What was radical exposure of social contradiction through a superior ironic vision becomes amused participation in the wished-for reconciliation of the concluding marriages. We might say that what appears as a narratological and epistemological honesty—only an individual, as we believe, can tell a story—here merges with a social and historical fantasy.

Flaubert's procedure is the opposite and for all its complications can be seen to be integrally related to his novel's refusal of happy personal and societal endings. Elsewhere I have argued that the book's scandalous narrative structure, that of a biased opening voice abruptly replaced by a mainly impersonal and virtually all-knowing narrator, parallels Marx's effort to overcome subjective, ideologically mystified modes of consciousness in favor of objective, "scientific" appreciations of reality.[17] The difficulty of this process is not minimized by Marx; so too the problem, the apparent impossibility of transcending the limitations of individual knowledge, is foregrounded early in *Madame Bovary:* "It would now be impossible for any of us to remember anything about him," says the initial voice of Charles (6, my translation). This impossibility is belied by the evocation of Charles's family and childhood that precedes it and by the remainder of the novel. Having inscribed a difficulty, even an impossibility, of narration, the novel nonetheless emerges. Note that this is not as contradictory as it might appear. The impossibility characterizes "any of us" (*aucun de nous*). The opening voice is not only subjective but collective, representing a markedly prejudiced group consciousness, a kind of class voice—bourgeois, provincial, but urban as well. In contrast, the major narrative will be largely impersonal and largely independent of class bias or identification.

An impersonal, classless, and omniscient narrative is to be sure not achieved absolutely. We have remarked the obscuring of the last meeting with Binet and the ambiguities created by the indirect mode, not to speak of the instances in which the narrative is rendered less univocal by such words as *perhaps* and *probably,* in which the narrator seems to formulate personal opinions. The subjective origin of narration and the participating imaginative activity of the reader are thereby, and inevitably, recognized.

But the individual and the imaginative are the starting points for perspectives that can become objective and historical, just as at a few points Flaubert's narration achieves the semblance at least of historical reality, notably in the description of Yonville (61–63), conveyed in the present tense and in impersonal form, historically, geographically, and geologically specific, aspiring to the status of real existence: "This is where [*On est ici*] Normandy, Picardy and the Ile-de-France come together"; "And nothing else has changed in Yonville since the events that we are about to relate [*que l'on va raconter*]." Elsewhere, without intrusive comment, narrative objectivity displays situations to which individuals, particularly the protagonist, are oblivious—including the class and economic aspects of the encounters mentioned earlier between Emma and the wet-nurse and Bournisien. Finally, at important points the narrator reveals full knowledge of the people and events that cause Emma's ruin in a structure paralleling Marx's arguments about the destructive economic activity that constitutes the hidden reality of bourgeois society.

Although dissimilar in almost all respects, Emma and Charles share an inability to confront the reality of such economic destruction. Emma's education is devoid of economic content, so it is a particular irony that among the wares Lheureux first displays for her are Algerian scarves, English needles, and coconut shell eggcups (90). This echoes in middle-class commercial terms the attractions of English nobility and exotic scenes in Emma's girlhood reading. Like her, Charles tends to put off thinking about the economic threat represented by Lheureux. Lheureux himself is a frightening embodiment of devotion to the profit motive; Marx could not have imagined worse. When he realizes that the riding crop for Rodolphe has compromised Emma, he exults, "Ah, I've got you!" (163), and when she comes to him before her suicide, he claims to be working like a slave (*nègre*), says he hardly lent her money out of charity (*pour l'amour de Dieu*), and dismisses her with a cruel "What do I care" (*Je m'en moque pas mal!* [254–55]). The scornful dismissal of religious values, Lheureux's propensity for an ethnically and racially biased "geopolitical" vocabulary (elsewhere involving Jews, Americans, and Arabs),[18] correspond to Marx's analysis of the tactics and disguises of the economic exploiter. Lheureux of course attends the funeral and barely keeps a dry eye.

Lheureux's—and even more Guillaumin's—activities are hidden from those they ruin and, to a considerable extent, from the reader; the "omniscience" of the narrator amounts to an obscuring, then revelation, of their destructive business, for *us*. Lheureux is first only a dry-goods dealer, then a somewhat sinister figure whose past is unknown, then more and more clearly an exploiting moneylender (68, 89, 163, 182–85). Emma ignores his questions about Tellier (90), and Homais is too busy at the fair to listen to Madame Lefrançois's story of how Tellier is being ruined by him (117). More "important" things are on the horizon in that chapter: political propaganda, sexual seduction. In our first reading, do we respond to the story of Tellier's fate as inattentively as Homais? Only during Emma's illness does the narrator explain that Lheureux's commerce and moneylending are intended to amass the capital for his investments and efforts to control transport (183), still later that he is also a pawnbroker (246). More

sinister is the indication that the sale of Charles's country property
has been hidden by Lheureux, becoming known only later (234–
36). Conscious by now of Lheureux's activities but not yet having
reached the end of the story, we here have a disturbing premoni-
tion. Still, the narrator reserves one of his clearest explanations
for the scene in which Emma makes her last effort with Lheureux:
"However, as a result of buying, not paying, borrowing, signing
promissory notes and then renewing them, so that they grew
larger each time they fell due, she had finally built up a capital for
Monsieur Lheureux, and he was now eager to have it to use in his
speculations" (253). A fundamental mechanism of capitalism at a
low level, an economic process at the expense of the human, is
what the omniscient narrator finally reveals.

The process is more surprising in the case of Guillaumin, mentioned only in passing throughout most of the second and third
parts. Were we alert, we might register that the source of Madame Lefrançois's information about Tellier's ruin is Théodore,
Guillaumin's servant. Much later we learn that Guillaumin fur-
thers Lheureux's investments (183) and that he draws up the two
powers-of-attorney that Emma obtains (220, 238). (The first notary in the book, of course, is the one who absconds with the
money of Charles's first wife, causing her death, a narrative
foreshadowing of the novel's underlying economic action [16].)
Still no mention of Guillaumin's involvement in the manipulation of Emma—until again on the last day, as she explains her
situation to him:

> Monsieur Guillaumin already knew about it, for he was se-
> cretly allied with the dry-goods dealer, who was always ready to
> put up capital for the mortgage loans that he was asked to
> arrange.
> He thereby knew (and better than she) the long story of her
> promissory notes, for small sums at first, bearing the names of
> various people as endorsers, made out for long terms, falling
> due on different dates and continually being renewed until the
> day when Lheureux, having gathered all the protests of non-
> payment, asked his friend Vinçart to institute the necessary
> legal proceedings in his name, not wishing to be regarded as a
> shark by his fellow townsmen [concitoyens]. (261)

Again the low-level financial activity, expanding into the wider areas of banking and real estate, is revealed. Marx would have smiled at the subversion of the personal and political ("friend," "fellow citizens"). The issue of knowledge is again stressed. The narrator reveals what he had withheld and what Emma has not glimpsed and will never know—and likely what we did not realize either. And the superior knowledge, as in Marx, concerns economic exploitation—to the death: "He therefore knew (and better than she) . . . ."

After Emma's death the profit motive is generalized as everyone takes advantage of Charles's situation: "Alors chacun se mit à *profiter*" (295). Correspondingly, the narrative mode of historical reality returns on the last page, the novel reemphasizing the economic and social transformations, with their grotesque impact on individuals, that are its true subject. In this later and more sombre historical period lucidly dissected, no dream of class reconciliation, no realization of desire that affords personal and societal satisfaction, is possible. The hypocritical Homais, who has ostracized Berthe, flourishes. Her fate after her father's death is described in the third-to-last paragraph of the book:

> When everything had been sold, there remained twelve francs and seventy-five centimes, which paid for Mademoiselle Bovary's trip to her grandmother's house. The good woman died that same year, and since Monsieur Rouault was now paralyzed, an aunt took charge of the child's upbringing. She is poor and sends her to work, to earn her living, in a cotton mill. (302, my translation)

The results of financial exploitation are stark: impoverishment, a family's destruction. The form of the writing brings this home. Whereas at the end of *Pride and Prejudice* the suddenly personalized voice humorously dismisses Mrs. Bennet and gladly projects its resolution of social conflict, here the impersonally objective vision flatly shows social and financial success for the Homais family in contrast to Berthe's utter degradation. Through the modulation of tenses, what was story seems to become truth; the suffering of Berthe and her aunt appears to become frightfully present in historical reality.

Three
LONDON AND
DUBLIN

James and Joyce are considered, though in different ways, as masters of the aesthetic, the former exemplary of a certain conception of the novel, the latter creator of a formal inventiveness that is perhaps too easily labeled modernist. Both are also deeply concerned with socioeconomic issues in works that transcend a colonial heritage and attain a cosmopolitan vision.[1] Discussion of *The Golden Bowl* (1904) follows consistently upon the analyses of the preceding chapter, in that James's last completed novel is dominated by problems of money, marriage, family, and class. In it we move in the circles of one of the "classes" Emma Bovary imagined in Paris—that of princesses and ambassadors, the wealthiest and highest levels of society. The marriage-money connection so central in *Pride and Prejudice* is correspondingly magnified, Adam Verver's millions and rented eighty-room summer house far surpassing the wealth even of a Darcy. But the pain of inappropriate marriage, present in the Bennets and in Wickham and Lydia and yielding suicide in *Madame Bovary*, is central to the unfolding of *The Golden Bowl* and the muffled anguish of its conclusion. An unhappy marriage is structurally and in human terms also vividly at the heart of *Ulysses* (1922), which, if not consecrated to the "lives of the submerged tenth" (646) that Leopold Bloom and Stephen Dedalus encounter in the cab shelter, nonetheless presents characters who live on the edge of poverty—we see somewhat more of Dilly Dedalus's misery than we do of Berthe Bovary's. *The Golden Bowl* and *Ulysses* treat the extremes of class and wealth and in ways that correspond closely not only to history but also to Marx's analysis of it.

The individuals whose fate so obsessively concerns James in *The Golden Bowl* are transparently linked from the outset in Prince Amerigo's meditations to the decline of European nobility, the power of the British Empire, and the wealth of American capitalism. The prince anticipates living a new and strange life amid American technology and is puzzled by the unfamiliar morality of Americans, comparing it to the "lightning elevator" in one of Adam Verver's fifteen-story buildings: "Your moral sense works by steam—it sends you up like a rocket" (48). This dimension of "historical allegory," which we detected in Austen and Flaubert, is also indicated by the obtrusive use of names and places—Amerigo, American City, Adam Verver, not to speak of Matcham and of Rance and Lutch (hailing from Detroit and Providence, hence minor comic versions of the international marriage quest). But from the opening page the prince sounds the historical note concerning "his London," which has replaced Rome as "the City to which the world paid tribute," and immediately in terms of the objects that are to play such a large role in the story—"objects massive and lumpish, in silver and gold, in the forms to which precious stones contribute, or in leather, steel, brass, applied to a hundred uses and abuses . . . tumbled together as if, in the insolence of the Empire, they had been the loot of far-off victories" (29).

As clearly as the jumbled implements in the storage room at Tostes, the items that the prince glimpses suggest large economic and political transformations, just as his intimate knowledge of the world's most powerful capital contrasts with Emma Bovary's provincial consciousness. But the "objects" in this so predictive opening page bristle with contradictions and dangers—concerning true quality, the possibility of abuse, the awareness, hardly explored in political and/or human terms, of conquest and empire. The narrator takes pains to indicate the "undirected thought" of the prince, "working at comparatively short range," and this mild criticism is perhaps augmented by the prince's decision at the end of the chapter to seek communion with a woman who is three times named an ass. Further, for anyone familiar with the history of the British Isles, who has read, say, *The Condition of the Working Class in England*, volume 1 of *Capital*, or *Ulysses*, the rapid, even "shallow," observation that Amerigo looks like "a 'refined' Irishman" (30) speaks volumes about oppression and prejudice and from a biased English point of view could virtually deprive him of stature and value.

Another limitation of Amerigo's vision is remarked by the woman he has loved, his future mother-in-law. Charlotte has observed that "below a certain social plane, he never *saw*"— whereas she prides herself on remembering beggars, servants, and cabbies, on distinguishing beauty in dirty children and admiring "type" in faces at hucksters' stalls (99). The remark sounds like a familiar criticism of James himself, who in *The Golden Bowl* is notably uninterested in seeing much below the richest levels of society. It is also suggestive about Charlotte, at the beginning poor and rather vulgarly delighted to proclaim herself so and whose appreciation of the lower classes is unpleasantly aestheticizing. Of course the observation concerns the shopman who tries to sell the bowl and is set in relation to other defects of vision. First is Charlotte's failure to notice the fault in the bowl, which Amerigo immediately perceives. Both moreover ignore the vendor's personal qualities, which— despite the anti-semitism that obscures his character—reveal themselves generously when he later repents of misleading Maggie, in the process hastening the downfall of Amerigo and Charlotte.

Obtuseness of various kinds—social, aesthetic, ethnic—is revealed in connection with the bowl during Charlotte's and Amerigo's exploration of London shops, at the very time however that the prince admires *her* "possession of her London," "her curious world quality," visible in Rome but "larger on the big London stage" (95). "Stage" is something of a giveaway, in view of the later use of the theatrical analogy to describe the devious relationships among the characters. But Charlotte's cosmopolitan element, together with her physical attractiveness, is the key to the magnetic quality of this splendid personage, and not only for the prince. In spite of her poverty, Charlotte Stant's background, education, travel, and linguistic flair appear to Amerigo as rare, rich, and precious, constituting a "small social capital" that, once she marries a millionaire, will become a big social capital indeed. To Amerigo, moreover, her gifts confer on her a special "race-quality," a phrase which, given the references to Irish and Jews, is not without resonance (64).

In spite of their blind spots hinted at so early on (not to speak of the much discussed "innocence" of the Ververs), Amerigo and Charlotte are inconceivable except on the international scene in a "world historical" context. For Marx, world historical consciousness is an alienated but promising state, an awareness of implication in global economic strife (world market, political and economic empire, domination by European and North American capitals not only of their respective countrysides but of the rest of the world). James's restricted ken, the socioeconomic situation of his characters, accounts for the limited nature of their "world quality." This can hardly be said of *Ulysses*, in which the main characters (not entirely excluding Molly), *because* of their more limited advantages, are extremely conscious of local and international conflict and in which even the "non-realistic" conventions often express such concerns—notably in "Aeolus," "Wandering Rocks," "Cyclops," "Circe," and "Eumaeus."

The Dublin of *Ulysses* is a provincial capital, inscribing Irish and English history, thereby also possessing its own "curious world quality."[2] Of Irish history the details are myriad, to the frustration of many a reader and the profit of many a producer of guides and notes. The monuments glimpsed throughout, the visits to graves of Irish leaders in "Hades," the underground visit to "the most historic spot in all Dublin," "the historic council chamber of saint Mary's abbey where silken Thomas proclaimed himself a rebel in 1534," the "old bank of Ireland . . . and the original jews' temple" (230)—they throng the consciousness of major and minor characters with their dose of nationalist obfuscation or unimpressive touristic glamour. Not to speak of Sinn Fein, Arthur Griffith, and Home Rule, Maud Gonne's fulminations against drunken English soldiers, Kevin Egan exiled in Paris, the Phoenix Park murders and Skin-the-goat, whose elucubrations we hear through the *longueurs* of the narrative in

"Eumaeus," or the ranting of the Citizen in "Cyclops," with its undeniable element of historical truth overwhelmed by prejudice and deflated by the gruff narrator of the chapter and by the interspersed parodic passages. What does it matter in all of this that Bloom's only contact with the Boer War was to have gotten unintentionally caught up in a street demonstration? Or that Molly Bloom's awareness of the issues in that conflict is limited to romantic regret for Gardner's death? Or that "Eumaeus" playfully inserts Bloom in "strict history" as the man who picked up Charles Parnell's hat during a scuffle, hence turning a Hegelian-Marxist formula ("history repeating itself with a difference") into another of the chapter's clichés (654–55)? The impact of local and international events may be glancing, but cumulatively they inform lives and consiousnesses—no more clearly so than in "Wandering Rocks," where the viceregal cavalcade spuriously "unites" the population of Dublin around the English political presence, producing reactions that range from fawning obeisance to hostile resentment.

Stephen and Bloom are noticeably absent from the enumeration of characters in the last section of that chapter, as they are also the figures who struggle to see through the obfuscations that surround the facts and issues of history. Throughout, Bloom is insightful about the manipulative role of religion and the flatulence of Irish patriotism ("Want to gas about our lovely land" [164]—bodily enacted on the last page of "Sirens"). In keeping with his education, Stephen is more intellectually penetrating about history and its burdens, at times however in sharp, even violent, encounters with representatives of the English view—Haines, Deasy, Carr.

The treatment of Haines conveys with scorn a vehement hatred of English domination. Haines is wealthy (Mulligan says his father prospered by selling "jalap to Zulus or some bloody swindle or other" [7]), university educated (he speaks Gaelic to the uncomprehending milkwoman), imperious ("This is real Irish cream I take it, he said with forbearance, I don't want to be imposed on" [249]), and supremely condescending ("We feel in England that we have treated you rather unfairly. It seems history is to blame" [20]). The last is in response to Stephen's angry admission to being "the servant of two masters," the "imperial British state . . . and the holy Roman catholic and apostolic church." Later, while teaching, Stephen meditates that history is "not to be thought away" (25), then sounds despondent in expressing to Deasy the famous thought "History . . . is a nightmare from which I am trying to awake" (34). In his mind he condemns both English and Irish, recalling Blake in response to Deasy's Anglo-Irish version of history (*"The harlot's cry from street to street / Shall weave old England's winding sheet"* [33]), later having a Rimbaud-like vision of his own ancestors as a "horde of jerkined dwarfs, my people," from whom he is alienated, speaking to no one, a changeling (45).[3]

These issues come to a head in the drunken clarity and violence of "Circe," in which Stephen articulates with determination the need for liberation. First from religion, taking the difficult step of overcoming guilt and saying "Shite!" to the ghost of his mother: *"Ah non, par exemple!* The intellectual imagination! . . . *Non serviam!"* (582). Then from English empire and militarism, somehow supported by Irish patriotism: "But I say: Let my country die for me" (591); "He wants my money and my life . . . for some brutish empire of his" (594); "The old sow that eats her farrow!" (595). He sums it up in a formula worthy of Dante or Blake (whom he quotes aloud, this time inserting Ireland for England) or Marx: "(*He taps his brow.*) But in here it is I must kill the priest and the king" (589). We may note the limitation of exclusive devotion to the "intellectual imagination," but the novel dramatizes throughout the dangers of mindless rhetoric and activism; killing in one's head the priest and the king and what they represent is perhaps the crucial and utterly prior need.

The Irish-English context is topically apt, historically necessary, and productive of insight and resolve. Resembling Marx's refusal to separate elements that are distant but ultimately related in a global perspective, the text of *Ulysses* at diverse points also cannot help echoing international economic relations and oppression of others by whites. In "Cyclops," newspaper articles and skits evoke the links between Manchester cotton magnates, Zulus and missionary activity in Africa (334), and the lynching of a black man in the American South: *"Black Beast Burned in Omaha, Ga.* A lot of Deadwood Dicks in slouch hats and they firing at a sambo strung up on a tree with his tongue out and a bonfire under him. Gob, they ought to drown him in the sea after and electrocute and crucify him to make sure of their job" (328). Racist language and the crude insight do not diminish the horror of the scene, which is all the more related to the action of the chapter in that within a dozen pages it will be a question of "crucifying" Bloom and of his criticism of all forms of racism and violence.

Another historical and geographic area of now almost obsessive concern is the Near and Middle East. Molly's birthplace, Gibraltar, allows her to be a source of Eastern exoticism in the book, expressed in her memories at the end and Bloom's imaginations of travel, notably in "Calypso." This is one way in which Joyce continues the Flaubertian critique of the ideologically formative role of literature—both Bloom and Molly unconsciously "quote" Coleridge's "Kubla Khan." But Molly has genuine memories of Gibraltar, her father did serve in overseas regiments, and Bloom's fantasy of the East is inevitably also related to advertisements for investment in plantations there. Depressed after the funeral and feeling the threat of Boylan and numerous ravenous males as well as a twinge of nostalgia for the former Josie Powell, Bloom is also aware of others: "A barefoot arab stood over the grating, breathing in the fumes. Deaden the gnaw of hunger that way. Pleasure or pain is it? Penny dinner. Knife and fork chained to the table" (157). Bloom's curious mind and attentiveness to the unfortunate here are the means by which Joyce, as opposed to James's technique in *The Golden Bowl,* seems to see "everything," in a notation that is clearly not "local" color, certainly not a mere *effet de réel.* The Arab on the Dublin street, like the "négresse" in Baudelaire's "Le Cygne" or the Arab in Rouen where Emma Bovary buys her incense, is a signpost of history, reminding us of conquest and dislocation, of future revenge and violence. How different is the Dublin Arab from "those handsome Moors all in white and turbans like kings" that Molly remembers (together with Jews) from Gibraltar (782).

But the foremost historical reality of ethnic and racial oppression in *Ulysses* is anti-Semitism. It is hard to overstate the attention that Joyce gives this issue, in a work published between World Wars I and II but whose action is set ten years before the beginning of the first. We recall that for Marx anti-Semitism is not a superficial but an integral aspect of the system he attacked, allowing those of the dominant religion to disguise their practice of economic oppression by ascribing that practice to Jews. With similar insight Flaubert has Lheureux, who to the end keeps his good name, counter Emma's worry about money with the response, "nous ne sommes pas des Juifs!" (90). (Later he claims not to be able to call off the banker Vinçart because he is more ferocious than an Arab). As we have hinted, the Jewish stereotype appears in *The Golden Bowl* as well, at times appearing to infect not only characters but narrative voice. Amerigo's brother has married a woman of "Hebrew race, with a portion that had gilded the pill" (39)—which apparently expresses only Amerigo's family's bias. In Brighton Charlotte perceives the purchase of the Damascene tiles as "some mystic rite of old Jewry" (173). But it is the narrator who characterizes Mrs. Assingham's somewhat tawdry exotic quality as combining the "eyes of the American city" and "the lids of Jerusalem" (50–51). As for the shopman, Maggie sees him as "a queer little foreign man" (406), but the prince and Charlotte call him a "little swindling Jew" (269). Disconcertingly, the surprise over his honesty is condescendingly expressed by the narrator, who remarks that he shows "a scruple rare enough in vendors of any class, and almost unprecedented in the thrifty children of Israel" (449).

The anti-Jewish note is a small but predictable element in a story in which non-Jews earn milions in ways that are not explained, marry for money, engage in infidelity, and inflict exquisite forms of anguish on one another. How much more blatant, yet paradoxically effective, is the dodge in the case of a Catholic population exploited by Protestants but wallowing in that exploitation through a virulent form of anti-Semitism.

First, inevitably, there is an economic component. For Haines England's number one problem is competition with German Jews; Deasy says England is in the hands of the Jews, whereas

Ireland has succeeded in keeping them out—a claim belied by the stereotypical figure of the Jewish moneylender, Reuben J. Dodd, whose case provokes the Citizen's ire. Note that the narrator of "Cyclops" condemns Blooms' late father's economic activities in similar terms and Bloom himself for not standing for a round of drinks: "There's a jew for you! All for number one. Cute as a shithouse rat" (341). Note also, early on, Stephen's Marx-like answer to the anti-Jewish phobia of the money-conscious Deasy: "A merchant . . . is one who buys cheap and sells dear, jew or gentile, is he not?" (34). As the language of the "Cyclops" narrator suggests, anti-Semitism is also expressed as a personal, almost visceral antipathy. Despite mild defenses of Bloom by Cunningham and Nolan, he is surrounded by mockery (for example, Mulligan's insults and homosexual innuendo in the library chapter), by references to bugs and fear of contamination and "*fetor judaicus*" (493)—"I'm told those Jewies does have a sort of a queer odour coming off them for dogs" (304). Not to mention "theological" aspects of prejudice—the Jews as lost to the light, as ritually murdering Christian children—and on and on.

Before this onslaught Bloom tends to submit, through disguise. He does not want to admit to Stephen that he is Jewish but thinks Stephen knows (643, 682). In the funeral carriage he illustrates to the letter Freud's analysis in *Jokes and Their Relation to the Unconscious* of the function of anti-Jewish stories and jokes among non-Jews but is thwarted of the punch line and thus of acceptance by the others (93–95). The butt of the story is Dodd, about whom Bloom later thinks, "Now he's really what they call a dirty jew," approving of rough treatment of the moneylender by the "wellmeaning old" judge Frederick Falkiner. Here Bloom submits to the "smokescreen function" of anti-Jewish feeling, since he accepts Sir Frederick's social standing and wealth, his "good lunch in Earlsfort terrace. Old legal cronies cracking a magnum. Tales of the bench and assizes and annals of the bluecoat school. I sentenced him to ten years. I suppose he'd turn up his nose at that stuff I drank. Vintage wine for them" (182–83). Finally, however, he is forced to take a stand against the Citizen ("And I belong to a race too . . . that is hated and persecuted" [332]). The Citizen's response hilariously reveals the

obfuscating function of anti-Semitism among those supposedly
devoted both to the Catholic faith and to the fight against English domination: "—By Jesus, says he. I'll brain that bloody
jewman for using the holy name. By Jesus, I'll crucify him so I
will" (342).[4]

Some conflicts of modern history are strongly visible in *Ulysses*,
if veiled in *The Golden Bowl*. Something of the same may be said,
as to amount of detail, of the treatment of money in the two
books. While James's novel is far less explicit than *Ulysses*, it is
equally obsessed by the theme.

Ulysses is highly concerned with the lives of economically marginal people. In spite of glimpses of those who are somewhat, or
enormously, better off, ranging from storeowners to millionaires
of the beer trade (and notably including Boylan), the book cen-
ters on characters who reckon money in small amounts, who
have intermittent or low-paying employment (or none at all), and
whose lives are correspondingly marred by alcoholism and family strife. An obvious instance is Dignam's death, with Bloom's
worry about the family, his son's thoughts after the funeral
("The last night pa was boosed he was standing on the landing
there bawling out for his boots to go out to Tunney's for to
boose more. . . . Never see him again" [251]), and Gerty Mac-
Dowell's reflections on her own dead alcoholic father. As this
last indicates, the Dignam story is easily generalized. On the way
to the funeral Bloom sees a boy "smoking a chewed fagbutt. A
smaller girl with scars of eczema on her forehead eyed him,
listlessly holding her battered caskhoop. Tell him if he smokes
he won't grow. O let him! His life isn't such a bed of roses!
Waiting outside pubs to bring da home" (71). Further, through
what has sometimes been thought to be the mean-spirited irony
of "Nausicaa," Gerty's economic and social limitations, her lack
of education and pathetic desire for elegance, are apparent. In
"Eumaeus" Stephen meets Corley, so desperate as to seek any
kind of work, even as a crossing sweeper; as mentioned, that
chapter glimpses a world of down-and-out men. The lot of
many women is no better, as we perceive through Bloom, excited by the combination of sex and wealth in the flash of silk

stocking and carriage (74), appalled by the effects of life on less fortunate women: the "shabby genteel" Mrs. Breen (158), the long-suffering Mina Purefoy and her multiple pregancies, wife of an "old bucko" praised by Costello for still being able to "knock another child out of her" (408), but also the young women in "Nausicaa"—"Sad however because it lasts only a few years till they settle down to potwalloping" (373).

None of this is irrelevant for the three major characters in *Ulysses*, all marked by penury and striving to rise above it. Stephen's "A.E.I.O.U." (190) is well known, as are his need for money and loose attitude toward it on paydays—he takes slips from the library on which to write his poems, tries to sell his ideas to Haines and others, but wastes his money on drink and in nighttown while ignoring offers of employment on the newspaper and planning to leave his teaching position. Early in the day he reflects on the wealth of his pupils' families, is scornful of Deasy's money, and recalls his time as a scholarship student, in a context of depression about his own and his uncle's family: "Houses of decay, mine, his and all. You told the Clongowes gentry you had an uncle a judge and an uncle a general in the army. Come out of them, Stephen. Beauty is not there" (39). Once more, the devotion to the aesthetic may strike us as insufficient, but Stephen here confronts the reality of his economic and social situation.

The depiction of that situation in regard to Stephen's immediate family is, however, more painful. With their mother dead, their father hanging about taverns, alternating between flattering barmaids and exercising his still beautiful voice, their older brother absent, what is the fate of Dilly and the others? Dilly is one of those poor children that Bloom notices: "Good Lord, that poor child's dress is in flitters. Underfed she looks too" (152). Later we see her sisters squabbling over a poor meal gotten on charity (226), and there is a painful scene in which Dilly scornfully extracts a few coins from her elusive father before Stephen meets her at the bookstalls. In this poignant meeting we realize the deprivation of Stephen's sister, her apparently not-to-be-realized desire for education (she has bought a French primer for a penny), Stephen's despair:

> She is drowning. Agenbite. Save her. Agenbite. All against
> us. She will drown me with her, eyes and hair. Lank coils of
> seaweed hair around me, my heart, my soul. Salt green death.
> We.
> Agenbite of inwit. Inwit's agenbite.
> Misery! Misery! (243)

How do beauty and the intellectual imagination square with this?
As with everything else, the book's open-ended conclusion does
not allow us to know if Stephen will undertake the ten years of
largely unremunerated labor necessary to produce a masterpiece (249), although we do learn in "Eumaeus" both that he
plans to quit his job and that he is still worried about how poorly
his sisters eat (617, 620). *Ulysses,* a work that in the figure of
Stephen and in the techniques of many of its chapters has
seemed to some to be obsessed with aesthetic explorations, nonetheless puts such artistry in painful relationship with economic
misery (and sexual discrimination, showing us not Shakespeare's
but Dedalus's sister).

Bloom and Molly are not quite so near to poverty. They eat
well, as we immediately observe, although Nosy Flynn attributes
that to assistance from the Masonic order rather than to Bloom's
earnings (177). A more likely explanation is Bloom's prudence—
as he appreciates Molly's superiority to other women beaten
down by child-rearing (373), so she recognizes that "he has sense
enough not to squander every penny piece he earns down their
gullets and looks after his wife and family goodfornothings"
(773–74). Still, he remembers buying used underthings for her
(160–61) and selling her hair—"Ten bob I got for Molly's comb-
ings when we were on the rocks in Holles street" (369)—and she
voices numerous complaints about his inadequate jobs and her
lack of servants, money, clothes, and other finery. Indeed the
book shows Bloom engaged in the sometimes demeaning, often
frustrating, and ever-recurrent activity of earning a living, significantly in the "modern art of advertisement" (683), for which
he dreams of creating "some one sole unique advertisement . . .
reduced to its simplest and most efficient terms not exceeding
the span of casual vision and congruous with the velocity of
modern life" (720).[5]

While Joyce here puts his finger on a phenomenon that has even greater bearing on our lives near the end of the twentieth century, Bloom pursues more mediocre versions, criticizing the bad ads he comes across, attempting to place the one for Keyes that will enable him to buy a petticoat for Molly, the sort of garment whose absence we later hear her lament: "If I net five guineas with those ads. The violet silk petticoats. Not yet. The sweets of sin" (260–61). As we follow him, we are aware not only of his sexual need but also that he has to be so concerned about finances, the smallest of earnings and expenditures, that he automatically notes the monetary value of virtually everything— unrented apartments, picture frames, Milly's job, the cost of a visit to her ("Might take a trip down there. August bank holiday, only two and six return. Six weeks off however. Might work a press pass" [67]), soap and meat, ladies' underwear: "Ladies' grey flannelette bloomers, three shillings a pair, astonishing bargain" (381). Although here his voice takes on the tone of an ad, Bloom resembles both Gerty and Molly, who often think of clothing in terms of price. Significantly, after Gerty's exhibitionism (underwear and all) leads Bloom to orgasm, he thinks, "Thankful for small mercies. Cheap too" (368), and wonders whether Boylan gave Molly money: "Why not? All a prejudice. She's worth ten, fifteen, more a pound" (369). Later Molly contradictorily is incensed that Bloom wants to turn her into a whore but fantasizes about using sex to obtain money (740, 745, 749, 780).

Bloom's apparent complacency unsuccessfully attempts to cover up his pain and again reveals his obsession with money. "Ithaca" 's listing of the day's puny budget, of his meagre assets in insurance, bank account, stock (and graveplot), its revelation of the suburban dreamhouse, which, like so many, he desires but will never own, reiterates the marginal nature of his economic activity. The imperative "Reduce Bloom," draws a response that shows how financially vulnerable he is, at the same time hysterically recalling all of those figures of suffering that in following him and Steven we have glimpsed, in "poverty," "mendicancy," "destitution," "misery": hawkers, duns, collectors, bankrupts, sandwichmen, distributors of throwaways, vagrants, and many others, down to the "aged impotent disfranchised ratesupported moribund lunatic pauper" (725).

Bloom's persistence doubtless will keep him and his family from this state, but the need to attend to every penny makes him see all of life in monetary terms, from religion ("And don't they rake in the money too?" [83]) to art (*Matcham's Masterstroke* [68–69] and his ideas for turning Stephen's various talents into paying jobs). His schemes for social reform, repeatedly burlesqued, finally also take a modest financial form—with people of "all creeds and classes *pro rata* having a comfortable tidysized income . . . something in the neighborhood of £300 per annum," provided, of course, that they work: "Where you can live well, the sense is, if you work" (644). The groggy Stephen retorts: "Count me out." This is amusing but also expressive of his determination, the ambiguities of which we have noted, not to submit to the order of labor and money.

Again, as hinted above, the financial and sexual are linked in Bloom's mind, not only in occasional reflections such as those already noted but in terms of prostitution, through encounters with prostitutes remembered by him (and by Stephen), and in "Circe," in Bella Cohen's "relieving office" (452), where Bloom has to safeguard Stephen's money. Stephen's quoting of Blake on England and Ireland as destroyed by the "harlot's cry" makes the sale of sex the central metaphor and reality—as in Marx and Engels as well as Blake—for a corrupt society. A remark by Zoe about Bella indicates how "mainstream" prostitution is: "She's on the job herself tonight with the vet, her tipster, that gives her all the winners and pays for her son in Oxford. Working overtime" (475). And Stephen expresses a withering view of the issue concerning the streetwalker outside the cab shelter, recalling his disagreement with Deasy: "In this country people sell much more than she ever had and do a roaring trade. Fear not them that sell the body but have not power to buy the soul. She is a bad merchant. She buys dear and sells cheap" (633).

If the sexual is invaded by the commercial, one of the attractions of *Ulysses* is its frank evocation of sex in its bodily, emotional, and psychological aspects.[6] Frank, but not unfettered, and hardly happy. If Bloom has a marvelous memory of Molly on Howth, combining love, sex, food, and nature (175–76), he is now most unhappy—it suffices to recall his pathetic correspondence with Martha, his expectation of his bath, the encounter with Gerty, the filial guilt and sexual humiliation of "Circe," and the disabling grief over his dead son, which leaves Molly deprived of fulfilling sex with him. Stephen, haunted by guilt and at the same time obsessed by sex ("And my turn? When?" [191]), is not much better off. In contrast, the exuberant sexuality of Molly (which has made some readers uncomfortable and has caused others to raise questions about representations of female sexuality by a male writer) provides satisfaction in its evocation of erotic pleasure, celebration of nature, and even a certain religious simplicity.

But Molly's sexuality is caught in the web of the socioeconomic and ideological forces that we have been discussing. Her physical need is great, and she complains about Bloom's infrequent and "unnatural" embraces (777) and expresses gratitude for Boylan's performance: "O thanks be to the great God I got somebody to give me what I badly wanted to put some heart up into me youve no chances at all in this place like you used long ago I wish somebody would write me a love-letter his wasnt much" (758). Here the sexual need naturally extends into larger realms—affection, communication, society. Sex is also an emblem of prestige and success, as Molly asserts her superiority to others: "see if they can excite a swell with money that can pick and choose whoever he wants like Boylan to do it 4 or 5 times locked in each others arms" (763). Finally, the sex with Boylan potentially opens up other experiences and pleasures of which Molly has been deprived. Not having had a concert in more than a year (she therefore is even more marginal than her husband), she looks forward to the tour: "O I love jaunting in a train or a car with lovely soft cushions I wonder will he take a 1st class for me he might want to do it in the train by tipping the guard"; "his father made his money over selling the horses for the cavalry well he could buy me a nice present up in Belfast after what I gave . . . it would be exciting going around with him shopping buying those things in a new city"; "he has plenty of money and hes not a marrying man so somebody better get it out of him" (748–49).

These are the desires of a lower-class Emma Bovary, not excluding the component of Eastern exoticism that Molly embodies. It is unclear from "Penelope" whether she has Spanish or Moorish blood or both, something that Bloom finds attractive, in Molly's explanation because of her being "jewess looking after my mother" (771, also 373, 745–46). We recognize a more blatant version of the stereotype that contributes mildly to Fanny Assingham's aspect of vulgarity, and it is significant that when Molly decides to give Bloom "one more chance" it is in connection with the desire for purchases that would allow her to dress the role: "Id have to get a nice pair of red slippers like those Turks with the fez used to sell or yellow and a nice semitransparent morning gown that I badly want or a peachblossom dressing jacket like the one long ago in Walpoles only 8/6 or 18/6 Ill just give him one more chance" (780). Here Joyce also has Molly imagine dressing the part for the harem or brothel dream that Stephen and Bloom have each separately had and that is marked by her unmistakable imagery (47, 217, 370). Coincidence? Jungian participation of the deeper self in some archetypal symbolism? Or "archetypal symbolism" as largely formed by the history and ideology that *Ulysses* throughout displays?

It is not sure that Molly will accede to Bloom's request to coddle him next day, since on the same page her anger at his idiosyncracies leads to shocking imaginations of humiliation for him, before her last suggestion that she will plan a good day for the morrow in case he brings Stephen home. She thinks of buying "those fairy cakes in Liptons I love the smell of a rich big shop at 7½ a lb or the other ones with the cherries in them and the pinky sugar 11d a couple of lbs of course a nice plant for the middle of the table Id get that cheaper in wait wheres this I saw them not long ago I love flowers Id love to have the whole place swimming in roses God of heaven theres nothing like nature" (781). This leads to Molly's celebration of nature and Gibraltar and Howth and Bloom and others and herself, and her final "Yes." Whether the "yes" is to be realized would depend presumably on commitments and acts by Bloom and Molly, and Stephen? (And perhaps Boylan?) In any event, though potentially as rich as Molly's final thoughts, the future that opens at the "end" of the book will require some of the cakes and flowers, and therefore some of the 7½d or 11d in terms of which Molly and her husband must always obsessively think.

A great distance gapes between the money-haunted characters in *Ulysses* and the world of *The Golden Bowl,* in spite of the Assinghams' frugality and the prince's worry about the mortgages on his ancestral properties (138), not to speak of Charlotte's initial poverty. She wonders about paying a penny for a bus and is so "very poor" that she cannot afford the £15 the vendor wants for the cheap gift supposedly intended for Maggie Verver (68, 105, 107). But once the prince's and her marriages take place, "Mr Verver's solvency" and the "bottomless bag of solid shining British sovereigns" the prince imagines at Matcham (243, 251) allow them and us to move exclusively, and without attention to financial detail, in the highest levels of society. The *bousculade* of the London scene, the season at Brighton or in the country at Fawns, may be treated with amusement, but Matcham, "a society so placed that it had only its own sensibility to consider—looking as it did over the heads of all lower growth" (249–50), is exposed in the persons of the adulterous Lady Castledean and her lover, Mr. Blint. At the opening of Part Third, Charlotte has reached the summit of this vapid social world, receiving a summons from royalty at the very time that she and Amerigo begin to maneuver into a position of realizing their love relationship (191–205). In retrospect we understand that this is also the beginning of their decline; to retain their moneyed ease they undergo the pain of separation so unbearably expressed in the prince's face on the last page.[7]

That Amerigo and Charlotte marry for money is apparent. He reflects on his marriage agreement as a business operation (30). If at that time he recalls joking with Maggie that he "cost a lot of money" (35), several years later his second affair with Charlotte is preceded by the serious if complacent reflection that Adam Verver "relieved him of all anxiety about his married life in the same manner in which he relieved him on the score of his bank account" (223). Although his wife swoons under his sexual

power, Amerigo uses this power as he habitually has with
women, to manipulate her, rather than out of passionate admiration or love. He thinks Maggie shallow, seeing her as does Mr.
Assingham—as "the young woman who has a million a year"
(80). Ironically, it is by resisting his sexual charm and developing
a complex and devious consciousness that Maggie succeeds in
separating him from Charlotte.

At the outset, though, Amerigo's advice to Charlotte is to
"marry some capital fellow" (66–67), "some good, kind, clever,
rich American" (150–51), and Charlotte tries, unsuccessfully, to
follow that advice, as Maggie explains to her father. Verver himself is inevitably "in the market" (129), pursued by the Rances
and Lutches of life, because of "his own special deficiency, his
unfortunate lack of a wife" (143). The echo of *Pride and Prejudice*
may not be accidental. Verver allows that he could "stand" another woman about, and Charlotte Stant instantly stands by (147,
also 96–97). Verver's proposal to her may be the least romantic
recorded in literature (174), but then he has never been ardent,
as the evocation of his first marriage to a "frail, fluttered creature," his admission to having never been jealous, and his liken-
ing of his collecting to the discovery of Cortez, unaccompanied
by female companion, all suggest (122–23, 477).[8]

The death of Maggie's mother and the companionship with her
father in his early collecting days explains the Ververs' closeness,
with elements of displacement and exaggeration that may make
of the American millionaire and collector (to anticipate a later
chapter) a muffled Goriot (113, 121, 171). That his collecting has
a libidinal component is implied by some of the language used to
describe it. Verver's realization that his future will be devoted to
acquiring art comes to him "with a mute inward gasp akin to the
low moan of apprehensive passion" (122). In a later analysis (160),
he is aware that he is "economically constructed," that the "aesthetic principle" in him is a "cold, still flame," the "lesson of the
senses" for him concerning the "plastic beauty" of art (rather than
a woman's body, we might think). The narrator closes this passage
with an ambivalent sexual analogy, significantly to suggest not
Verver's erotic life but his collecting, which has not troubled "his
economy at large." And, although Verver has been charmed by

the long music-filled evenings alone with Charlotte at Fawns, the object that he wants to handle "tenderly" is not her but the Damascene tiles, which—together with the high figure he pays for them—mediate his proposal to her (172–73). No wonder that his failure as a husband and sexual partner is in a variety of ways criticized by Charlotte and Amerigo (and Mr. Assingham) in explanation of their liaison (191*ff*., 202, 233–37, 292).

But it is a matter neither of putting all the blame on Verver nor of joining in the critical pastime of justifying him and his daughter.[9] Adam's proposal has nothing to do with sexual love; rather it is designed initially to relieve Maggie of worry and later to take advantage of Charlotte's "social utility" (317). But Charlotte and Amerigo are equally manipulative, and dishonest to boot. Adam and Maggie Verver speak of purchasing and value and being taken on approval (182, 186–87), the prince and Charlotte of bargains, quotations, expense, return for services rendered, contracts (204–7, 241). *The Golden Bowl* is even more extreme than *Pride and Prejudice* in presenting personal relations in financial terms.

The monetary analogy is pervasive and often just that, an analogy, as when Fanny's analyses are compared to adding up a bill (214) or when Charlotte uses the expression to be "sold" (93) to indicate the disappointment she would have felt had the prince refused to spend the morning with her in London shops. That James uses the phrase in his preface to describe the reader's disappointment in bad prose (24) suggests that the analogy is not merely incidental. We might feel that this clandestine meeting, of which Maggie later learns, is the first step in a process by which Charlotte is indeed sold. Frequently, too, the money metaphor describes the social function of individuals, even the social scene itself, as when Amerigo thinks of Fanny's matchmaking in terms of profit, remuneration, and assets (41) or when Charlotte is viewed as performing "the duties of a remunerative office" to the point of accepting the arid aspects of the social scene as "false pieces in a debased currency" (240–41).

But money can also represent success or failure in what is most passionately desired. Charlotte's announcement that Amerigo and she will stay over for lunch at Matcham appears to him as "the chink of this gold in his ear" (260). Even were we to accept money as an appropriate figure for the anticipated pleasure of sexual love, we later must be disturbed by more extended developments of the analogy to describe the relations among what the preface calls the "more or less bleeding participants" (8). As Maggie and Charlotte look in on Verver from the terrace at Fawns, Maggie feels that her stepmother is extracting a price, "a sum of money that she . . . was to find" (464). And in the last two pages, having dispatched Charlotte, Maggie imagines her victory over Charlotte and the prince in terms of money—an amount to be paid, a speculation concerning a number, payment in full from a proffered money bag at the expense of Charlotte. What deformation of consciousness and compassion (which Maggie is supposed to feel for Charlotte) is expressed by this compulsive financial metaphor, so at odds with the traditional tragic vocabulary of "pity and dread" with which the work ends? Such a (concluding) passage is close indeed to Marx's insistence on the prostitution of the human to the monetary in modern society.

The Golden Bowl also strikingly recalls other aspects of Marx's writing on money—namely, his dissection of the fetishism of precious metals, of various systems of exchange, and particularly of what he calls the dazzling, absurd money-form. His arguments about value are also relevant to James's novel, in financial, personal, and—since Verver is such a collector—aesthetic realms. The widely noted motif of Amerigo as a possession, a "representative precious object" (35, 121), is initially formulated by the prince himself in terms of value (43–44). He ruminates that the marriage agreement seems to supppose in him some "essential quality and value." The immediate image of this value is that of a medieval coin, wonderfully embossed, worth a great deal in modern money but "of a purity of gold no longer used," hence susceptible of "finer ways of using it" than the monetary. Here the allure of precious metal, the glamorous past, the fusion of the aesthetic and the monetary, are all present. So is the notion of something superior to current monetary usage, an essential and finer quality, a supreme use-value, uncontaminated by profit-making. But as the prince attempts to understand, "morally speaking," the value that the strange Americans ascribe to him, he can only return to the realm of modern money: "Who but a billionaire could say what was fair exchange for a billion? That measure was the shrouded object." As we have been seeing, money, accumulated in enormous amounts, is insistently the measure of value and desire throughout. Later, scornfully and it turns out self-deceivingly, Amerigo thinks of Verver as paying attention to him only as to his "amount," like "the figure of a cheque" (245).

But the prince precipitates the pursuit of money that leads to the trampling of affective values in the novel, a possibility we might already glimpse in his reaction when seeing Charlotte at Fanny Assingham's. Charlotte "owns almost nothing in the world," but she is the "person in the world . . . whose looks are most subject to appreciation," according to Fanny (54–55). At the end, illustrating Marx's argument about owning and being, Charlotte possesses Verver's millions but is hardly any longer appreciated—the prince calls her stupid (533). At the beginning, though, when she comes into Fanny's house (58–59), Amerigo's reactions make it clear that he has known her sexually, as he "appreciates" the various parts of her body, in a response which, we have seen, is not shared by her sexless future husband. Like Verver imagining Maggie as a carving of a nymph on an ancient vase (154), however, Amerigo in the early scene also thinks of Charlotte as incarnating a lost beauty: her arms have "the polished slimness that Florentine sculptors, in the great time, had loved, and of which the apparent firmness is expressed in their old silver and old bronze" (59). In the later passage Verver is bemused by the coexistence of images of nymph and nun to characterize the "prim" Maggie as well as by his tendency to think of persons and works of art in equivalent terms. Amerigo has less clarity in perceiving Charlotte's "sylvan head of a huntress" simultaneously in relation to "his notion, perhaps not wholly correct, of a muse." The slight disclaimer by the narrator might be linked by us to the fact that Charlotte first appears to Amerigo as "a cluster of possessions of his own," items or relics in a cabinet. A sense of possession, an objectification, precedes sexual and aesthetic appreciation (although, to be fair to the prince, relics also imply reverence). Quickly, too, Charlotte's body is seen as a wonderful "instrument," having "attachments," "something intently made for exhibition, for a prize." The collector's instinct is visible, and the word *attachments* adds mechanical overtones to the aesthetic sense of *instrument*. Finally, the prince cannot resist the money analogy, which supplants the sexual and, suggestively, the natural:

> He knew above all the extraordinary fineness of her flexible waist, the stem of an expanded flower which gave her a likeness also to some long, loose silk purse, well filled with gold pieces, but having been passed, empty, through a finger-ring that held it together. It was as if, before she turned to him, he had weighed the whole thing in his open palm and even heard a little the chink of the metal. (58–59)

The imagery prepares later passages noted above—the chink of gold Amerigo hears at Matcham, the money bag proffered to Maggie on the last page. Perhaps even more significantly, the description of Amerigo's appreciation of Charlotte conveys a bodily, erotic quality which, form appropriately "embodying" theme, is instantly transformed by the writing into the monetary.

Charlotte as much as Amerigo is later perceived as a precious object by the "great American collector" (171), who however certainly is not such an object himself. Although his daughter sings his praises (484–85), he is "a small, spare, slightly stale person, deprived of the general prerogative of presence," with a "concave little stomach" and a quaintly monotonous style of dress, although "strangely beautiful" eyes (141–42). How this person could have had such a successful "economic history" is a mystery to the narrator, who imagines his brain in the past as a white-hot "workshop of fortune," where the "acquisitive power" assured the "perfection of machinery," "the necessary triumph of all operations." Although amiability has "been known to be the principle of large accumulations," Verver's success is ascribed to a lack of "variety of imagination," an inscrutable monotony (112–13). Verver himself recalls the fascination of "transcendent calculation and imaginative gambling," also the "vulgarity" of getting in or out of the market first. Finally he views "acquisition of one sort as a perfect preliminary to acquisition of another" (124). He is driven by "the idea (followed by appropria-

tion) of plastic beauty" (160). He wants to avoid "vulgarity," but
it is suggested that he appreciates the "look" of authenticity as
much as authenticity itself (121, 126). Tantalizingly, he is the
only one who does not see the bowl. But there is good reason to
view him as a supremely vulgar acquisitor, storing countless
works in warehouses, vaults, banks, and safes like a pirate (36),
basking like Alexander amid the spoils of Darius (40), having
realized that "the business of his future" is to "rifle the Golden
Isles" (122), wishing to transport the church at Fawns "in a glass
case, to one of his exhibitory halls" (129). Many have regretted
that a real American millionaire has realized such a wish as Adam's. His goal, to release grateful millions "from the bondage of
ugliness," is hardly treated kindly either when it is called "the
religion . . . the passion for perfection at any price" (124–25).

Moreover, despite attempts to defend the Ververs, the novel
irremediably shows them treating Amerigo and Charlotte as
objects, however precious. The paragraph about the prince as
"representative" precious object concludes that works of art surrounding Verver, "as a general challenge to acquisition and
appreciation, so engaged all the faculties of his mind, that the
instinct, the particular sharpened appetite of the collector, had
fairly served as a basis for his acceptance of the Prince's suit"
(121). Here the "accepted monomania" (171) that leads him to
the Damascene tiles takes on a less genial tone. As for Verver's
desire to satisfy himself simultaneously about Charlotte and the
tiles, the narrator this time takes a critical stance: "Nothing
perhaps might affect us as queerer, had we time to look into it,
than this application of the same measure of value to such
different pieces of property as old Persian carpets, say, and new
human acquisitions; all the more indeed that the amiable man
was not without an inkling, on his own side, that he was, as a
taster of life, economically constructed" (159–60). Verver is still
amiable, and the narrator apparently diffident, but the queer-
ness of acquiring people like property, in this economic construction of human relations, is exhibited.

The beautiful, horrible, last meeting of the four characters
(540–41) pointedly reasserts the gratification and suffering connected with the themes of acquisition, precious objects, and

money that we have been pursuing. Maggie is united with her father in "abiding felicity" (despite his departure), in part through the mediation of a work of art. The Florentine "treasure" that had been his wedding gift to her now seems to contain him and his love "as if the frame made positively a window for his spiritual face": "In leaving the thing behind him, held as in her clasping arms, he was doing the most possible toward leaving her a part of his palpable self." Here a "thing," an object of aesthetic acquisition, has been irradiated with love, and what could be seen as an alienating need for possession becomes humanized.

But the dehumanizing result of aesthetic accumulation dominates in the Ververs' view of the room and of their respective mates. The furniture and art, "objects," " 'important' pieces," are supreme and noble, with "the whole nobleness" including the "two noble persons," "who fairly 'placed' themselves, however unwittingly, as high expressions of the kind of human furniture required, aesthetically, by such a scene." The note of class deceit is not absent (just before, Maggie and her husband had seemed to her to be "distinctly *bourgeois!"* [537]). More importantly, Amerigo and Charlotte, human furniture, unwittingly continue to contribute to Verver's "triumph of selection." Or, as he says to Maggie: *"Le compte y est.* You've got some good things." Clearest of all, the "diffident" narrator whose comments we have occasionally noted intervenes devastatingly here: "Though, to a lingering view, a view more penetrating than the occasion really demanded, they also might have figured as concrete attestation of a rare power of purchase." What the prince vaguely apprehended at the outset has been made overwhelmingly clear by the end: the celebration of the aesthetic and the misuse of persons, two forms of acquisition, are rooted in that original accumulation, the money of the amiable Adam Verver.

Against a sociohistorical background glimpsed in *The Golden Bowl* though evident in *Ulysses,* James and Joyce depict the delusions of social, sexual, ethnic, and national bias and reveal human values as deformed in different segments of society by the need for, and the accumulation of, money. In spite of Marxist criticisms of these "modernist" writers, it seems instead that their works are consonant with Marx's analysis of the deprivation of the poor and the alienation of the rich. Even on formal grounds, the accusations of excessive attention to technique (James on "the endless worth for 'delight,' of the compositional contribution" [9], Joyce's formal innovations), and of "fragmentation" of the inner person (stream of consciousness and "oblique" "point of view" [7,8]), especially as formulated by Lukács, seem off the mark. What follows is a more nuanced appreciation of form (although certainly not isolated from thematic considerations), organized for the sake of focus around James's preface and the strategically situated and structured "Aeolus" chapter.

There is matter in the preface to justify the claim that James overestimates the value of works of literature and of the literary profession—pompous formulations about the "pretension of performance by a series of exquisite laws," on "the creative power otherwise so veiled" (7), on novels as a "superior and more appreciable order" than many "vital or social performances" in our dispersed lives (25–26). But the portentous vocabulary surrounds the argument that literature represents a superior use of responsibility, conduct, and freedom (25), enunciated first in relation to James's preference for "indirect" narrative tactics, not "my own impersonal account of the affair in hand, but . . . my account of somebody's impression of it" (7–8). This opposes "the mere muffled majesty of irresponsible 'authorship' " that he might maliciously have found in Stephen Dedalus's pronouncements about the genres in *Portrait of the Artist as a Young Man* or Joyce's practice in *Ulysses*. Absolutizing literature and viewing life as performance gives us pause, but the insistence on the author's ethical implication in the work rings true, in formal and thematic terms, for *The Golden Bowl*.[10]

James's satifaction with form in his best works ("so many close notes . . . on the particular vision of the matter itself that experience had at last made the only possible one" [17]) seems justified in the case of *The Golden Bowl*, a novel in which "we see very few persons," but "see about as much of them as a coherent literary form permits." His "small handful of values" (char-

acters in his view being both "intrinsic" values and "compositional" resources) are worked to the fullest in a novel that,
despite its unfolding over a period of years with artfully man-
aged gaps, delays, and mysteries, is indeed highly coherent (9–
10). Even considering its focus on three protagonists and its use
of the unities and Homeric parallels, *Ulysses* requires other perspectives to be viewed as "a coherent literary form," something
like Northrop Frye's all-inclusive work of narration in a perspective of ideological criticism. The books, however, share the feature of unhappy marriage and correspondingly problematic
endings. And, despite the technical "ingenuity" (10) of both
writers, as well as the contrary class limitations of the characters
in the works, the novels have that stature that James also requires for successful fiction. They are general, comprehensive,
and exemplary (19, 26)—as everything argued earlier in this
chapter proves, Marx's ideas in my view serving to enhance our
awareness of these qualities.

Moreover, in keeping with James's insistence on the author's
ethical responsibility, *The Golden Bowl*, through what it shows and
through narrative comment, constantly places its characters in a
critical moral perspective with regard to money, social position,
and the exploitation of others to those as well as to "aesthetic"
ends. The "use" of people is much discussed in the novel, in a
minor way in the case of Fanny and horrendously in that of
Charlotte and Amerigo. Maggie's vision of the latter two pushing
the family coach, containing herself, Verver, and the principino,
well represents the situation in which Charlotte has been " 'had
in,' as the servants always said of extra help" (315). The avidity of
Amerigo and Charlotte, and Verver's unromantic proposal,
have been mentioned, but not the strange arrangement in which
Maggie by telegram in effect gives permission for the marriage.
Some of the most disturbing formulas (among many) on all of
this concern the Ververs' enjoyment of their "purchased social
ease" (331) and their later less tranquil conversation on Charlotte and why they had wanted "to get her for?" Maggie answers,
"Oh yes—to give us a life" (364)!

The tranquility with which this use of others is discussed by
the Ververs is chilling. So is the deceit engaged in by all—the

initial dishonesty of Amerigo and Charlotte, the deception practiced by the others in response. Lies and silences eventually engage all in a painful masquerade in which all essentially know
what is happening. Maggie and Fanny see "high decency," form,
taste, and finally Charlotte's "mastery of the greater style" (290,
519, 531, 547) in this fascinating behavior, but the inhuman
damage is remorselessly stressed—in Charlotte's shriek and Amerigo's grimace (496–99), in the imagery of steel hoop (396), gilt
cage (454), prison (498, 526), and silken noose (493, 522).

Ironically, in view of this later imagery, Charlotte and the
prince had thought that in their affair they were rediscovering
their freedom (208, 220–28, 268–69). And troublingly, Maggie's
exhilaration at her victory over them is inseparable from her
awareness that they have instead lost all independence, her compassion accompanied by her own sense of freedom—freedom to
be always with the prince despite his suffering (430, 452, 490,
498–99, 546–47).

Traditional values, truth and freedom, are shown in compromised form in *The Golden Bowl.* So much more so is the more
fundamental and inclusive ideal of ethical behavior itself. At the
outset the prince intends to be "much more decent as a son-in-
law than lots of fellows" (30), and the narrator's comment about
his use of English does not completely erase the impression of
lightness that the formulation carries with it. Amerigo also insists
to Maggie that he doesn't lie (37)! Evidently such initial "beautiful intentions all around" (291) that Fanny perceives in the main
characters are not enough to ensure morally justifiable behavior.
I extend Fanny's "all around" to include the Ververs, because
they are shown to hold to a view of conduct that does not differ
basically from that of Charlotte's and Amerigo's.

The prince enunciates the view with nervous sententiousness
in his first re-encounter with Charlotte: "My dear friend . . . it's
always a question of doing the best for one's self one can—
without injury to others" (67). This ethical commonplace, attacked by Marx in its political form in "On the Jewish Question"
as the key to the egoism of bourgeois society, indeed takes on a
sinister aspect when, strong in their sense of the injury done to
them, the two embark on that intimacy "of which the sovereign

law would be the vigilance of 'care,' would be never rashly to forget and never consciously to wound" (246). Later, after Matcham, Maggie is aware in the prince—where it is a matter of not offending Verver (whose wife is Amerigo's mistress!)—"of the felt need of not working harm!" (343).

But the Ververs at Fawns before their summons to Charlotte also "each knew that both were full of the superstition of not 'hurting.' " The narrator adds that they "might precisely have been asking themselves, asking in fact each other . . . whether that was to be, after all, the last word of their conscientious development" (135). In spite of their subsequent growth in consciousness (not conscientiousness), the answer to this question appears to be "yes." At the opening of Book Second, Maggie sees "the possibility of some consequence disagreeable or inconvenient to others" (304) as the only constraint on her freedom of response. Near the end she reasserts her desire not to hurt others: "I don't at all want . . . to be blinded, or made 'sniffy,' by any sense of social situation"; "One must always, whether or no, have some imagination of the states of others—of what they may feel deprived of." In contrast to earlier mild self-criticism, Verver here responds that he is not selfish (472–76). Contrary to the claim to concern for others and awareness of social difference (concerning Lutch and Rance), the silent subtext of the discussion is the decision to take Charlotte away to America. As a wife with her back to the wall, Maggie is justified, we may feel, in causing and even enjoying the torment that Amerigo and Charlotte experience. But the concern for others she so pompously announces, in this universe of interpersonal strife, is left very much in tatters in the process.

We need to extend the argument to include the puzzle of Verver as "amiable" millionaire. In the passage just described, Maggie recalls her and her father's reflection in the wake of Matcham on their original decision to bring Charlotte "in." During their discussion at that time (361–62) Verver had talked of their immorality and selfishness, of being "all careless of mankind," in a "kind of wicked selfish prosperity perhaps, as if we had grabbed everything, fixed everything, down to the last lovely object for the last glass case of the last corner, left over, of my show." To Maggie's "pleasantly echoed" question, "The immorality?" he answers:

> Well, we're tremendously moral for ourselves—that is for each other; and I won't pretend that I know exactly at whose particular expense you and I, for instance, are happy. What it comes to, I daresay, is that there's something haunting—as if it were a bit uncanny—in such a consciousness of our general comfort and privilege.

The reader might be excused for impatience at this pleasantly hypocritical statement, in which morality is circumscribed to Marx's individual monad and immediate family—the father-daughter couple against all. Hypocritical it is, on two levels. In the following pages, through distortions and lies, Charlotte emerges as the person "at whose particular expense" the Ververs have been happy. But there is a more fundamental explanation of their comfort, which is hardly "uncanny," of their ability to purchase every "last lovely object." They are happy at the expense of those from whom Verver has profited ("by devious ways," as he vaguely and at only one point recalls [124]), specifically from his past workers. Nothing in this novel, or perhaps anywhere in James's writing, explicitly "authorizes" this reading, which, however, in a Marxist perspective is the inevitable and accurate one.

That such considerations are not foreign to the book, as well as the intricacy and aptness of James's formal structuring of it, are apparent from the scene in which the Ververs first decide to invite Charlotte to Fawns, a scene to which the two passages just discussed of course refer. Characteristically, the earlier passage (139–56) begins with the Ververs' contentment in their fortune and ease, a kind of "helplessness in their felicity." The narrator, however, draws our attention to the importance of the moment and to the possibility that they are insufficiently aware of that importance: "But mightn't the moment possibly count for them— or count at least for us while we watch them with their fate all before them—as the dawn of the discovery that it doesn't always meet *all* contingencies to be right?" Thus warned, we may be alerted to the significance of what follows: the description of

Verver's "stale person" but his inevitable place in the marriage "market," Charlotte's failures in her effort to marry, whereby she remains poor if admirable in Maggie's eyes. The Ververs' banter about her is anything if not condescending: "It [Maggie's wealth] ought to make me—if I were in danger of being a fool—all the nicer to people like Charlotte"; "Well, she mustn't be wasted. We won't at least have waste"; "But one can always, for safety, be kind . . . one feels when that's right." The issue of using Charlotte also crops up for the first time: "I should always, even at the worst—speaking for myself—admire her still more than I used her." The irony of Maggie's words as the story unfolds is matched by that of her giving Charlotte credit for courage in an unhappy love for "somebody I'm not acquainted with," together with her realization that she herself has never suffered: "Do you realize, father, that I've never had the least blow?"

The Ververs are depicted as affably capable of using others, unknowingly preparing suffering for themselves as well. We grasp some of this because of the narrator's warning, but it becomes clearer once we know the end, which justifies James's insistence in the Preface on rereading (as well as viva voce reading), on reading as a docile submission (do we agree?), one that nonetheless constitues an "*act* of re-appropriation" (14–15). Reading *The Golden Bowl* involves submersion in an extremely intricate text, in which patience and attentiveness are at a premium, to my mind a process far more trying than that of reading *Ulysses* (recalling the reaction to James's last novel by a distinguished colleague—"What a dull read!"—as well as Stéphane Mallarmé's judgment, in response to the charge of obscurity, that his contemporaries did not know how to read).[11]

The cooperative activity of narrator and reader is insistently marked, sometimes in affected fashion, as the narrating "I" explicitly multiplies his metaphors (304) or "our" attention to Verver becomes "tender almost to compassion" (111). As noted, the narrator consistently emits judgments, sometimes concerning elements that *seem* minor, sometimes on evidently crucial manners. We saw an example of the former regarding Prince Amerigo's musings on his marriage contract in the opening pages of the book. Similarly, at the opening of Book Second,

Maggie's architectural image of her situation produces this comment: "Maggie's actual reluctance to ask herself with proportionate sharpness why she had ceased to take comfort in the sight of it represented accordingly a lapse from that ideal consistency on which her moral comfort almost at any time depended" (303). The growth from this limited awareness to the prince's "fear of her fifty ideas" at the end (527) is prodigious.

Maggie's fifty ideas show her to be in the long run a wizardess in the possession of the complex states of awareness that exalt Fanny Assingham, that the prince mistakenly thinks are impossible for his wife and father-in-law, and that James's preface celebrates as the goal of literature, the "fun" for author and reader. The ultimate form of such finer consciousness is represented by those silent interactions that abound in the novel, early on in the "communion" between Amerigo and Fanny into which a spectator "might have read meanings of his own" (50). Later there is the "mute communication" between Maggie and Verver that we might "prematurely" take as critical (131) but that does quickly lead to the decision to invite Charlotte. After Matcham, these unarticulated communications become more frequent and more intense, with characters (rather than narrator and reader) interpreting the thoughts of others, often to the point of imagining whole speeches, as on the evening of Amerigo's tardy return— "Some such words as those were what *didn't* ring out" (312). This process focuses on Maggie, in her duel with Charlotte and in her increasing mastery of Amerigo. The latter phenomenon is notable after Fanny breaks the bowl, when there occurs between husband and wife a silent and "unprecedented moral exchange over which her superior lucidity presided" (428). Increasingly these silent communications also punctuate Maggie's interactions with her father. Knowing "by the warning of his eyes" not to express her thought directly (480), Maggie gets Verver to understand that Charlotte must be taken away, and this is followed by the "snatched communion" between them, in which unasked questions concerning Charlotte's "shriek of a soul in pain" are imagined and Verver's look conveys shame, pity, anguish, until "blushing to his eyes, he turned short away" (496–97).

Within the action of the novel, therefore, the Preface's "maturer mind," "speculative interest," "intellectual 'sport,' " "intenser lights of experience," and the "immense array of terms, perceptional and expressional," that evoke them (17–18), have a horrible content of human conflict. And "communions" are most often hideously painful. Although in its evocation of external things, expressive of wealth and exalted class, the novel does intermittently "bristle with immediate images" (11)—just as through the consciousness of Bloom *Ulysses* is filled with the objects of another socioeconomic sphere—nonetheless the overwhelming impression in *The Golden Bowl* is of isolated consciousnesses, locked in combat. The bipartite structure of the book corresponds. Jameson's labeling of James's narrative method as "privatized" seems an appropriate characterization of the work's silent speeches, a kind of *sous-conversation* expressive of estrangement and struggle. *The Golden Bowl* does not finally celebrate such ambiguous finer consciousness, just as in its dissection of its characters it avoids Fanny Assingham's identification of morality with "high intelligence" (87). As for the reader, there is much insight, gained through the strain and exaltation of the book's narrative mode. Reading in *The Golden Bowl* is an alienation that provides knowledge.

The Golden Bowl exhaustively mines a single narrative mode. *Ulysses* by contrast is a "chaffering allincluding most farraginous chronicle" (423), not least in its bewildering variety of formal conventions. "Aeolus" is pertinent as the first chapter to introduce "intrusive" modes against the preceding norm of objective narrative flowing abundantly into interior monologue; the chapter also prepares much that follows, thematically and formally. Its congruence with Marx is considerable, particularly with the much criticized but suggestive fragment in the *Grundrisse* on myth, technology, and literature (245–46). Marx there values myth highly as an imaginative shaping and mastering of nature, which however is superseded by actual control of nature through technology.

That myth can be so thoroughly evacuated is subject to debate, and might be debated extensively in relation to *Ulysses;* "Aeolus," where the Homeric underpinning seems arbitrary and ironic, might illustrate Marx's view of the issue.[12] Beyond irony is the question of the impact of the technology of journalism on consciousness and the creation of literary forms. Marx makes the obvious point that traditional epic is incompatible with the printing machine, and his question "What becomes of Fama alongside Printing House Square?" interestingly accords with Joyces's writing in "Aeolus," where newspaper technology and expression (and bombastic mythology) inform the minds of the characters and the pattern of our reading.

Hence Bloom's problem is to communicate concerning the Keyes ad amid the noisy machinery (before attempting to reach Keyes through other means of transport and communication, phone and tram). His initial reaction combines prudence and cliché: "Machines. Smash a man to atoms if they got him caught. Rule the world today." He also notes the skills involved in producing a paper: Murray's skill with scissors and paste, Nannetti's proofreading, the typesetter's backward reading and dexterity: "Seems to see with his fingers." "Almost human," the machinery does "its level best to speak," thereby interrupting human communication: "Slipping his words deftly into the pauses of the clanking he drew swiftly on the scarred-woodwork" (117–22). The innerness that characterizes Bloom elsewhere (despite his openness to external stimuli) is inflected by the technological environment. But as usual he has a good deal of insight: "Funny the way those newspaper men veer about. . . . Weathercocks. Hot and cold in the same breath. Wouldnt know which to believe. One story good till you hear the next" (125). Or, in O'Molloy's words: "Sufficient for the day is the newspaper thereof" (139). This slightly funny modification of the biblical text become proverb reminds us that, as Bloom is bombarded by the sounds of the presses, we follow him through the formalized interruptions of the headlines, which contribute some amusement, some insight, and much proverbial cliché: GENTLEMEN OF THE PRESS (116); HOW A GREAT DAILY ORGAN IS TURNED OUT (118); INTERVIEW WITH THE EDITOR (146).

Bloom's efforts relate "Aeolus" to the socioeconomic preoccupations of the book. WE SEE THE CANVASSER AT WORK (119) and also see Stephen as "bullockbefriending bard" (132), bearer of Deasy's letter about foot-and-mouth disease and the Irish cattle trade. Stephen's presence provokes a job offer: "He wants you for the

pressgang," says O'Molloy (135). As the latter prepares to render
an example of Irish oratory, Stephen thinks, "Noble words coming. Look out. Could you try your hand at it yourself?" (142). He
resists the temptation. In the newspaper office both he and Bloom
act characteristically in regard to money, Bloom timidly trying to
get repayment for a loan (119), Stephen inviting the newspaper-
men for a drink, thinking: "I have money" (143).

Other resonant issues come to the attention of Bloom and
Stephen through the rantings of those in the office, and to us
through the headlines as well. Events in the world, disasters and
assassinations, are naturally known to the journalists. The conflict with England is evoked through patriotic speechifying. Recalling the ethnic themes discussed earlier, Bloom is impressed
that the Italian Nannetti is integrated in Irish society to the point
of holding office: "More Irish than the Irish" (118–19). By contrast, despite parallels between Irish and Jew under English and
Egyptian oppression, Bloom himself is treated rudely in Crawford's response to Keyes: "He can kiss my royal Irish arse" (147).
This may appear to support national pride but clearly forgets
who is politically subject to whom. If the professor approves a
similar insight by Bloom (124), and Crawford expresses the
more apt "You and I are the fat in the fire" (131), the two
nonetheless indulge in the balderdash about Irish history that is
so debilitating throughout. With Nelson's column just outside,
the professor carries on about the Irish propensity for lost
causes: "We are liege subjects of the catholic chivalry of Europe
that foundered at Trafalgar" (133). And Crawford turns an
event in the Irish-English conflict, the Phoenix Park murders,
into a celebration of *newspaper* history, creating a kind of mythology of journalism around the figure of THE GREAT GALLAHER:
"Gave it to them on a hot plate . . . the whole bloody history";
"That's press. That's talent" (135–37). In response, Stephen
thinks, "Nightmare from which you will never awake," where I
take the "you" to designate Crawford and the others. The
changes from his earlier statement to Deasy indicate Stephen's
growing awareness of the entrapping coils not only of history but
of falsifying versions of it.

Counterpointed with some of the headlines (in this case the

redundancy and cliché of Crawford's ranting as suggested by
LINKS WITH BYGONE DAYS OF YORE [139]), stream of consciousness
thus continues to play a major role in "Aeolus," to the point that
a single word conveys Bloom's sense of separation and desire for
acceptance:

> —Of course, if he wants a par, Red Murray said earnestly, a
> pen behind his ear, we can do him one.
> —Right, Mr Bloom said with a nod. I'll rub that in.
> We. (117)

Lukács, who seems unaware of any other mode in *Ulysses,* is right
to link inner monologue with alienation, to the extent that the
separate sequences of three chapters each that precede "Aeolus"
have shown both Stephen and Bloom as embattled personalities,
preoccupied with personal and familial tensions, worried about
success or failure, in tension with others. In "Aeolus," amid the
noise and concern about money, Bloom recalls fleetingly his dead
father, and Stephen recalls the strophe he composed in "Proteus,"
where among other things he had been thinking of his mother,
sex, and death. Significantly, "Aeolus" is the first chapter to bring
about a near intersection of the two, at the same time that it
intrudes the headline convention on the inner monologues.[13]

Stream of consciousness reappears strongly in "Lestrygon-
ians," where Bloom feels threatened by Boylan and other men,
and "Scylla and Charybdis," where Stephen does intellectual
battle in the library. Even in chapters in which different modes
intrude and dominate, stream of consciousness brings us back
to the individuality of Stephen and Bloom—in "Wandering
Rocks," "Sirens," and the second half of "Nausicaa." In the first
two of these, the mixture of stream of consciousness and indirect monologue (*erlebte Rede*) allows secondary and even more
minor characters such as Conmee, Richie Goulding, and Stephen's father to look like fools; in the first half of "Nausicaa"
heavily ironic erlebte Rede is foregrounded to produce a personality that is almost entirely formed of the clichés of a certain
kind of reading. If the passage is subject to a feminist critique,
Bloom as male protagonist hardly fares heroically in the chapter, where the return to his voice reemphasizes how solitary his

sexual act has been. Similarly, the singing in "Sirens" may seem to effect the union of "Siopold!" (276), but this is undercut by Bloom's cool reflections on how music produces such feelings. In any event he has chosen to sit apart in another room—"See, not be seen" (265). This proximity which is really isolation is generalized in the narrative mode of "Wandering Rocks." There the unifying thread of the viceregal procession and the separate sections on different individuals could be seen as paralleling the Hegelian-Marxist categories of civil and political—for Marx, the political being a delusion, the civil a realm of isolated warring individuals.

But the book famously moves its two male leads into ever closer connection and toward the recumbent Molly (another source of the feminist critique). Bloom glimpses Stephen on a couple of occasions early on. We have seen that each separately runs across Dilly and that Bloom listens to Si Dedalus in "Sirens." They literally cross paths in the library, before the drunken noncommunication of "Oxen of the Son" and "Circe." "Circe," and to some extent the concluding pages of "Ithaca" and all of "Penelope," allow for an expansion of the waking self into the realms of the pre- and subconscious and the mythic, revealing the primordial dialectic of psyche, family, sex—and death. (Nonetheless, as we saw, the sociopolitical violently reasserts itself in the person of Private Carr.) The fact that the discussion between Stephen and Bloom is deflected by the verbiage of "Eumaeus" and the vast impersonality of "Ithaca" accords with the psychosomatic states of the participants and with the perhaps fleeting nature of their meeting, Joyce allowing the reader to imagine what may ensue in the future. But Bloom's "searching ordeal" in "Circe" ("To drive me mad! Moll! I forgot! Forgive! Moll!" [514, 541]), his defense of Stephen and almost unbearably moving hallucination of Rudy, and Stephen's confrontations with his mother's ghost and Private Carr are spiritual triumphs that must have some positive results. Further, the clarity of "Ithaca" allows for sharper insight, for example, Bloom's view of Stephen's "predominant qualities": "Confidence in himself, an equal and opposite power of abandonment and recuperation" (673). Finally, despite Molly's flaws, with the return of interior monologue in "Penelope" we indeed encounter an intrinsic value and a compositional resource, a rounded character in more than one sense of the phrase.

We might think of these meanings garnered in pursuing the modulations and transcendences of interior monologue as the products of a "working through" in the psychoanalytic sense. Much else in *Ulysses* constitutes an ideological working through, with "Aeolus" being the apt point of departure for a number of features to be studied in this connection. First, there is the contrary of the individual mind, the totalizing perspective that in "Wandering Rocks" seems to encompass the entire city and its inhabitants before leaving behind the sociopolitical and veering off to the infinite perspectives of "Ithaca." "Aeolus" begins IN THE HEART OF THE HIBERNIAN METROPOLIS, with a hint of global perspectives through the postal system—"for local, provincial, British and overseas delivery" (116). For the first time in HELLO THERE, CENTRAL!, if fleetingly, the narrative attains the citywide scope necessary for a chapter like "Wandering Rocks": "At various points along the eight lines tramcars with motionless trolleys stood in their tracks, bound for or from Rathmines, Rathfarnham, Blackrock, Kingston and Dalkey, Sandymount Green, Ringsend and Sandymount Tower, Donnybrook, Palmerston Park and Upper Rathmines, all still, becalmed in short circuit" (149). Here as elsewhere it is clear that Lukács was wrong in his argument that Dublin is inessential to *Ulysses*. The growth beyond narrowly subjective perspectives is linked to the "content" of the city and to the totalizing views that are the key to that content. Hence before telling his parable, Stephen thinks: "Dublin. I have much, much to learn" (144).[14]

Other elements in "Aeolus" recall the ideological critique through parody of various modes of discourse that Marx practiced as brilliantly as Flaubert. Approached in such a perspective, the chapter can give us a view of much in *Ulysses* that has appeared to be stylistic trickery for its own sake as instead highly motivated. "Aeolus" is a laboratory for the study of forms that later threaten to take on overwhelming proportions.

As we have seen, journalism and political oratory are highlighted. But they are surrounded by an array of other modes of expression, some of them included in the list preceded by the

headline OMNIUM GATHERUM—law, the classics, the turf, literature, the press, advertising, and vocal music (135). Examples of
forensic oratory, the language of racing, literary allusions, the
headlines, and Bloom's ad, references to opera, and lines from
Irish patriotic songs do crowd together in "Aeolus," and intrude,
often massively, in later chapters.

  We should add to these the actual phrases in Hebrew, Greek,
Latin, and French that occur in "Aeolus," most easily comprehensible and related to the issues under discussion—Irish-Jewish
parallels, the lost radiance of the Greeks, the dominance of empire for Romans and English. No Irish can be spoken, which
lends a point to the headline HIS NATIVE DORIC (126) in relation
to Taylor's oratory at a meeting concerning the restoration of
the Irish language. The speech itself is an example of bombast:
the professor belches in the middle of his rendition, and Stephen, moved by an earlier speech (140), dismisses Taylor's as
"dead noise" (143). Moreover, the phrase "native Doric," echoed
in "Sirens" as a prelude to Dollard's singing of "The Croppy
Boy" (282), is significant. It refers both to the language of the
Dorian Greeks and to rustic English and Scottish dialects at the
end of the nineteenth century. Particularly as describing Irish
oratory and song expressed *in English,* it implies both the reality
of British dominance and the elusiveness of native expression or
authentic insight among the multifarious modes of utterance in
"Aeolus."

  Especially if we add to those already noted these others:
Lenehan's repertory of foolish expression—mock Latin and
Franglais, riddle, limerick, baby talk; Burke's version of archaic
language and literary allusion; " 'Tis the hour, methinks, when
the winejug, metaphorically speaking, is most grateful in Ye ancient hostelry," "Lay on, Macduff!" (143–44); and the reiteration
of the clichés of master codes, national, ethnic, and religious:
AND IT WAS THE FEAST OF THE PASSOVER; ERIN, GREEN GEM OF THE
SILVER SEA; O, HARP EOLIAN; THE GRANDEUR THAT WAS ROME;
KYRIE ELEISON!; ITALIA, MAGISTRA ARTIUM; FROM THE FATHERS
(122–23, 127, 131, 133, 139, 142).

  In amplified form the features enumerated above, alone or in
combination, are relevant for the unconventional modes that

make several later chapters difficult but rewarding reading. The combination of archetypal codes, journalistic and other forms of cliché, and parody explains many of the effects of boredom, hilarity, and insight in "Cyclops," "Nausicaa," and "Eumaeus." The music in "Aeolus" threatens to impose its form on language and lucidity in "Sirens," where in combination with political eloquence it is finally stopped, not by a belch but by a fart. And if the obsession with Shakespeare causes stylistic quirks in "Scylla and Charybdis," "Oxen of the Sun" parodies the entire literary canon of English before degenerating into the nonsense, baby talk, mockeries of language and dialects and nationalities, racing slang, and everything else that could be a drunken expansion of Lenehan's performance in the newspaper office.

All of this does not have the limited function of demonstrating Joyce's virtuosity. As the self expands beyond the stream of consciousness in the "unconventional" chapters treated earlier, so also must it be grasped that sociopolitical realities cannot be glimpsed except through the exhibition of the various discourses in which they disguise and impose themselves. That these discourses attain monstrous proportions in later chapters attests to their formative and controlling power, which needs to be revealed and deflated. Such is the price of Stephen's "Nightmare from which you will never awake"; "Dublin. I have much, much to learn"; "But in here it is I must kill the priest and the king."

Such also is the price of his parable (144–50), whose scope is far more inclusive than his devotion to the aesthetic, his morbid poem or the epiphanies that he now mocks (40), and whose importance is stressed by the fact that he repeats it to Bloom in "Ithaca" (685*ff.*). Bloom characteristically sees in it potential for "financial, social, personal and sexual success" in terms alien to Stephen, but this is followed by a quite forthright exchange between the two on Jewishness, exile, and accomplishment. The exchange is especially significant since Bloom just misses the parable in "Aeolus," in fact interrupts it with the business that provokes Crawford's K.M.R.I.A., disrupting as well Stephen's stream of consciousness. The reaction of the others to the parable is also delayed briefly by the notation of trams stalled at points throughout the city. Stephen's ironic and incisive "vision"

thus emerges within the conflicts and discrepancies of internal
and external worlds, individual and supraindividual perspectives. Nonetheless he forges ahead with it: "On now. Dare it. Let
there be life."

The thematics of Stephen's parable are expressive of his experiences earlier and in the newspaper office and of the work as a
whole. There is Irish religion and repressed sexuality—the Dublin vestals, wise virgins, Lourdes water, and passionist priests,
Crawford's uneasy reaction to Stephen's description of the old
women pulling up their skirts and sitting down on their striped
petticoats, the ugly if funny physicality of their eating and drooling and spitting. Then, too, calling Nelson the "onehandled adul-
terer" takes advantage of glorious and not so glorious aspects of
the admiral's life to link sexual infidelity with military and political conquest. Amid the nonsense about lost causes and Catholic
chivalry, only Stephen emphasizes the importance of the monu-
ment: the women want to see "the views of Dublin from the top
of Nelson's pillar." Ironically, the totality of the Hibernian metropolis is visible only from the perspective of the symbol of
English domination. Only after hearing the title do the others
recognize that from what they have been saying and from his
earlier reflections he has made a parable of religious-sexual and
political oppression.

Like so much else in *Ulysses,* the parable also exaggerates certain features to the point of parody—notably the pretension of
realist or naturalist fiction to exhaustive detail—in the headlines
DEAR DIRTY DUBLIN and LIFE ON THE RAW, Stephen's thought,
"Dubliners," and the details about the women, their names, beliefs, and expenditures: "They buy one and fourpenceworth of
brawn and four slices of panloaf at the north city dining rooms
in Marlborough street from Miss Kate Collins, proprietress." But
we have seen that such exaggerated specificity characterizes the
treatment of Bloom and others throughout the work and recall
also that in "Wandering Rocks" the totalizing perspective is capable of recounting every detail, the precise content of minds as
well as of pockets and bags. Stephen's amusing reproduction of
the nineteenth-century motif of rising above the city in order to
comprehend it thus moves us—as does "Aeolus" as a whole—

along the path from individual consciousness to more comprehensive perspectives.

The parable although brief, hints at other characteristics of *Ulysses* as a whole. There is the mixture of direct presentation of experience and proto-erlebte Rede: "Glory be to God. They had no idea is was that high." The abrupt ending causes Crawford to ask, "Finished?" He has other questions: "Where did they get the plums?"—echoed by the headline, WHAT?—AND LIKEWISE—WHERE? This reminds us that the text of the novel sometimes interrupts itself to raise questions as a reader would, most clearly in "Nausicaa": "But who was Gerty?" (348). The conventions of narrating and reading fiction are counted among the forms of discourse that the fictional work highlights and exposes.

The parable also epitomizes *Ulysses* in the effects it produces—insight into oppression and a laughter that can be grim but also liberating. Stephen reminds the professor of Antisthenes, disciple of the sophist Gorgias, who was the son of noble and bondwoman, wrote a book praising Penelope's beauty over Helen's, and of whom it was said that "none could tell if he were bitterer against others or against himself." The accusation of sophistry, the issues of family and class conflict, the role of Penelope, the sense of pervasive bitterness—these are relevant for Stephen and for Joyce. Indeed, if Stephen's listeners are "tickled" at the end, they are also "weary" and "grim." Nonetheless laughter and insight predominate—in Stephen's "young laugh as a close," and in the professor's reiterated appreciation:

> —I see, the professor said.
> He laughed richly.
> —I see, he said again with new pleasure. Moses and the promised land. We gave him that idea.

But perhaps the most liberating humor is present in the headlines that accompany Stephen's parable, emblematic of the many ways in which throughout *Ulysses* language and form "take off" from the representational function and seem to caper wildly. Earlier headlines vary among those that convey socioeconomic themes (THE CROZIER AND THE PEN [118]), some that read like actual headlines (MEMORABLE BATTLES RECALLED [127]) or that suggest the falsification of journalistic writing (WITH UNFEIGNED REGRET IT IS WE ANNOUNCE THE DISSOLUTION OF A MOST RESPECTED DUBLIN BURGESS [118]), others that have headline form but not content (WHAT WETHERUP SAID [126]), and those that are whimsical and bizarre, a foretaste of those accompanying the parable (ONLY ONCE MORE THAT SOAP [123]). The headlines commenting on the parable are not without their element of clear meaning—on the sexual, political, literary, and religious themes of the book. But by their length, headline format, overdone alliteration, mixture of high-flown language with vernacular and slang, they take on their own zany substantiality: DIMINISHED DIGITS PROVE TOO TITILLATING FOR FRISKY FRUMPS. ANNE WIMBLES, FLO WANGLES—YET CAN YOU BLAME THEM?

This is a far cry from *The Golden Bowl,* which eludes comedy, ending not with laughter but with soundless shrieks, grimaces, and the Aristotelian formula for tragedy. In James's novel the moral act, the act of freedom, consists in rigorous adherence to a single coherent mode, which affords lucid insight while mimicking in its form the condition of alienated consciousness that it depicts. I hope to have shown that the range of what is thus depicted expands in the contexts furnished by Marx and Joyce. And to have shown also that the novel transcends the fetishism of literature in James's preface by its dissection of the inhuman results of aesthetic acquisition among the Ververs and their mates.

Ulysses is comparably honest in its depiction of Stephen's quest for the intellectual imagination in a context of filial guilt and familial impoverishment. The socio-sexual-political meaning of his parable, and related themes that are present throughout and that we have discussed extensively, also demolish the accusation of excessive formalism in his case. Unlike James's writing in *The Golden Bowl,* the structural innovations of many chapters in *Ulysses* allow for what I have called a psychological and ideological working-through. The effect of this working-through is at least to challenge the absolutizing of isolated selfhood, which, despite the closeness of the *sposi* (Maggie and her father!), persists in *The Golden Bowl,* while at the same time exposing the imprisoning discourses that contribute blatantly or insidiously to the society of conflict represented in Joyce's book.

The last point of course we experience directly as readers. Whereas *The Golden Bowl* perpetuates throughout the mode of communication in which a reader-listener responds to the words or voice of a single communicator-narrator, in *Ulysses* we are submitted to *forms* of reading that are essentially different, and first of all in the interrupting headlines of "Aeolus." Reading in *Ulysses* is an expansion that is arduous and liberating.

But it is not a matter of "accounting for" everything that is strange or bizarre in *Ulysses*. The work retains its ineluctable element of the arbitrary, of parody pushed to its limits and thus creating new forms, in keeping perhaps with the conceptions of romantic irony and romantic novel evoked in chapter 1. *The Golden Bowl* is a work of painful consciousness of socioeconomic and personal estrangement clearly consonant with Marx's analyses. Even closer to Marx perhaps, Joyce's more encompassing book has to be appreciated for what it is: supreme anatomy, preciously liberating irony.

Four

VAUTRIN'S HUNDRED

Le Père Goriot and *Absalom, Absalom!*[1] together repre-sent a longer historical span than the novels studied thusfar. They are works which the thought of Marx allows us to see not in terms of simple "influence" (though I believe there is also that) but in terms of literature's deployment of history in what Michel Foucault has called "the space of a dispersion."[2] Foucault's emphasis on the concept of discontinuity may help us to highlight the historical convergence of these novels regarding not only "content" but also their very different formal features— Honoré de Balzac's projective narration in *Goriot*, William Faulk-ner's extraordinarily repetitious and retrospective writing in *Absalom*. Further, if complexity of form, especially in Faulkner's book, is related to the increasingly problematic nature of the effort to represent history through fiction, other issues pursued earlier—the economic, familial, and sexual—also have a height-ened intensity, particularly in the form of homosexual and de-monic themes.

Despite their differences, there is a surprising convergence between *Le Père Goriot,* composed between September 1834 and January 1835 and whose action unfolds in the autumn and win-ter of 1819–20, and *Absalom, Absalom!*, published a century later almost to the year (1936). In Faulkner's book, Quentin Comp-son, first in September 1909, then in January 1910, initially in Mississippi with the elderly Miss Rosa Coldfield and his father, later at Harvard with his Canadian roommate Shreve McCannon, attempts to puzzle out the story of Thomas Sutpen. As we eventually learn, this story begins early in the nineteenth century and continues in Mississippi from the 1830s until the Civil War and beyond, with suggestive connections with France and the French West Indies as well as refigurings of characters, situations, and themes from *Goriot*.

In the genealogy that Faulkner provides at the end, all the characters listed are dead, except Jim Bond, Sutpen's sole (and mulatto, and idiot) descendant, and Shrevlin McCannon, who has completed his studies at Harvard and participated in World War I: "Captain, Royal Army Medical Corps, Canadian Expeditionary Forces, France, 1914–1918. Now a practising surgeon, Edmonton, Alta." (477). These are the last words we read, and in them this most obsessively retrospective of narrations opens into a present and a future that are very nearly our own. But not before its sole competent survivor returns in some sense to the France from which in an important measure *Absalom* derives— which is a way of saying that between them *Goriot* and *Absalom* encompass many of the major historical events of the modern Western world.

We can rehearse some of these features of history in *Goriot*. First, the enfeeblement of provincial nobility, and Eugène de Rastignac's typicality in confronting the new urban-based societal and economic modes. Despite the luxury of Parisian nobility under Louis XVIII the waning of the ancien Régime is signaled by the withdrawal of Madame de Beauséant, last daughter of "the quasi-royal house of Burgundy" (273). The novel also evokes the economic as well as political impact of the French Revolution (the story of how Goriot made his fortune); the history of empire, defeat, and restoration (Madame Couture and other war widows, the former Napoleonic prefect who coaches Rastignac during his first try at gambling, the presentation of Goriot's daughter Anastasie de Restaud at court); and, implicitly, the end of the restoration and the beginning of the July Monarchy. Other significant features appear as well: increased centralization in bureaucracy (Poiret) and police (the chief of police under the name of Gondureau); new forms of economic activity, particularly banking and land speculation (Taillefer and Nucingen, whose wife—

Goriot's other daughter, Delphine—desires to penetrate the sphere of Madame de Beauséant, a representation of the struggle between traditional and finance aristocracies).

Faulkner's novel takes up where Balzac's leaves off and overlaps it, not least in Sutpen's French connection: slaves who speak a form of French, a captive French architect, trips to New Orleans, all finally explained by the revelation that it was in Haiti that he first tried to make his fortune. As Rastignac indicates to Monsieur de Restaud, his family's fortune was compromised in the ruin of the *Compagnie des Indes* (84), so that he and Sutpen are distantly related through the French colonial exploitation of the West Indies. Other features of Sutpen's story evoke the history of English and Scotch immigrants in the Virginia mountains and the slave economy of Tidewater Virginia; land swindles against American Indians and the establishment of plantations in Mississippi; the conflict between this patriarchal slave system and Northern industry; the year-by-year events of the Civil War and its disastrous consequences for Sutpen and those like him; the burden of history for those alive in the first decade of the twentieth century; and—deftly, at the end—the even more obscenely destructive wars of our own century.

Within this historical continuum are set the figures that obsess authors, narrators, and readers. In Balzac: the young Rastignac, his initiation and corruption, the nearly incestuous dimension of the relationships between him, Père Goriot, and Delphine, and the temptation and illumination represented by the homosexual criminal Vautrin. In Faulkner, displaced versions of such personages and relationships: Sutpen, whose design is strikingly similar to Vautrin's, despite his initial "innocence"; his son Henry, initiated into the corrupt French city, this time New Orleans, by Sutpen's son of a first marriage, Charles Bon, who at the end is revealed to have negro blood; indeed, a pervasive incestuous theme involving race and sex, brother and sister, son and father, more extreme than in *Goriot* and comparable to that other astonishing work of urban social analysis and gothic sexual imagination, *La Fille aux yeux d'or (The Girl with the Golden Eyes)*.

At the center of Faulkner's story, Sutpen is a compelling refiguring of Balzac's Vautrin. Vautrin's demonic qualities, fierce look, disguise of wig and dyed sideburns, brick-red hair, robust body and hands covered with "a vigorous growth of fiery red hair," the wound and "chest as shaggy as a bear's back," thick with "reddish, coarse hair" that arouse "a sort of horror, mixed with disgust" and that he has Rastignac touch, together with increasingly more direct hints about his homosexuality, his physical strength, and his ability to shoot the ace of spades from a card at thirty paces (39, 125), are recapitulated in Sutpen—in his "solitary furnace experience," the "big frame . . . with a short reddish beard which resembled a disguise and above which his pale eyes had a quality at once visionary and alert, ruthless and reposed," his display of riding "at a canter around a sapling at twenty feet and [putting] both bullets into a playing card fastened to the tree" (36). Although Sutpen is not a homosexual, the mixture of animal physicality, moral exaltation, and sexual ambivalence that characterizes Vautrin is apparent in him as well— in the recurrent scenes of fighting with his slaves ("a white one and a black one, both naked to the waist and gouging at one another's eyes as if their skins should not only have been the same color but should have been covered with fur too" [31]), in the virginity that he claims to have kept until his first marriage, and in the wounds that he showed Quentin's grandfather, General Compson: "he showed Grandfather the scars, one of which, Grandfather said, came pretty near leaving him that virgin for the rest of his life too" (317).

Another similarity in Vautrin and Sutpen is that they have mysterious, perhaps criminal, pasts and are thought capable of anything, even murder. Vautrin's cover story is that he is a retired merchant, and at the outset no one cares to question that story. Miss Rosa thinks Sutpen disreputable because he has no known lineage; the townspeople arrest him on the assumption that his lavish furnishings must have been gotten illegally. There is also the unlawful or at best shady business deal carried out with the help of the otherwise scrupulous Coldfield—which is never explained. Later, when Sutpen has become successful, his power remains obscure to most, so that they invent an underworld or supernatural role for him:

from the ones who believed that the plantation was just a blind
to his actual dark avocation, through the ones who believed
that he had found some way to juggle the cotton market itself
and so get more per bale for his cotton than honest men could,
to the ones who believed apparently that the wild niggers
which he had brought there had the power to actually conjure
more cotton per acre from the soil than any tame ones had
ever done. (87)

Vautrin is a criminal, as we learn when he is arrested—Jacques
Collin, alias Cheat-Death, treasurer of the Society of Ten Thousand, an original form of organized crime at war with society. It
is one of the similar features of structure in these different works
that the revelations about Sutpen also come late, in chapter 7, in
which Quentin repeats the story of his life that Sutpen told General Compson on two occasions separated by a thirty-year interval. Here we learn for the first time of Sutpen's birth in what was
to become West Virginia, his "fall" into the world of Tidewater
Virginia, the insult that made him resolve to make his fortune by
going to Haiti, where he became the overseer of a French plantation owner, was wounded while quelling an uprising, married
the owner's daughter, but soon repudiated her and their son,
Charles Bon. Hence we realize that all of Sutpen's efforts in
Mississippi represent his second attempt to realize his design, an
effort frustrated by the coming on the scene of Bon, and, with
greater historical inevitability, by the Civil War, after which, as
Rosa remarks, Sutpen's Hundred is reduced to just about Sutpen's *One* (210).

How astonishingly Sutpen's second version of his design corresponds to the idea that Vautrin describes to Rastignac, in his
"offer that nobody would refuse [*une proposition que personne ne
refuserait*]":

My notion is to go and live the patriarchal life on a great estate,
say a hundred thousand acres, in the United States of America,
in the deep South. I intend to be a planter, to have slaves, earn
a few nice little millions selling my cattle, my tobacco, my tim-
ber, living like a monarch, doing as I like, leading a life unimag-
inable by people here where we live crouched in a burrow
made of stone and plaster. . . . I possess at this moment fifty

thousand francs, which would give me scarcely forty niggers. I need two hundred thousand francs, for I want two hundred niggers to carry out my idea of the patriarchal life properly. Negroes, you see, are children ready-made that you can do what you like with, without a nosy Public Prosecutor coming to ask you questions about them. With this black capital, in ten years I shall have three or four millions. If I succeed no one will say to me, "Who are you?" I shall be Mr Four-Millions, American citizen. (131)

Balzac's Vautrin says this in December 1819, in anticipation of departure in 1820, the year that according to the Chronology in *Absalom* Sutpen leaves home (although the date 1823 is mentioned earlier [299]). Speaking from within the alienation of Paris, one of the giant cities at the center of the world economic system, Vautrin desires what Sutpen achieves, patriarchal sovereignty in the far-flung non-European world.

The brutal exploitation of slaves inherent in this "idea" is echoed and exposed in *Absalom* through General Compson's somber reflections on Haiti: "high mortality was concomitant with the money and the sheen on the dollars was not from gold but from blood"; "a theater for violence and injustice and bloodshed and all the satanic lusts of human greed and cruelty"; "a soil manured with black blood from two hundred years of oppression and exploitation until it sprang with an incredible paradox of peaceful greenery and crimson flowers and sugar cane sapling size and three times the height of a man and a little bulkier of course but valuable pound for pound almost with silver ore" (312–13). Here Quentin's grandfather redefines Sutpen's "innocence" and "courage" as "unscrupulousness," and his comments could recall Marx except that he does not apply them to the slave system in Mississippi within which he himself prospered and for which he fought.

Of course Vautrin's goal, to achieve a new identity, so that no one will ask him who he is, and his equation of great wealth with an *American* identity, is also what Sutpen, despite the resistance of the Jefferson community, acquires: "He was the biggest single landowner and cotton-planter in the county now. . . . He was not liked . . . but feared. . . . he was accepted; he obviously had too much money now to be rejected or even seriously annoyed any more" (86–87). Here we encounter a New World realization of what Vautrin explains to Rastignac as a general principle, something like Marx's dissection of the concept of the "primitive accumulation": "The secret of great fortunes with no apparent source is a forgotten crime, forgotten because it was properly carried out" (136).

But Vautrin's "idea," in addition to suggesting the evils of conquest, violence, and racial enslavement that are at the base of Sutpen's wealth (and that he displays and perpetuates in his periodic physical triumphs over his slaves), contains a further contradiction that is central to the drama of the South and the Civil War. His desire to use black "capital" to achieve "patriarchal" sovereignty, recalling justifications of the South against the industrial North (and parallel skirmishes in Faulkner criticism), points to the conflict of differing modes of production that in large measure the Civil War represented. In *Absalom* the only surviving "document," Charles Bon's letter to Judith, expresses, indeed embodies, this fundamental conflict:

> *if I were a philosopher I should deduce and derive a curious and apt commentary on the times and augur of the future from this letter which you now hold in your hands—a sheet of notepaper with, as you can see, the best of French watermarks dated seventy years ago, salvaged (stolen if you will) from the gutted mansion of a ruined aristocrat; and written upon in the best of stove polish manufactured not twelve months ago in a New England factory.* (160)

Bon's letter contains meditations on temporality, the immobilization of time that the war seems to represent, and redundancy but also on time as history and the impact of history on individuals. Its personal augury that he and Judith are among those "*doomed to live*" (163) is negated by Henry, but not his insight into the economic conflict. Writing in "*this year of grace 1865,*" he sees that the very materials that he uses epitomize the conflict. His letter encapsulates part of the historical-economic continuum that is inscribed in discontinuous form in these two novels—reaching back to the aftermath of the Revolution in the mid-1790s in France, evoking the ruin of Southern aristocracy, suggesting the

inevitability of the destruction of Vautrin-Sutpen's dream before
the economic growth of modern industry: *"manufactured not
twelve months ago in a New England factory."* Faced with events of
such scope, might not Vautrin too have ended like Sutpen, "running his little crossroads store with a stock of plowshares and
hame strings and calico and kerosene and cheap beads and rib-
bons and a clientele of freed niggers" (226–27)?

But Vautrin, who is described as having insight into everything, "ships, the sea, France, foreign parts, business, men,
events, the law, great houses and prisons" (40), as possessing a
kind of criminal world-historical consciousness, has the "luck"
to be arrested. His later career, in *Splendor and Misery of Courtesans,* after further crimes, disguises, and the successful seduction of Lucien de Rubempré, ends after Lucien's suicide in
Vautrin's going over to the side of the law and becoming chief
of police, from which he retires tranquilly "around 1845." What
an allegory of the ability of bourgeois society to absorb subversive elements![3]

In contrast, Sutpen, who begins in the furthest reaches of
isolation and at the end is still trying to understand the "error" of
his design, appears as a victim of overwhelming historical forces.
Bon's letter is preceded by the words Judith is supposed to have
said to Quentin's grandmother:

> Because you make so little impression, you see. You get born
> and you try this and you dont know why only you keep on
> trying it and you are born at the same time with a lot of other
> people, all mixed up with them, like trying to, having to, move
> your arms and legs with strings only the same strings are
> hitched to all the other arms and legs and the others all trying
> and they dont know why either except that the strings are all in
> one another's way like five or six people all trying to make a
> rug on the same loom only each one wants to weave his own
> pattern into the rug. (157)

Judith's desperate awareness of being caught in the trammels of
circumstances that no individual can dominate has a parallel in
Mr. Compson's suggestion of personal and familial time being
overtaken by the historical:

Because the time now approached (it was 1860, even Mr Coldfield probably admitted that war was unavoidable) when the destiny of Sutpen's family which for twenty years now had been like a lake welling from quiet springs into a quiet valley and spreading, rising almost imperceptibly and in which the four members of it floated in sunny suspension, felt the first subterranean movement toward the outlet, the gorge which would be the land's catastrophe too, and the four peaceful swimmers turning suddenly to face one another, not yet with alarm or distrust but just alert. (89)

And a similar insight is expressed by Rosa, as she observes Sutpen after the war, struggling "*now not with the stubborn yet slowly tractable earth as . . . before, but now against the ponderable weight of the changed new time itself as though he were trying to dam a river with his bare hands and a shingle*" (202). Superseding Rosa's demonic version of Sutpen's story and tragic interpretations proposed by Mr. Compson and Sutpen himself, such passages present him (with Rastignac, Goriot, and Vautrin) as a representative figure of inevitable economic history.

That the economic is fundamental to Balzac's fiction and that Balzac is close to Marx in this respect have long been recognized. Marx's view of the fiercely competitive nature of bourgeois society and of the denaturing of human relations by money is everywhere paralleled in *Goriot*. The narrator describes the faces of the Parisian underclass in the Pension Vauquer as "coins withdrawn from circulation" (36) and shows Rastignac in his first encounter with Delphine as already imagining his future behavior: "If Madame de Nucingen takes an interest in me I will teach her to manage her husband. The husband deals in the money-market [*fait des affaires d'or*], and with his help I might pick up a fortune in one stroke of business." And the narrator adds: "He did not state this baldly to himself in so many words, he had not the subtlety yet to sum up [*chiffrer*, to figure the cost of] a situation, estimate its possibilities and calculate its chances [*l'apprécier et la calculer*]" (150). Vautrin's dissection of contemporary society ("your social disorder" [125]), marriage, career, and the legal system tells a similar story, that of egotistical struggle for power, domination, money. Big and small, rich and poor alike are governed by financial avidity. Madame Vauquer extracts the utmost from her lodgers, and she and the rest, including church officials, intensify this pursuit at Goriot's death. At the beginning, Madame d'Ambermesnil tries to beat out Madame Vauquer for Goriot's wealth, and Michonneau later bargains for a larger fee for betraying Vautrin. According to the latter, Taillefer murdered his partner during the Revolution, and it is through the murder of Taillefer's son that Vautrin proposes to make the fortune of Rastignac and himself. Delphine explains Nucingen's dishonest real estate manipulations late in the book. Ajuda-Pinto abandons Madame de Beauséant for "two hundred thousand livres a year" (97). And on and on.

The most pathetic case is of course that of Père Goriot, who goes from ease to sordid poverty and agonizing death through his daughters' manipulations. Even on his deathbed he is pressured to provide the money which he no longer has. When Anastasie returns to get her father's signature, Rastignac whispers to Delphine: "She came back for the endorsement" (261), and later he says of Anastasie: she has discounted (*escompté*) "her father's very death into cash" (276). Goriot in his anguish cries out: "Money is life itself, it's the mainspring of everything" (248); "Money buys everything, even daughters" (284). Eugène throws as much blame as possible on Anastasie and wants to exculpate Delphine, but even he has to recognize her—and therefore his—contribution to this "elegant parricide" (270).

Throughout, Vautrin has predicted that unless he chooses the path of revolt, Rastignac will have to make his fortune through an advantageous marriage or liaison. At the end, Eugène confronts the opportunity to begin his career with Delphine (which in later novels will give him the financial, social, and political success that he desires):

> His gaze fixed almost avidly upon that space that lay between the column of the Place Vendôme and the dome of the Invalides; there lay the splendid world that he had wished to penetrate. He eyed that humming hive with a look that seemed to suck out its honey in advance, and said these grandiose words: "It's between us now!"

> And as a first act of throwing down the gauntlet to Society, Rastignac went to dinner with Madame de Nucingen. (304, my translation)

Comments by the narrator have stressed the moral ambiguity of Eugène's behavior, despite his admirable qualities and acts. The ambivalence is maintained in this beginning disguised as an ending, through the vocabulary describing the almost sexual quality of his avidity, the implied irony in the word "grandiose," and the fact that his defiance, far from being an act of revolt, reveals an intention to join society, use its weapons and tactics, and reach its summit.

Rastignac's ambivalence as a protagonist is linked to the economic and social world that the novel depicts. But this is also true of Goriot. This victim has himself been a victimizer, as we discover from the story of how he made his fortune. Rastignac learns the story from the duchesse de Langeais, then from the man who bought Goriot's business. Langeais says that Goriot was

> President of his Section during the Revolution; he was in the know about the notorious famine, and laid the foundation of his fortune at that time by selling flour for ten times as much as it cost him. He had as much flour as he wanted. My grandmother's land-steward sold it to him for immense sums. This Goriot no doubt shared the loot, like all of those people, with the Committee for Public Welfare. (101, my translation)

This is complemented by the "reliable information" obtained from Monsieur Muret:

> Before the Revolution Jean-Joachim Goriot was an ordinary workman employed by a vermicelli-maker. He was a skilful and thrifty man, and enterprising enough to buy his employer's business when by chance the latter fell a victim to the first upheaval in 1789. He established himself . . . and had the great good sense to accept the Presidency of his Section so that his business might have the protection of the most influential persons of those dangerous times. This judicious action laid the foundation of his fortune, which he started to build up in the days of the famine, real or artificial, during which the price of grain soared to dizzy heights in Paris. Most people fought to the death for bread at the bakers' doors, while others went quietly

without any fuss to the grocers, to get hold of Italian past foods. During this year, Citizen Goriot amassed the capital which later enabled him to carry on his business with all the advantage which a solid backing of money gives to its possessor. (111–12)

Notice first the intersection of history, chance, and talent. Chance made his employer a victim of the Revolution, but Goriot had the qualities to take advantage of the situation. Then there is aristocratic class bias. Langeais's grandmother made "immense sums" in dealing with Goriot, but the duchess scornfully speaks of the trickery of "those people" with the Comité du Salut Public. Still, Rastignac's final version shows that Goriot did have the sense to protect his business politically. Finally, Goriot profited enormously from the fear, suffering, and perhaps even death of many people. Though not literally a crime, his first year's business certainly constituted a "primitive accumulation" that allowed his later success. And the text goes on to describe his business acumen, knowledge of grains, prices, and crops, and his worldwide commerce, from Sicily to the Ukraine.

So the Christlike father (*Christ de la Paternité* [235]) was at the outset a profiteer and a capitalist. Even more interesting, he exemplifies the alienation that Marx claimed to threaten even the exploiters in the capitalist system. "His dealings in grains seemed to have absorbed all his intelligence. . . . Take him from his specialty . . . and he became once more the uncouth, slow-witted workman, incapable of following an argument, insensible to all the pleasures of the mind" (112). Here the commercial has debased the human, except in Goriot's love for his daughters, which however is marked by a similar exaggeration. Concerned about Victorine but indifferent to the murder of her brother, capable of imagining kidnapping Restaud's son to protect Anastasie (shades of Vautrin), Goriot is indeed a specialist of paternal love for daughters. After his wife's death "paternal feeling developed to the point of mania in Goriot: the wealth of affection which death had frustrated was transferred to his two daughters, and at first they fully satisfied all his emotional needs," before rejecting him as political and social fashions change (113). In the novel, Goriot most clearly exemplifies Marx's arguments about

the dominance of the economic and its degradation of the human in terms of intelligence, sensibility, emotion, and relations
among human beings, even family members.

Money is not mentioned on every page of *Absalom*, but it has its
role as necessity, instrumentality, and alienation. Sutpen from
the outset realizes that money is essential to his design, which
explains his trip to Haiti: "I learned . . . that there was a place
called the West Indies to which poor men went in ships and
became rich, it didn't matter how" (302); "So when the time
came when I realized that to accomplish my design I should
need first of all and above all things money in considerable quantities and in the quite immediate future . . . I went to the West
Indies" (303–4). Sutpen's instrumental view of money—does he
not feel that he can put aside his first wife through a financial
arrangement and does he not remark of the design: "To accomplish it I should require money, a house, a plantation, slaves, a
family—incidentally of course, a wife" (329)—is criticized by General Compson, and Shreve, and Faulkner critics as immoral, as
reducing life to abstract calculation. According to Rosa, when
arriving in Jefferson, Sutpen obviously was "accustomed to having money and intended to have it again and would have no
scruples about how he got it" (20). He has enough Spanish coins
to buy his ten square miles of land and eventually becomes the
biggest planter in the region.

If money is an alienating instrumentality for Sutpen, it takes
on an alluring intensity for some secondary characters. There is
Bon's legal guardian, transformed by Shreve into a fabulous
embodiment of the money drive:

> *Today he finished robbing a drunken Indian of a hundred miles of
> virgin land, val. 25,000. At 2:31 today came up out of swamp with
> final plank for house. val in conj. with land 40,000. 7:52 p.m. today
> married. Bigamy threat val. minus nil. unless quick buyer. . . . Doubt-
> less conjoined with wife same day. Say 1 year . . . Son. Intrinsic val.
> possible though not probable forced sale of house & land plus val. crop
> minus child's one quarter. Emotional val. plus 100% times nil. plus
> val. crop. Say 10 years, one or more children. Intrinsic val. forced sale
> house & improved land. . . . Emotional val. 100% times increase
> yearly for each child plus.* (375–76)

But there is also Coldfield, whose religion and probity combine with close attention to his low-level commercial dealings as store owner. He frees his slaves but docks them for the meals they do not have to prepare on occasions when he visits Ellen at Sutpen's Hundred. According to Quentin's father, he uses religion as "a demand balance of spiritual solvency, exactly as he would have used a cotton gin in which he considered himself to have incurred either interest or responsibility" (58). As Cleanth Brooks remarks, the character might have come from a reading of Richard Henry Tawney.[4] Interestingly, Coldfield's daughter Rosa, that most belated of children and most deprived of sexual gratification, is also excluded from the use of money. Mr. Compson recalls that "at that time Miss Rosa actually could not count money, change, that she knew the progression of the coins in theory but that apparently she had never had the actual cash to see, touch, experiment and prove with" (93), her father retracing her steps on shopping days to pay for the items she had taken from each store. So the Coldfields combine moral probity, religion, and a very special relation to the money system. There is also the scandal of their providing respectability for Sutpen through marriage and economic and legal support, as Coldfield hires the wagons to transport Sutpen's outrageously luxurious furnishings and signs his bond after his arrest.

Critics such as Brooks have discussed the relation between Sutpen and Coldfield, but we should also consider the one between Sutpen and General Compson, his only friend, the source of most information about him, who lends him seed cotton to get his start and even offers a loan of money. Sutpen gains a semblance of respectability from Coldfield but also from Compson, who represents professional training (the law), social status, and money in Jefferson. The novel does not comment on this complicity, except perhaps indirectly in the burden of memory that the general's grandson is made to bear. But it is striking that, despite the town's resistance, Sutpen is aided by a pillar of organized religion (Coldfield is a Methodist steward) and by a prominent figure of "legitimate" social and financial standing. The distinction between legitimate and criminal breaks down; at the origin of illicit wealth is a crime, in this case

that of the whole system, embodied as much in General Compson as in Sutpen.

As this argument suggests, the economic in *Absalom* as in *Goriot*
needs to be approached not only in terms of the monetary but
through such broader categories as class, mode of production,
and the country-city-world market nexus.

The German Ideology presents the conflict of city and country as
one of the elemental divisions of labor in human history—and
we might think it reflected in the contrast between Balzac's urban novel and the work of America's great "regional" writer.
Among Balzac's urban-provincial, North-South works, *Le Père
Goriot* is unusual in rigorously excluding the province from the
narrative action. Eugène de Rastignac exchanges letters with his
family, listens to Vautrin's analyses of provincial society and to
Bianchon's reference to a newspaper that has an early edition
for the provinces, and goes home on vacation. But we as readers
do not follow him; in fact we never leave the city. The narrator
laments the evils that are specific to the French capital, celebrates
its special pleasures, comments on the unique nature of love
there, and involves us in evocations of its many places and facets.
He wonders at the outset whether his story can be understood
elsewhere: "Will it be understood outside Paris? One may doubt
it" (27). Later the police chief tautologically expresses the special
and specialized fascination of the city: "Paris is Paris, you see!
That explains my life" (209).

But Paris has its comprehensible historical significance. Vautrin suggests that it differs from other European capitals in being
more hospitable to new money (133). Rastignac is presented as
typical in historical and economic terms; he is "one of those young
men" (34) from poor provincial noble families who have come to
Paris to profit from the new social and economic circumstances.
Vautrin explains to him that he represents a large historical phenomenon, one of twenty thousand, perhaps fifty thousand,
young men coming from the provinces (Vautrin understands,
saying, "I know all about it, I have lived in the South"), many to
study law, aspiring to the limited number of positions of attorney-
general (only twenty for all of France [126–29]).[5] Eugène's abandonment of his law studies and his liaison with Delphine can thus

be read in terms of an underlying political and economic allegory, whereby impoverished provincial nobility reinvigorates and reenriches itself by alliance with the new urban money of bankers and real estate speculators (itself drawing on still other sources of capital, city-centered but deriving from world trade, since Delphine's dowry comes from Goriot's business).

Nor should we take the division between rural and urban as absolute in Faulkner's novel. Marx—and Vautrin—know that Paris implies not only the depleted provinces but the colonies and the United States as well. The sign of a comparable recognition in *Absalom* is the architect, gotten from Martinique but whose "frock coat and . . . flowered waistcoat and . . . hat . . . would have caused no furore on a Paris boulevard" (39). Similarly, if the Mississippi of the 1830s is a thoroughly rural environment, shapeless in its immensity, so that the mob at Sutpen's wedding disperses to "taverns twenty and fifty and a hundred miles further on along nameless roads" (68), as Sutpen's story progresses we see Jefferson grow in size and glimpse on the horizon the distant big cities of the American South, particularly Memphis, where prospective brides shop for a trousseau and men go for business or prostitution.

More fascinating still is the French city of New Orleans, where Sutpen goes on mysterious business and where Charles Bon takes Henry. Mr. Compson's reconstruction of this incident is a decadent, enfeebled version of what happens between Rastignac and Vautrin. Henry makes a pathetic Rastignac, the Mississippi boy in "countrified clothes" who has perhaps never even been to Memphis, "the provincial, the clown almost," tempted by Bon, a younger, more effete, less powerful figure than Vautrin, yet one who is insistently characterized as "the seducer," as French, and as of ambivalent sexuality (118–20, 132).

Despite the differences, the content of the seduction is the same as that offered to Rastignac in Paris—money, power, sexual experience beyond imagination:

> the purlieus of elegance . . . the architecture a little . . . femininely flamboyant and . . . opulent, sensuous, sinful; the inference of great and easy wealth measured by steamboat loads in

place of a tedious inching of sweating human figures across
cotton fields; the flash and glitter of a myriad carriage wheels,
in which women . . . appeared like painted portraits beside
men in linen a little finer and diamonds a little brighter and in
broadcloth a little trimmer . . . than any Henry had ever seen
before: and the mentor . . . telling Henry, "But that's not it.
That's just the base, the foundation." (136–37)

The economic dimension of New Orleans is not developed in
relation to the personal story of Sutpen and his family, yet this
passage suggests the historically important limitation of plantation productivity and wealth as opposed to international sea
trade and the accumulation of money in the city. (After all, the
capture of New Orleans and Northern control of the entire Mississippi after the Seige of Vicksburg were major causes of the
South's loss of the war.) Instead, Bon's Marxlike "base" and
"foundation" refer to the system of octoroon chattelry to which
Bon exposes Henry and which is maintained by a select group of
murderous individuals, not Vautrin's *Société des Dix Mille* but "the
thousand . . . white men" (142). Mr. Compson does recognize
the economic basis of the institution, since he has Bon describe
white prostitution as a vulgar "economic matter," whereas the
octoroons "are more valuable as commodities than white girls"
(144–45). But far more insistent in the lurid imagination of
Quentin's father is Bon's explanation of the sexual attraction of
the mixture of white blood with "a female principle which existed, queenly and complete, in the hot equatorial groin of the
world long before that white one of ours came down from trees
and lost its hair and bleached out—a principle apt docile and
instinct with strange and ancient curious pleasures of the flesh"
(144). Here we see that the scenes in New Orleans serve primarily to inject into the Anglo-Saxon sexual morality and Mississippi
system of "ladies, women, females" (that is, white virgins, white
prostitutes, and black slaves) that Mr. Compson analyzes elsewhere (135), a myth of African sexuality that could come straight
out of the French nineteenth century and that has a great deal to
do with the distortions of family, sex, and race that we will treat
shortly.

In spite of the differences I have noted, Henry and Bon's interaction provides insights like those of Vautrin and Marx into the relationships among country, city, colonies, and the money-sex system. Surprisingly, Faulkner's book reveals an even deeper (or "longer") stratum of economic history than *Goriot*, something like Marx's sequence of prehistoric and historical modes of production in relation to class conflict.

Sutpen's "innocence" comes from his upbringing in the mountains, where a sense of property close to Marx's conception of tribal ownership, preceding the advent of private property, pertained. It is as if Faulkner had in mind this passage from *The German Ideology:*

> The first form of ownership is tribal . . . ownership. It corresponds to the undeveloped stage of production, at which a people lives by hunting and fishing, by the rearing of beasts or, in the highest stage, agriculture. In the latter case it presupposes a great mass of uncultivated stretches of land. The division of labour is at this stage still very elementary and is confined to a further extension of the natural division of labour existing in the family. The social structure is, therefore, limited to an extension of the family; patriarchal family chieftains, below them the members of the tribe, finally slaves. The slavery latent in the family only develops gradually with the increase of population, the growth of wants, and with the extension of external relations, both of war and barter. (151)

Though immigrants from the British Isles, the Sutpens have regressed in their mountain isolation to a nearly prehistoric form of society, the earliest stages of what Marx describes—vast stretches of uncultivated land, isolated family units with their simple division of functions, surviving by hunting and fishing, lacking tribal structure, slavery, or agriculture, and having virtually no communication with the outside world:

> he was born . . . where what few other people he knew lived in log cabins boiling with children . . . men and grown boys who hunted or lay before the fire on the floor while the women and older girls stepped back and forth across them to reach the fire to cook, where the only colored people were Indians and you only looked down at them over your rifle sights, where he had

never even heard of, never imagined, a place, a land divided
neatly up and actually owned by men who did nothing but ride
over it on fine horses or sit in fine clothes on the galleries of big
houses while other people worked for them; he did not even
imagine then that there was any such way to live or to want to
live, or that there existed all the objects to be wanted which
there were, or that ones who owned the objects not only could
look down on the ones that didn't, but could be supported in
the down-looking not only by the others who owned objects too
but by the very ones that were looked down on that didn't own
objects and knew they never would. Because where he lived
the land belonged to anybody and everybody and so the man
who would go to the trouble and work to fence off a piece of it
and say 'This is mine' was crazy; and as for objects, nobody had
any more of them than you did because everybody had just
what he was strong enough or energetic enough to take and
keep. . . . So he didn't even know there was a country all divided and fixed and neat with a people living on it all divided
and fixed and neat because of what color their skins happened
to be and what they happened to own. (275–76)

Astonishingly, Sutpen experiences a rapid transition from communal property to the system of private ownership of land and
things, class differentiation accepted even by the oppressed, and
slavery. Suddenly he is in the world of what Marx calls "*object-
bondage*" (72), a point relevant for the luxury of the furnishings
he acquires (and for the narrator of Balzac's object-laden urban
world, who, decades before *Madame Bovary*, worries about the
impeding of narrative movement by the necessities of description [32]).

Sutpen's penetration of the society in which he finds himself,
while incomplete and primitive, is perceptive. He discovers, without always naming them, some of the categories of "political
economy," not only property but class and labor. After the insult
by the negro slave, he suddenly perceives himself and his people
as the rich man has seen them all along:

the boy outside the barred door in his patched garments and
splayed bare feet, looking through and beyond the boy, he
himself seeing his own father and sisters and brothers as the
owner, the rich man (not the nigger) must have been seeing

them all the time—as cattle, creatures heavy and without grace, brutely evacuated into a world without hope or purpose for them . . . a race whose future would be a succession of cut-down and patched and made-over garments bought on exorbitant credit because they were white people, from stores where niggers were given the garments free. (293)

The youth cannot use the word *class,* but his realization here is precisely that of belonging to a whole group of poor whites, not slaves but free—"free" in Marx's ironic use, free to possess virtually nothing, to live practically below the level of the human. There is a suggestion too of what the young Sutpen senses elsewhere, concerning violence by poor whites against slaves: "you knew that you could hit them. . . . But you did not want to, because they (the niggers) were not it, not what you wanted to hit" (287), an indication of how racial difference masks class conflict. Finally, on returning to his home, Sutpen sees his sister's submission to the female part of what Faulkner very nearly calls "alienated" labor: "her back toward him, shapeless in a calico dress and a pair of the old man's shoes unlaced and flapping about her bare ankles and broad in the beam as a cow, the very labor she was doing brutish and stupidly out of all proportion to its reward: the very primary essence of labor, toil, reduced to its crude absolute which only a beast could and would endure" (294–95).

Sutpen's decision to fight the class of owners on their own terms ("So to combat them you have got to have what they have. . . . You got to have land and niggers and a fine house" [297]) of course leads him to duplicate all the evils he has glimpsed. Class domination—he gets to the top of the owner class, and is it not fitting that he is killed by a member of the class of poor whites, his retainer, Wash Jones?[6] And racial slavery—is this not why he repeatedly must vanquish his slaves in actual physical combat? And the patriarchal concept of pure genealogy and progeny that goes along with feudal Southern society, his dream of "fine grandsons and great-grandsons springing as far as eye could reach" (339), from which, for reasons of racial purity, he excludes his first son, who returns to destroy the whole scheme.

As this last indicates, and as their titles emphasize, the economy of these two novels is also that of the patriarchal family, that other great division of labor, whose potential to enslave the female we have noted in *The German Ideology* and in Faulkner's depiction of Sutpen's original family. As remarked earlier, Marx and Engels argued that this enslavement increased in nineteenth-century society and saw the sexual system, comprising marriage, infidelity, and prostitution, as an arrangement for male power and communal ownership of women. Disturbing propositions, and markedly consistent with *Goriot* and *Absalom*.

Indeed, *Goriot* depicts marriage as an economically denatured arrangement that regularly becomes a *ménage à trois*, or rather *à quatre*. It is not that sexual energy does not exist—on the contrary, it is constantly appraised, not only in the young (Rastignac's reactions to Victorine and both of Goriot's daughters) but even in older figures, among them Michonneau and Goriot. But desire, affection, and love do not exist between marriage partners, except in Goriot's dedication to his late wife and in Rastignac's nostalgia, before engaging himself fully in the Parisian hell, for the idyllic relations of his provincial family. In Paris, by contrast, Vautrin claims that forty-seven out of sixty marriages are based on economic calculations, and his argument that you can sooner find the moneylender than the lover in the hearts of Parisian women is born out in Eugène's experience. La duchesse de Langeais remarks that "our marriages . . . have become very sorry farces" (100–101), and the narrator makes a similar historical judgment, attributing the errors of wives to "society, as it is at present constituted" (168). Even the noble Madame de Beauséant has a lover, whom her husband accepts because he has a mistress; Eugène witnesses a horrible though silent scene between husband and wife. Early on, Anastasie's lover is coolly accepted by her husband. The narrator, Delphine, and Goriot himself explain Nucingen's indifference to Delphine and his attentions to his mistress, as well as Delphine's mistreatment by her lover, de Marsay.

In all of these arrangements women have considerable power, and Eugène can succeed only by alliance with an imposing female figure. But at the end this strength gives way before the dominance of men. Beauséant and Langeais are betrayed; Nucingen retains control of Delphine's money; neither daughter is permitted by the husbands to attend Goriot's funeral; Anastasie is reduced to "complete prostration" by her husband, who asserts her duties to him and his child, her submission to husband and son (292–93).

As suggested earlier, the ambivalence of the attractive young protagonist Rastignac resides largely in the fact that he must work within the system, that he has the choice of marrying for money or of becoming the officially recognized lover of a married woman. The scheme regarding Victorine is appalling. It involves murder, yet Eugène participates almost to the end. It also entails manipulation of a young, abandoned, and innocent girl, and Eugène plays his part so well that he is shocked by his effect on her. All the while Vautrin presides, mockingly explaining to Victorine what her womanly duties will be while degrading her: "I would rather not let that man see me like this; he says things which stain the soul, and his looks make a woman feel as if she were being undressed" (205, my translation).

If Eugène withdraws from the scheme for ethical reasons, he is helped along at the crucial moment by obtaining his bachelor's apartment at Goriot's expense, a costly watch complete with his family arms, and an enticing note from Delphine. Goriot makes his contribution officially a loan, and Delphine overcomes Rastignac's scruples with arguments about the conditions for success in modern society, so that Rastignac is free to enjoy the sense of ownership of his new possessions. Moreover, his fidelity to Goriot is sustained and does much to balance his moral compromises. More importantly, although greatly postponed, the union of Rastignac and Delphine is consummated, and is successful, and leads to a partnership of pleasure, gratitude, and love:

> Everything was changed in his life. The woman . . . had confiscated everything to her profit. The circumstances in which Rastignac and Delphine had come together seemed expressly designed to afford them the keenest pleasure [*jouissances*] in each other. Their well-prepared passion had grown through what kills the passions, through enjoyment [*jouissance*]. When he possessed this woman, Eugène realized that until then he

had only desired her; he loved her only on the morrow of his happiness. Love is perhaps no more than gratitude for pleasure [*plaisir*]. It did not matter whether this woman was abominable or sublime, he adored her for the pleasures [*voluptés*] which he had brought her as a dowry, and for those which he received. (272, my translation)

In its emphasis on sexual pleasure, this passage indicates the satisfying and reciprocal nature of Eugène and Delphine's lovemaking, something that we as readers, in our libidinal investment in the book, have long anticipated. But Barbéris is right to note the calculated notion of this satisfaction, its long delay, the sequence desire-pleasure-gratitude-love.[7] The union of Delphine and Eugène, although genuine (and in later novels enduring), is based on a bargain, as the economic vocabulary makes clear. Their love is an exceptional instance of a satisfying erotic-personal-financial relationship within the degraded sexual system that *Goriot* reveals.

Other significant features of this system involve distorted relations between parents and children, suggestions of incest, and the theme of male homosexuality. Fathers and their offspring are highlighted, here as in *Absalom*. The maternal function is either eliminated through death (Goriot's and Taillefer's wives), marginalized (Eugène's family), ineffectual (Madame Couture, Anastasie at the end), or nonexistent (Langeais, Beauséant, Vauquer, Michonneau, and, very importantly in this novel at least, Delphine). But a trio of powerful father figures indirectly confront one another in exacerbated relations with their children. Taillefer's repudiation of Victorine in preference for his son and her devotion to her father and Goriot's sacrifices for his daughters and their destruction of him read like a Hegelian set of oppositions on the theme of the alienated family. In the figure of Goriot, fatherhood is absurdly magnified and thereby discredited. Rastignac finds Goriot sublime in his assertion that fathers have godlike pleasures. But in his delirium at the end the old man wants his daughters brought to him by the police, urges passage of laws to prevent the infidelity to fathers represented by marriage, and argues that his fate threatens the destruction of society: "Justice is on my side, everything is on my side, nature, law. I protest. The fatherland will perish if fathers are trampled underfoot. The thing is clear as day. Society, the whole world turns on paternity, everything crumbles if children do not love their fathers" (286, my translation). And Goriot is right; in a society supposedly based on a benevolent concept of fatherhood and fatherland, exploitation seems to be rather the rule than the exception. Balzac's novel reveals an agonizing crisis of family and society.

This elephantiasis of paternity is linked to transferences that can become nearly incestuous and to homosexual themes. Goriot believes that Rastignac loves his father and mother, but Eugène's exchange with his family is exclusively with its female members; his father is barely mentioned, is kept in the dark about the money sent to Rastignac, and is never at any time contacted by his son. Instead Rastignac takes to calling Goriot "père." And Goriot uses him to provide Delphine with the sexual satisfaction that she has not had and to draw closer to her himself. He intrudes uncomfortably in their relationship, proposing to live upstairs from Eugène's apartment, so that he can see Delphine in "her morning quilted gown, picking her steps daintily like a little cat" (195). He conducts himself with her as childishly as a young lover, and Eugène senses the violence of their conflicting passions. The hyperpaternal Goriot has to be removed before the young love of Delphine and Eugène can be consummated. But so does another strange father, Vautrin.

Shortly before undertaking *Goriot,* Balzac completed *La Fille aux yeux d'or.* After a masterful sociological analysis of Paris, he introduces de Marsay, later Delphine's lover, to a bizarre sexual experience. Without detailing the story, we can note these elements: two people, de Marsay and his half sister, who unknown to each other are children of the same father by different liaisons but who instantly recognize this fact due to their physical resemblance; lesbianism versus phallic power, but also suggestions of hermaphroditism and a kind of incest; a woman with golden eyes as opposed to de Marsay's dark half sister; multiple allusions to the non-French origin of the girl with the golden eyes, including Spanish, Asian, Creole; heightened sexual experience followed by murder. It is perhaps too much to see a connection between this story and Goriot's complaint, "You do not know what it is to see the . . . gold of a look change suddenly into" lead (287); but de Marsay is a link between the two women and Goriot's blond and brunette daughters, whereas the themes of unknown children of the same father, race and recognition, multiple forms of sexuality, and murder are in the background even more of *Absalom* than of *Goriot*.

A hint of this is provided in the description of the Pension Vauquer, whose sign reads not *"Lodgings for Ladies and Gentlemen, etc."* (29), but *"Pension bourgeoise des deux sexes et autres"*—*"Quality Lodgings for Both Sexes and Others."* This is in keeping with the freedom with which hypotheses are formed about the sexual propensities of Goriot and others. But it is not until Vautrin's homosexuality is revealed to Michonneau that anyone has suspicions about him and not until her venomous remarks after his arrest that Eugène receives "a flood of hideous light into his mind" (224). Earlier he had wondered about the fascination exercised on him by Vautrin. Yet Vautrin had been very clear, as in another passage that needs retranslation: "Poussons chacun nos pointes! La mienne est en fer et ne mollit jamais." *Pointes* evokes swords, but since the verb *mollir* means to weaken, literally to get soft, the translation "and I never yield it" obscures its evident phallic meaning (183).

In addition to suggesting homosexual relations, Vautrin offers Eugène riches, protection, fidelity, friendship, even love. It is not for nothing that he calls himself "votre papa Vautrin," frequently adopting a paternal tone and kissing Rastignac on the forehead just as Goriot does. All of this is incompatible neither with women and marriage (with Victorine) nor with Vautrin's special sense of posterity, as he offers to make Rastignac his heir: "If I have no children (which is likely: I am not anxious to replant myself here through cuttings of my stock), I will bequeath my fortune to you" (182, my translation). As in *Splendor and Misery of Courtesans,* in which Vautrin is Lucien's lover and fake spiritual father (in his ecclesiastical disguise) and in which there are also rumors that Lucien is Vautrin's natural son, Vautrin here redefines the paternal in homosexual terms. His patriarchal dream of Southern plantation sovereignty includes not only economic relations but also the personal and the sexual. *Goriot* reveals a *fatherly* economy in which the family is as dehumanized as Marx and Engels argued, in which parental and filial roles are played in insanely destructive ways, in which heterosexuality is countered by incestuous and homosexual themes. Vautrin exposes all this, then by his arrest is removed (a homophobic gesture, and one of ideological recontainment?). Only then, and with the death of Goriot, can the union of Delphine and Eugène occur.

It is instructive to pursue such themes in *Absalom*, which also displays disconcerting familial and sexual configurations.[8] Fulfillment for the female characters is virtually absent. Sutpen's first wife is barely mentioned in his narrations to General Compson. His second wife, Ellen, is empty-headed in happiness and brought to near catatonic immobility, then death, in the face of disaster. His daughter, Judith, lives out an existence of tragic virginity, as does her aunt Rosa (whose mother died in giving birth to her). At the opening of the book, Quentin smells "the rank smell of [her] female old flesh" (4); at the end he learns of her coma and death. Those of mixed race, Bon's octoroon wife and Clytie, fare little better; the former quickly disappears from the story after Bon's death, the latter lives to burn down the Sutpen mansion, killing herself and Henry and causing Rosa's death. Others, Wash Jones's daughter, granddaughter, and great granddaughter (no mention of a wife for him), also end badly—the first supposedly in a Memphis brothel, the other two murdered by his own hand. We get few glimpses of the marriage between General Compson and his wife, except to learn that she became hysterical at the mention of Bon's letter, and Quentin's neurotic mother from *The Sound and the Fury* is absent from this novel. Perhaps the amusing story of Rosa's aunt, first presented as a man-hater but who escapes out a window of Coldfield's house and who remains faithful to her horse trader husband, suggests the slim possibilities for female happiness.

Female sexuality, if it finds expression at all, is brutally submitted to the male. I mentioned Mr. Compson's analysis of the three castes of women and his evocation of New Orleans chattelry. Sutpen's use of women for progeny, in the absence of any sense of love, or for mere physical gratification, is equally flagrant. His first wife is put aside as not "adjunctive or incremental to the design" (300), which we have seen includes "incidentally of course, a wife" (329)—so much for Ellen, too. The sexless Clytie is the child of one of the female slaves Sutpen originally brought with him, deliberately, according to Mr. Compson: "He probably chose them with the same care and shrewdness with which he chose the other livestock—the horses and mules and cattle— which he bought later on" (73). The same calculation appears in his proposal to Rosa: "*The bald outrageous words exactly as if he were consulting with Jones or with some other man about a bitch dog or a cow or mare*" (210); later it leads to his own death at the hands of this very Jones.

In contrast to the suppression of the female, male sexuality, of an ambivalent sort, is highlighted. The most intensely bodily passages in the book are exclusively male. Even though he breeds with several females, we see Sutpen's body only in the scenes of his fighting with his slaves—violent, naked male-to-male contact. This gives a point to Wash's reiterated "I'm going to tech you, Kernel" (360). And we should not forget, in the second part of the book, the sexualized descriptions of Shreve, "his naked torso pink-gleaming and baby-smooth, cherubic, almost hairless, the twin moons of his spectacles glinting against his moonlike rubicund face" (227); "naked to the waist, in the warm and rosy orifice above the iron quad" (271); "Shreve . . . in his spectacles and nothing else (from the waist down the table concealed him; anyone entering the room would have taken him to be stark naked)" (272). The erotic economy, so to speak, of Faulkner's book is as distorted as the social world it depicts and corresponds closely to Marx and Engels on marriage and to Irigaray's argument that the essential structure of modern society is that of (clandestine) male homosexuality (which surfaces, though without being explicitly admitted, in such works as *Absalom*).

Incestuous and androgynous themes, glimpsed in Balzac, are accordingly heightened in *Absalom,* with the exotic mixture of races in *La Fille aux yeux d'or* taking on catastrophic historical significance. John Irwin's demonstration of the parallels between Quentin's attraction to his sister, Caddie, in *The Sound and the Fury,* unmentioned in *Absalom,* and his fascination with Henry, who murders his sister's lover, need not be repeated here. Ever in character, it is rather Mr. Compson who most of all imagines incestuous, homosexual, and androgynous relations among Bon, Henry, and Judith. His reflections on brotherly desire flow into suggestions of bisexuality:

> In fact, perhaps this is the pure and perfect incest: the brother realizing that the sister's virginity must be destroyed in order to have existed at all, taking that virginity in the person of the brother-in-law, the man whom he would be if he could become, metamorphose into, the lover, the husband; by whom he would be despoiled, choose for despoiler, if he could become, metamorphose into the sister, the mistress, the bride. (119)

For Compson, the whole complex relationship could only have begun in Bon's love for Henry, "seeing perhaps in the sister merely the shadow, the woman vessel with which to consummate the love whose actual object was the youth" (133). But this homosexual version of the origin is enlarged by the fact that, from the outset, he views the couple Henry and Judith as androgynous— "that single personality with two bodies both of which had been seduced almost simultaneously by a man" (113).

Still, the male-to-male dimension is reasserted in the next to last chapter as the two students imagine not the relations among Bon, Henry, and Judith but the plight of Bon in his rejection by Sutpen. At times they conceive of him as wishing only a sign of recognition: "*I am your father. Burn this*" (408); "*You are my oldest son. Protect your sister; never see either of us again*" (433). But elsewhere he wants that bodily contact, that touch with the father that is shown in the few moving embraces between Sutpen and his "legitimate" children that the text records: "*I will just touch flesh with him*" (435); "Because he knew exactly what he wanted; it was just the saying of it—the physical touch even though in secret, hidden—the living touch of that flesh warmed before he was born by the same blood which it had bequeathed him to warm his own flesh with, to be bequeathed by him in turn to run hot and loud in veins and limbs after that first flesh and then his own were dead" (399). Here the magnification of fatherhood, and the anguish of rejection by the father, are more acute than in *Goriot*. This physical contact of male with male, guaranteeing the son's identity and with it all future posterity (Sutpen's own goal)—this contact of male with male is the anguished need of the patriarchal economy that Faulkner's novel exposes.

As Eric Sundquist has shown, the themes of father and son and the taboo on incest are rendered immeasurably tragic by being fused with the historical realities of slavery and miscegenation that Faulkner's book confronts. The Sutpen tragedy is compounded when, though able to "pass" as white, Bon's son by his morganatic marriage with the octoroon chooses in desperate rebellion a black identity and marries a fullblooded black woman, described by Mr. Compson through offensive racial stereotypes: "a coal black and ape-like woman," a "black gargoyle," who is "kenneled" like "something in a zoo" (257, 259, 262). Quentin recounts in chapter 6 the compassion that his father and grandfather express for Bon's *son*. But the caricature by Mr. Compson of the native African woman and the fact that their offspring is one of Faulkner's many idiots perpetuates the obsession with miscegenation that animated all parties, pro- and antislavery, before the Civil War, and persists. Shreve's closing "You've got one . . . nigger Sutpen left" (471) and the conflagration that destroys Sutpen's house are ironic, melodramatic testimonies to the sexually and racially alienated nature of the patriarchal urge in the American setting, whose evil this novel reveals but in no way dissipates.[9]

In the preceding sections I have demonstrated, through the mediation of Marx's thought, the intersections of *Le Père Goriot* and *Absalom, Absalom!* in the closely linked fields of history, economy, and family. None of this has been "merely" thematic. But I want to conclude by stressing individuality and convergence in relevant formal features, arguing that these works are also *structural* counterparts. Elements to be highlighted are the depiction of time and the claim of these novels to be representations of historical truth; the means of discovering such truth, including the roles of informants, "mouthpieces," and narrators; and the instability of what is so revealed, particularly in terms of reconciliations and endings.

Both works are preoccupied with time and history, fairly recent but overwhelmingly disruptive history in *Goriot,* older and tragic history, the burden of the dead South, the "dead time" (21) mentioned frequently in *Absalom.* For well-known reasons (including twentieth-century experience of the psyche and experiments in "modernist" form), the representation of time is much more complex in Faulkner's writing than in Balzac's. There is also a specifically American reason for this, expressed in Eric Sundquist's argument that the extraordinarily repetitive quality of *Absalom* and its split into two narrative moments reflect both the burden and the contradiction of U.S. history. Shreve says as much within the novel, in regard to himself, Northerner and Canadian: "We dont live among defeated grandfathers and freed slaves . . . and bullets in the dining room table and such, to be always reminding us to never forget" (450). Earlier I made much of Marx's sentence about how the "tradition of all the dead generations weighs like a nightmare on the brain of the living" (595). Although the sentence corresponds to both form and content in *Absalom,* we should not forget that it was written to describe events in mid-nineteenth-century France—that is, the very decades toward which the end of *Goriot* opens. In their treatment of time and history, these two novels, the one mainly projective and the other highly retrospective, are indeed counterparts.

I do not need to repeat here the exhaustive study by critics of the role of time in *Absalom,* but I can summarize major features. First, there is the passage of time in the various tellings of the story, as Rosa drones on, Quentin with his father later waits for it to get dark, and the chimes mark the passing hours in the Harvard dorm room. On the other hand, narrators and characters often feel that time has stopped, as in Quentin's metaphor of the connecting pools in which the same event ripples on forever (326) and his reaction as Miss Rosa talks in chapter 1:

> It (the talking, the telling) seemed (to him, to Quentin) to partake of that logic- and reason-flouting quality of a dream which the sleeper knows must have occurred, stillborn and complete, in a second, yet the very quality upon which it must

> depend to move the dreamer (verisimilitude) to credulity—
> horror or pleasure or amazement—depends as completely
> upon a formal recognition of and acceptance of elapsed and
> yet-elapsing time as music or a printed tale (22–23).

This describes Quentin's sense of the cessation of time during Rosa's speech. Its reference to music, literature, and the Aristotelian categories of verisimilitude, pleasure, horror, and amazement also suggest our reactions, the dreamlike transformation of time that we as readers experience in this work, which, in a very different way from Balzac's, is at once novel, non-novel, and tragedy.

In spite of various immobilizations of time, *Absalom* nonetheless also evokes its successiveness, particularly as history, in the litany of dates and battles that delineate the conflict between North and South and the defeat of the latter, first in Mr. Compson's version and later in Shreve's and Quentin's reconstruction in chapter 8. But the pursuit of the past means that time in the book is primarily retrospective, involving several kinds of memory, as when in chapter 6 Shreve asks Quentin to retell the experience of finding the Sutpen graves with his father—this conscious memory being followed suddenly by a deep flashback to a time when, as a much younger boy, Quentin had gone out to the Hundred and encountered Clytie and Jim Bond. Nonetheless time has its projective dimension too, as when the wisteria associated with Rosa in chapter 1 mixes with Mr. Compson's cigar smoke at the beginning of chapter 2 and is projected by the narrator toward that time when "five months later Mr. Compson's letter would carry up from Mississippi and over the long iron New England snow and into Quentin's sitting-room at Harvard" (where it is indeed recalled [34, 217]). Sometimes the temporal sequence is not logically regressive *or* successive: I accept Cleanth Brooks's argument that Rosa's reference to light and wisteria (178) indicates that chapter 5 occurs before Quentin's discussion with his father that evening in chapters 2, 3, and 4.[10]

This last remark can serve as a pointer for the elaborate manipulation of temporal dimensions in Faulkner's narrative strategy—especially repetition, initiated by the "twice-bloomed wistaria" (4), exemplified by the double narration of key events and the multiple evocations of innumerable details; and also delay, for example, Bon's letter, shown at the opening of chapter 4 but not read until the end of that chapter, as well as more significant events, including the meeting between Sutpen and Henry and Quentin's meeting with the dying Henry (at the end of the last two chapters). Yet, in spite (or because) of such convoluted narrative procedures and their suggestion of the complexities of the temporal, Quentin and Shreve transcend time for themselves and the reader in chapter 8, creating a persuasive representation of what historically happened.

After recalling the involutions of time in *Absalom,* it is instructive to pursue a similar analysis of *Goriot,* which, while much more straightforward, has its temporal particularities. As already suggested, time in *Goriot* moves primarily forward. It is presented as an essentially continuous succession of days, weeks, and months from autumn 1819 to February 1820, a short time in which a great deal happens. The sequence involves the encounters and revelations (some comic, for example, the first visit to Anastasie) that allow Rastignac to discover the nature of Parisian society as well as Goriot's story and to begin his own adventures. Occasionally time drags, and days and weeks go by with little progress. At other important points, events succeed one another quickly, as on three mornings marked by the fact that Rastignac or someone else oversleeps; once, following his first appearance at Madame de Beauséant's ball, at a time when something of Goriot's true situation is becoming visible; then, after being drugged by Vautrin, on a long day that sees the Taillefer murder, recognition of Victorine by her father, Eugène's wrestling with his conscience, Vautrin's arrest, and then also Rastignac's first evening with Goriot and Delphine in his new apartment; finally, when he succeeds in making love with Delphine at the time when her father nears death. As the last shows, in the concluding movements of the novel time seems to speed up, and the temporal notations more and more become hourly:

> The evening before he had been obliged to leave Delphine at one in the morning, but that night it was Delphine who left him to return home at two o'clock. He rose rather late next day, and

> waited for Madame de Nucingen, who came to breakfast with
> him about noon. . . . Getting used to all the elegant things that
> belonged to him was one long festival. . . . However, about four
> o'clock the two lovers called Goriot to mind. (264–65)

The incessant forward movement of time is related to what I
have called the novel's projective quality, not only in its "conclusion" but also at other moments in the text in which Rastignac's
and others' futures are suggested. We learn that Ajuda-Pinto later
regretted his marriage; at one point Eugène utters a witticism of
the sort "in which he later in life excelled" (119), and of his first
social success it is said that "he was to remember it to the end of his
days" (172). *Goriot* narrates events in a fixed period of time but
opens, expectantly and without resolution, to an as yet unexperi-
enced future. Balzac's dating of the book as September 1834 on
the last page extends that future at least into the early years of the
July Monarchy; and the connections of *Goriot* with other novels in
the *Comédie humaine* implicitly carry that movement further forward in history. Time progresses rapidly in the few months of the
novel; by its form, moreover, the book is not limited to those
months and seems to draw us into a vaster future.

But only after having rid itself of a certain anchoring in the
past, which considerably impedes the beginning of the flow of
events noted above. This past is inevitably the historical one of
revolution, empire, and restoration, amusingly (for us) summa-
rized by Madame Vauquer after Vautrin's arrest, as she sees
herself virtually without boarders on this day that is "among the
most extraordinary days in the history of the Maison Vauquer"
(210, my translation): "We've seen Louis XVI have his accident,
we've seen the Emperor fall, we've seen him come back and fall
again; but that's all in the order of possible things, whereas
middle-class boarding-houses are firmly settled: you can do without a king but not without your dinner" (238, my translation).
What is amusing (and potentially attractive) is Madame Vauquer's insistence on the priority of *personal* history; yet we have
seen to what extent Balzac makes the lives of his characters a
function of political and economic events. Goriot arrives at the
pension in 1813, and the first signs of his radically diminished

resources, when he moves to a cheaper room and goes without firewood during the winter, appear two years later, when, as Madame Vauquer notes, Napoleon returns and falls again; thereafter, during the restoration, Goriot's situation gets steadily worse.

But the relationship between personal fate and (inter)national history is usually not so clear, as is suggested in Madame Vauquer's other remark that the day of Vautrin's arrest has aged her by ten years (239). On the opening page the narrator indicates that she has been running the pension for forty years before 1819, and this is the final version of the text. But Balzac had earlier written thirty years, which is what Madame Vauquer herself claims (203). Did she start ten years before the Revolution or in the very year 1789? Inattention on the part of the author, vanity on the part of his character—or rather the sign of an insistent, not fully clarified, indeterminate relation between the literary work and the convulsions of history initiated by the Revolution? Critics have remarked comparable indeterminacies in *Absalom*.[11]

The confusion is only one aspect of a general obscurity and sluggishness that affects the temporal in the opening movement of *Goriot*. After all, this is a work (still in the final version) whose narrator speaks of the action as beginning at four different points: "In 1819, the time when this drama begins" (27); "At the time when this story begins" (34); "And so towards the end of November, 1819" (54); "Such was the general situation in the boarding-house at the end of November 1819" (57). Here there is only the slightest progress from a notation of the year to the month, first "towards" the end of November, then "at the end" of that month. Importantly, it is not until Rastignac has learned the story of Goriot's past that the "prologue" (*l'exposition*) of the work is completed ("So ends the prologue of this obscure but terrible Parisian tragedy" [115]) and that the action can truly begin.

Aside from the importance of Goriot's past, this impeding of narration comes from the narrator's layering tactic of describing the *quartier*, then the pension, then giving thumbnail sketches of the boarders, followed repetitively by fuller descriptions. In addition, most of the characters, not only Goriot, have a murky past—suppositions are formulated concerning Poiret, Michonneau, Vauquer, and Vautrin. Finally, the effect of time within the pension is palpably perceived as burdensome and sordid; time exists as the force that renders things vulgar and decrepit:

> This room . . . was formerly painted in a color unrecognizable today. This paint forms a background on which successive layers of dirt have traced fantastic figures. Sticky sideboards line the room and are covered with chipped, stained carafes. . . . Here is encountered the indestructible furniture, banished everywhere else, but placed there like the debris of civilization. . . . In order to describe to what point these furnishings are old, cracked, rotten. . . . (31–32, my translation)

Time of course is measured here not in hours or days but in years. Before the speedy events of Rastignac's initiation can begin, the novel must clarify this time, this sordid sluggishness of the past, and wrest itself from its grasp. For this to be accomplished, several scores of pages are required.

But this slowness of time and retarding of events are minor in comparison with *Absalom*. Once begun, Balzac's story unfolds quickly through several well-known devices: Eugène's "education," which is completed by the end, and his function in uncovering Goriot's story; the availability of sources of information on Goriot and of personages capable of educating the young man; the removal of Vautrin, Beauséant, and Goriot before Delphine and Eugène's union; the earlier role of Vautrin and Beauséant as mouthpieces for Balzac in his dissection of society; and the intrusive commentary of the narrator.

Much attention has been paid to the Balzacian narrator, with his constant aphorisms and generalizations, his complex analyses of motivation and action.[12] For our purposes, what is most interesting about the narrative voice is its contribution to the central moral ambiguity of the novel, the question of the legitimacy of Rastignac's behavior. Numerous passages express criticism of that behavior, presenting it as an example of the lax morality of the epoch (150), showing Rastignac rolling morally in mud (176), exposing the self-serving aspect of his love for Delphine. But others justify the young man, picturing him as absolved by angels, asserting that in finally resisting Vautrin his integrity emerged like an iron bar (216). At times the narrative voice loses objectivity and identifies with the experience of the student, as in this effusive generalization after Eugène receives the money from his family:

> The whole of Paris is his. Age when everything is gleaming, when everything sparkles and flames! age of joyous strength from which no one, man or woman, profits! age of debts and sharp apprehension that multiply every pleasure tenfold! He who hasn't frequented the left bank of the Seine, between the rue Saint-Jacques and the rue des Saint-Pères, knows nothing of human life! (119–20, my translation)

That this may express Balzac's personal opinion is not the point; rather it is of interest in illustrating how the critical narrator can at times invest himself enthusiastically in the personage of Rastignac—an ambivalence, an ethical mixed message, that characterizes the narrative as a whole.

This last passage implicitly evokes a reaction from the reader, as the narrator does directly throughout, by numerous addresses, imperatives, exclamations, questions, suppositions. And this is true from the outset, in the famous reflection on this period of "doleful literature" and egotistical indifference to those crushed by the juggernaut of "civilization," an indifference in which we as readers are pointedly included:

> That's how you will act, you who are holding this book in your white hand, who are settling into a softly cushioned armchair, saying to yourself, "Perhaps this one's amusing." When you have read of the secret misfortunes of old Goriot, you will dine with unimpaired appetite, holding the author to account for your insensitivity, taxing him with exaggeration, accusing him of poetry. Ah! recognize this: this drama is neither a fiction nor a novel. *All is true,* so veritable that each person can recognize its elements in himself, in his own household, in his heart perhaps. (28, my translation)

Here the narrator's implication of the reader in the story of Goriot's secret is linked to an affirmation of the fundamental truthfulness of the work. (*All is true* appears in English and apparently was thought by Balzac to derive from Shakespeare.) This claim to the veracity of an innovative literary form, not fiction, not novelistic in any trivial sense, but having the emotional truthfulness of great tragedy, concerns immediately the personal and the familial (either could be meant by the expression *chez soi; père Goriot* means "father Goriot" as well as "old Goriot"). But it also concerns the historical, specifically the modern urban, with suggestions of class, security, and economic well-being. Indeed, the economic vocabulary (*mettre sur le compte de, taxer*) suggests all of that aspect of societal reality that will follow in the book and that we have previously analyzed.

A painful historical context in relation to the creation of unconventional literary forms, the investment of narrator and involvement of reader, secrets and the effort to unravel them, the role of informants, mouthpieces, and narrator in that effort, and the claim of fiction to embody personal and historical truth—all of these elements are exacerbated in *Absalom*. In Balzac's book, Rastignac (unlike the other boarders, whose indifference to Goriot's plight parallels Marx's argument about the atomization of nineteenth-century society) obtains correct information on Goriot from reliable sources. The fact that Muret is nowhere else mentioned in the *Comédie humaine* has made the ease of Rastignac's investigation seem contrived to some. Rather we could argue that the success of the inquiry, which closes the prologue and opens the action, underlines the accessibility of history and the transparence of possible courses of action (as compromising as they may be). In *Absalom*, by contrast, two university students, at a remove of more than forty years, attempt to reconstruct a tragic past. Their informants—until we learn of Quentin's meeting with Henry—are not the business connection and the society notable but the daughter of the one and the son of the other. Significantly, their inquiry is not a prologue to action; the difficult task of interpreting the past *is* the action of the novel. Indeed the catastrophe of familial and national past is so extreme that one of the students will never "act" as an adult—he is to commit suicide within a few months.

The difficulty of the historical enterprise in *Absalom* derives from distance in time, the inaccessibility of individual motivation, simple lack of knowledge. Rosa, a marginal participant and witness, frequently admits her lack of certainty: "But I was not there" (33); "*I never saw him. I never even saw him dead*" (181); "*I do not even know of my own knowledge that Ellen. . .*" (183). Mr. Compson, who lacks essential information that Quentin later obtains, is reduced to complaining that it "just does not explain," in the effort to understand the past on the basis of "a few old mouth-to-mouth tales" and letters "without date or salutation or signature" (124, 160). Accompanied by Judith's comment about pieces of paper and scratches on tombstones as anonymous communications to strangers, conveying only the fact of *someone*'s past existence (158), the letter could be seen as a Foucault-like *non*-document.[13] The pervasive formula, "nobody knows," "nobody knew," over and over expresses the elusiveness of the facts of the story— concerning what exactly was said between Henry and Sutpen that led him to renounce his father, the business deal with Coldfield, the degree of Judith's awareness of the affair between her father and Wash's granddaughter, what—if anything—occurred between Sutpen and his first wife in New Orleans, and—most fundamentally—Bon's knowledge about his father: "Nobody ever did know if Bon ever knew Sutpen was his father or not" (235).

This remark, made by Quentin in chapter 7, indicates that a substantial portion of the italicized passage at the end of the following chapter, in which we seem to witness the revelation by Sutpen to Henry, then by Henry to Bon, that Bon is Sutpen's son whom he rejected because of the taint of black blood, is an imaginative reconstruction—at the very least, there is no certainty that *Bon* ever knew these things. But, according to General Compson, the meeting between Sutpen and Henry did take place; Sutpen did play what he called his "last trump card" (341–42, 345). Moreover, there are indications that the version in chapter 8 is substantially correct, based on the fact that Quentin obtained new information, never known to the other informants, the night he and Rosa went out to the Hundred (332, 342). His earlier claim to the positive value of distance in time in understanding the past ("*No. If I had been there I could not have seen it this plain*" [238]) therefore ceases to seem paradoxical. We realize that in the meeting with Henry, Quentin learned something— what and how the text does not tell us, and it remains elusive despite the debates of critics—that informs the passage at the end of chapter 8.

The book's overall structure (the discussions with Rosa and Mr. Compson, the revision of that material with Shreve, the inverted sequence of the revelations in chapters 8 and 9) hence leads us to question, then to appreciate, the validity of the story as represented in the next to last chapter. Another key feature is the dialogic nature of that chapter, the doubling and fusing of Quentin and Shreve, so that it is unimportant who is talking, and so that we as readers often cannot tell which one it is. The effect of this is progressively to remove the content of the story from the limitations of either of the individual consciousnesses and voices that imagine and tell it. Hence the last passage in italics simply emerges—discontinuously, first from a reflection of the narrator on Quentin and Shreve as stereotypes of the South- erner and Northerner, and takes the form of a historical narra- tion within parentheses, situated in the voice of no particular speaker: "(—*the winter of '64 now, the army retreated across Ala- bama* . . . [433]). Then, after an interruption by Shreve, there is a "meld" from the narrator's description of the two students into a direct evocation of that past scene:

> They were both in Carolina and the time was forty-six years ago, and it was not even four now but compounded still fur- ther, since now both of them were Henry Sutpen and both of them were Bon, compounded each of both yet either neither, smelling the very smoke which had blown and faded away forty-six years ago from the *bivouac fires burning in a pine grove, the gaunt and ragged men sitting or lying about them, talking not about the war yet all curiously enough (or perhaps not curiously at all) facing the South where further on in the darkness the pickets stood—the pickets who, watching to the South, could see the flicker and gleam of the Federal bivouac fires.* (438–39)

In the moving scenes that follow, the past tense quickly gives way to the present, and we see directly the meeting of Henry and his father, their embrace and conversation (including "*Henry.* . . .

My son" [441]), then finally the revelation: "*—He must not marry her, Henry. His mother's father told me that her mother had been a Spanish woman. I believed him; it was not until after he was born that I found out that his mother was part negro*" (443). After a transitional passage we follow, again in the present tense, the exchange between Henry and Bon, which includes Bon's answer to Henry's plea, "*You are my brother*": "*No I'm not. I'm the nigger that's going to sleep with your sister. Unless you stop me, Henry*" (446). With Bon's repetition of that threat, the italics break off and we return to the voice of Shreve: " 'And he never slipped away,' Shreve said" (447).

This remarkable sequence thus enacts, as present and as outside the limits of any individual consciousness, the past. More than the ancient and elementary forms of history (chronology and genealogy) that Faulkner appends to the novel, with their implication of the book's aspiration to historical validity, chapter 8 works its way up to a recuperation of the past, to a representation through fiction of historical reality. Marx's words, representation (*Darstellung*) and appropriation (*Aneignung*), apply closely. As much as in *Goriot*, in *Absalom* the fictional mode succeeds in becoming a depiction of historical truth.[14]

Quentin and Shreve's version is also legitimized by Faulkner's narrative tactics, in particular by the role of the presiding narrative voice. In the first part of the novel, Faulkner's narrative practice looks very different from Balzac's in *Goriot*, for the narrative voice is not highlighted, functioning almost exclusively to set up the situations in which the individual tellers, Rosa and Mr. Compson, give their versions. The effect of this is to make the "informants" take on some of the qualities of "narrator" and "mouthpieces" in *Goriot*. Hence the expressions of opinion, bias, generalization, and conjecture, as well as appeals to an interlocutor, take place between the characters within the novel. So Mr. Compson analyzes the exploitation of women while expressing antifemale attitudes and reports his father's indignation about oppression in Haiti without reflecting on its relevance for Mississippi. So also he conjectures, generalizes, and appeals for responses from Quentin: "Have you noticed how so often when we try to reconstruct the causes which lead up to the actions of men and women, how with a sort of astonishment we find ourselves now and then reduced to the belief . . . that they stemmed from some of the old virtues?" (150). Later the exchanges between Shreve and Quentin—"For God's sake wait"; "All right. . . . Go on"; "Wait, I tell you!"—intensify the reactions that a sole narrator might produce in a reader. Finally, it is the character Quentin, and with him the reader, who in his imagination obsessively *sees* many of the central scenes: Henry and Bon arriving at Sutpen's Hundred before the murder, Henry bursting into his sister's room, Quentin's visit to the Hundred as a boy, the ride out to the Hundred that night, and his fateful meeting with Henry.

Whereas in the first portion, and still often in the second, all of this happens through the interactions of the characters, nonetheless in the second part of the book the narrative voice itself becomes progressively more insistent. At increasing length, the narrator emits opinions about youth, time, innocence, virginity, why the South lost the war, and so on. At one point at least, the narrator's involvement and exaltation augment to the point of endangering lucidity. Commenting on the ease of Quentin and Shreve's identification with Henry and Bon, he asserts that details of place and person do not matter—"so long as the blood coursed—the blood, the immortal brief recent intransient blood which could hold honor above slothy unregret and love above fat and easy shame" (369). This devotion to blood, honor, and love may reflect the ideas of Henry and Bon, and perhaps of Quentin and Shreve. But this is also an instance of the narrator's identification with and celebration of values that the novel as a whole shows to be intimately linked to the tragedy of Sutpen and the South. More subtly perhaps than the narrator in *Goriot*, Faulkner's narrative voice displays its own kind of ideological inconsistency.

Still, the major role of the narrator is to legitimate the interpretation of the two students. Although not very different from "Sutpen's morality and Miss Coldfield's demonising," their effort takes place in a setting dedicated to the "best of ratiocination" (350), earlier described as "this snug monastic coign, this dreamy and heatless alcove of what we call the best of thought" (323). Here not only is the students' reconstructive activity praised, but in a rare gesture to the reader the narrator invokes *us* as a collectivity situated on the margins of their collaboration. True, they may be arbitrary (the lawyer, who was wounded at Pittsburgh Landing); they even run the risk of complete unreality ("the two of them creating between them, out of the rag-tag and bob-ends of old tales and talking, people who perhaps had never existed at all anywhere" [378—79]). But the narrator repeatedly asserts that their version is "probably true enough" (419), "probably right" (420) and finally justifies them in the celebrated bonfire passage, with its play on Bon's name and foreshadowing of the fire at the end of the book.

Here the narrator says that Shreve need not have spoken of love, since he and Quentin were thinking only of that:

> all that had gone before just so much that had to be overpassed and none else present to overpass it but them, as someone always has to rake the leaves up before you can have the bonfire. That was why it did not matter to either of them which one did the talking, since it was not the talking alone which did it, performed and accomplished the overpassing, but some happy marriage of speaking and hearing wherein each before the demand, the requirement, forgave condoned and forgot the faulting of the other—faultings both in the creating of this shade whom they discussed (rather, existed in) and in the hearing and sifting and discarding the false and conserving what seemed true, or fit the preconceived—in order to overpass to love, where there might be paradox and inconsistency but nothing fault nor false. (395)

In spite of the continuing activity of imagination ("creating"), the presence of paradox, inconsistency, preconception, and mistakes ("faulting"), it is finally claimed that there is nothing essentially false in this Faulknerian *All is true*. Through the communion of voices the estrangement of solitary individuals is mitigated. Quentin and Shreve have the role, the duty, of accomplishing this, and the larger, societal dimension of their activity is noted through another reference to all of us, to a collective "you." They rake the leaves, we—you—get the bonfire at the end—as we do. Through the implications of the metaphors, a nightmarish reality (Bon's death, the burning of Sutpen's house, and all they represent of the horrors of slavery, destructive sexuality, and murder) is "overpassed." There are suggestions of gathering up, burning away, and thus dissipating the past, references to forgiveness, love, unity. Unlike the union of Eugène and Delphine, with its allegory of class and economic mingling and rejuvenation, this verbal marriage intimates the effort of confrontation, cooperation, and reconciliation necessary for America to transcend its historical past.

"Historical" refers not just to Southern but to all American history. Faulkner—perhaps in a development of *Goriot*'s North-South symbolism—has the reconciliation occur between "Shreve, the Canadian, the child of blizzards and of cold," and Quentin, "the Southerner, the morose and delicate offspring of rain and steamy heat" (432). Earlier, the narrator had extended this North-South motif into a geographical, biological, and religious figure of unification paralleling that of marriage:

> the two of them . . . both young, both born within the same year: the one in Alberta, the other in Mississippi; born half a continent apart yet joined, connected after a fashion in a sort of geographical transubstantiation by that Continental Trough, that River which runs not only through the physical land of which it is the geologic umbilical, not only runs through the spiritual lives of the beings within its scope, but is very Environment itself which laughs at degrees of latitude and temperature, though some of these beings, like Shreve, have never seen it. (322)

This is the unified vision of our land that is struggled toward in the reconciling "marriage of speaking and hearing" carried out by the two youths, one Southern, one Northern, and in which we as readers participate.

But *Absalom*'s reconciliations need to be "deconstructed" and are largely deconstructed by the novel itself. We have seen how little the end of *Goriot* is a conclusion and the extent to which it is purchased at the cost of the revelations about Goriot's profiteering and insane familial drives, the expression then removal of Vautrin's subversiveness, the moral ambivalence of the career on which Rastignac embarks. The problematic features at the end of *Absalom* are even more flagrant.

First, despite Rosa's important contribution, her repeated struggle against what "*they* [the men] *will have told you doubtless already*" (166), the narrative economy of *Absalom* is otherwise overwhelmingly male. Ellen and Clytie are mute, and Judith's one speech shows her as unable to comprehend the meaning of events. But the testimony of General Compson, through his son, and of Henry is transmitted to the male couple Quentin and Shreve. Nor should we forget the insistently sexualized descriptions of Shreve's body. Indeed, in this overpassing, the only satisfying love and marriage is the verbal one between the two students. If not explicitly so in thematic terms, the novel is narratologically homosexual, as well as patriarchal (all the references to everyone sounding like Quentin's father). *Absalom* displays the destructiveness of the patriarchal order but perpetuates the essential *form* of that order, the privileged and intimate communication between males.

Second, we should question the lateness of key revelations in both novels. Postponement, an honored tactic of narrative suspense, contributes much to the interest of *Goriot* and *Absalom* but is in some profound sense ideologically overdone. Why, despite increasingly obvious hints, does it take so long for Vautrin's homosexuality to be openly revealed—requiring even police testimony and his arrest? An unavowed homosexual potential in Rastignac is thus suggested (and repressed), but the mystery surrounding Vautrin's sexual nature may also be thought of as preparing his rapid evacuation from the scene. The mystification of the homosexual in *Absalom* is more extreme, since it is never admitted, except perhaps in Mr. Compson's reflections on Bon and the Sutpen children—but never about Sutpen himself or about Quentin and Shreve. A homosexual tendency is therefore displayed but not avowed. And what of the great secret of Bon's black blood? The novel gives us clues about it all along, but somehow no character can respond to these clues until the end. Even for us as readers, long after we *must* have understood, the "revelation" comes only near the end. The fear of miscegenation in American history is thus suggested, and powerfully so; but the theme is also mystified, maintained in its tabooed status, by such narrative procedures.

Finally, the marriage in chapter 8 does not hold up. At the end Quentin compulsively relives the meeting with Henry that "waking or sleeping . . . was the same and would be the same forever as long as he lived" (465)—he who is soon to commit suicide and who ends the narrative proper by responding to Shreve's taunts about the South: "*I dont. I dont! I dont hate it! I dont hate it!*" (471). On that last page, too, Shreve points out what is obvious, that the ledger has not been cleared, that "You've got one nigger left. One nigger Sutpen left," hence pointing to the legacy of slavery that shadows American society still. Indeed, Shreve's own closing comment about blacks "bleaching out," while flippant, is unavoidably racist.

Shreve is the last person mentioned at the end of the genealogy, the only person—with Jim Bond—still alive in the indeterminate "now" of the work's last sentence. The chronology and genealogy of course visibly undermine the possibility of closure—when the book apparently ends, it still goes on. Somewhat differently, the last page of *Goriot* opens to a future, which—as we saw from the perspective of Marx's *Eighteenth Brumaire*—turned out to be calamitous. That is, though it is true that the novels are formal counterparts, in the texture of their writing straining toward the middle decades of the nineteenth century, the one through exuberant projection, the other through anguished retrospection, it is nonetheless the case that Faulkner's book also has its forward-looking dimension. Shreve, we learn, has experienced the trial of World War I. In the "now" of 1936 and beyond, the Aryan burliness and racist remark of this one white survivor of *Absalom* thrust us into the even more horrendous present and future, the middle—and later?—decades not of the nineteenth but of our own century.

Five
A MUTUAL,
JOINT-STOCK
WORLD

*I*n terms of historical scope *Le Père Goriot* and *Absalom, Absalom!* may be thought to frame the works treated earlier. Following study of them, *Moby-Dick* is a suitable concluding work for this book.[1] It is American, still familiar to our experience; written in the middle of the nineteenth century (1851), it exhibits striking resemblances to many elements in Marx. Its treatment of history and related issues retains a high degree of actuality, whereas the range of its references to global economic developments makes it in this respect the closest of our novels to Marx's work. This is reflected in its encyclopedic form, as suggested in chapter 1—in its simultaneous comprehensiveness and "careful disorderliness" (469). *Moby-Dick* also concentrates and augments sexual, exotic, demonic, and visionary elements only glimpsed in works like *Madame Bovary* and *Ulysses*, and present in melodramatic form in *Goriot* and *Absalom*. Readers of French literature will recognize in these labels the significance of writers like Nerval, Baudelaire, and Lautréamont, with whom we shall see that Melville also has affinities and whom a longer book might have studied in detail.

In myriad ways, often thought to be self-contradictory, *Moby-Dick* expresses the impulse to leave the realm of the sociohistorical, so privileged in a Marxist perspective. But we have seen that for Marx the contradictions of the religious order are closely related to those of the societal and economic spheres.[2]

In the infinite trance, the "opium-like" reverie of "The Mast-Head" (250–57), news and gazettes, domestic and commercial afflictions, even concern for one's next meal become irrelevant, until individual identity is lost, becoming "diffused through time and space." But the chapter concludes with a warning about accidental death amid such pantheist experience (although the experience of the "mysterious, divine Pacific" later produces adoration of Pan [594]); moreover, "The Mast-Head" also includes nineteenth-century political references, as we shall see.

Other instances of the "mystic mood" are too intermittent to assuage Ahab's sorrow and lead Ishmael to reflect that their meaning is to be discovered only in death (602). Numerous philosophical musings on Plato, Kant, and Spinoza, among others, reinforce this concern with the finite, the strong sense of human mortality expressed from the outset concerning the fictitious usher and sub-sublibrarian (75, 77–78). Examining funeral monuments before his dangerous voyage, Ishmael reflects on the paradoxes of religious faith and practical existence ("Life Insurance Companies pay death-forfeitures upon immortals"), then asserts that, as for his body, "it is not me" (130–31). This does not prevent him elsewhere from rejoicing in his body (456–57). Another body that he praises belongs to the Polynesian Queequeg, whose serenity in the face of deathly illness reveals his "immortal health," in a passage accompanied by oceanic and cosmic motifs and revealing finally that Queequeg's tattoos represent "a complete theory of the heavens and the earth, and a mystical treatise on the art of attaining truth"—the key to which has unfortunately been lost (587–93).

Ahab's reaction—"Oh, devilish tantalization of the gods!"—is in tune with the book's reiterated expression of the difficulty of the act of interpretation,[3] especially in obtaining knowledge about ultimate realities. Ishmael has more equanimity, entertaining doubts but also "divine" and "heavenly" intuitions (482). Moby-Dick becomes a focus for such concerns, for Ahab (262), but also for Ishmael, in that the ambiguous whiteness of the whale is experienced in terms of the primeval and the numinous, evoking "reverence and awe," "a certain nameless terror" (291). In Ishmael's view, the "mighty god-like dignity inherent" in the brow of the whale makes "you feel the Deity and the dread powers more forcibly than in beholding any other object in living nature," an opinion that leads to reflections on hieroglyphics and the disappearance of a sense of religious myth—"in the now egotistical sky; on the now unhaunted hill" (454–55). When Moby-Dick finally appears, he is described (in sexually seductive terms) as divine: "The grand god revealed himself" (656–57). Fearsome and seductive, the whale as embodiment of the sacred is a figure of fundamental and unsettling ambivalence. Accordingly, the cabin boy Pip's encounter with the divine brings madness, defined by Ishmael as an indifference equal to God's (526). Ahab's monomania eventuates in an equally mad encounter with the fundamental fiery force of the universe: "Defyingly I worship thee!" (616–17).

Though diabolical in the ritual with the pagan harpooners (600), Ahab's "religion" has some disquieting points of contact with the conclusion of Father Mapple's sermon (143), particularly with the sentence on the joy of the lonely prophet: "Delight is to him . . . who against the proud gods and commodores of this earth, ever stands forth his own inexorable self." Ahab's life is agony rather than delight, and he struggles against the divine, although also against those who hold earthly power; yet in his sense of his "queenly personality" (616) and in his "sultanism" (243–44), he is not unlike Father Mapple's version of the prophet's superiority to "the boisterous mob." Mapple's prophet and Ahab both suggest the book's ambivalence on democracy, a theme we will discuss. But Mapple is also inconsistent on the issue of selfhood, since he goes on to evoke the prophet's address to God: "I have striven to be Thine, more than to be this world's, or mine own." God to be sure is known chiefly for his "rod," and early in the sermon there is a reference to the sins of Gomorrah and Sodom (137). Ishmael, whose homosexually tinted relations with Queequeg frame the chapter on the sermon ("The Counterpane" and "A Bosom Friend"), makes no comment on Mapple's discourse. Here, as in the other instances noted in this necessarily brief survey, it is clear that the religious impulse is insistently present and also deeply contradictory.

Different registers of the temporal in the work suggest a similar difficulty in integrating personal, religious, geological, and historical concepts and experiences of time. One of the aims of the book, visible in its marshaling of evidence about whales from the earliest periods and from all regions, is to bring us out of the limited time-space frame in which we habitually live. Sometimes this is done through references to biblical time, for example, concerning "antique Adam who died sixty round centuries ago" (130). Or else scientific, specifically geological, notions of time are introduced, in relation to whale fossils (377), man's aboriginal awe of the sea (380), the temporal limitations even of the entire human race—since "time began with man" and "preadamite traces" of whales suggest that they will exist "after all humane ages are over" (568–69). The geological perspective reduces the significance of the human as much as do the Pascalian reflections of Joyce's "Ithaca." In such a perspective, the traces of human history, of religions, nations, and governments, pale in importance. During the flood the whale "despised Noah's Ark"; once, too, "he swam . . . over the site of the Tuileries, and Windsor Castle, and the Kremlin" (574). The admonition seems all the more relevant today.

At least one passage combines sacred and scientific measures with the existence of the individual in historical and calendar time. The "mistifying" spout of the whale has existed for "six thousand years—and no one knows how many millions of ages before," right "down to this blessed minute (fifteen and a quarter minutes past one o'clock P.M. of this sixteenth day of December, A.D. 1850)" (477)—where the time of composition of the work is intruded. At the outset, Ishmael had been deliberately vague about the time of the events to be narrated: "Some years ago—never mind how long precisely" (93). But shortly after, in a proto-Joycean use of theater bills and newspaper headlines, he situates the voyage in 1840–42 (98). Juxtaposing his trip ("Whaling Voyage by One Ishmael") with a presidential election and with an English defeat in the first of the Afghan wars ("BLOODY

BATTLE IN AFFGHANISTAN") is hardly a way of dismissing the significance of American and international history. Again, there is a sense in which the history sketched by the headlines is still with us, has changed little in a century and a half, presents the same problems and dangers. The powerlessness of the individual in the face of this history is also underscored by Ishmael, though in ahistorical terms. He dismisses his belief that he undertook the voyage out of "unbiased freewill" as a delusion, invoking instead Providence and the Fates as responsible. Despite the pull of sacred experiences and the perspectives of religious and geological time, the horizon of political, economic, and military history is glimpsed from the opening chapter.[4]

Two great problems of American history—conflict with and decimation of indigenous populations by the settlers, and black slavery—are repeatedly, and somewhat ambiguously, evoked in *Moby-Dick*. One of the "pagan" harpooners is the "unmixed" Gay Head Indian Tashtego, whose "unvitiated blood of . . . proud warrior hunters" is celebrated, although already in a way that preludes the demonic paganism of Ahab's quest. Having Indian, Oriental, and Antarctic qualities, Tashtego is both attractive and fearsome to the white mind: "To look at the tawny brawn of his lithe snaky limbs, you would almost have credited the superstitions of the earlier Puritans, and half believed this wild Indian to be a son of the Prince of the Powers of the Air" (215). An earlier invocation of the reader has reminded us, in regard to the name of the ship, of the extermination of such noble savages: "*Pequod*, you will no doubt remember, was the name of a celebrated tribe of Massachusetts Indians, now extinct as the ancient Medes" (164). At other points, warfare between whites and Indians appears as an analogy of the primary themes of the work— conveying Ahab's unsociability and the courage of those who hunt down destructive whales (250, 305). In these instances the reference is apparently accidental but conveys contrary sympathies in the white-Indian struggle, in one case understanding of the Indian Logan, whose family had been massacred, in the other justification of the destruction of Rhode Island tribes. Such mixed sympathies are perhaps also visible in the juxtaposition of passages suggesting how easily white men may become

savages (376) with another in which Ishmael misuses the phrase
"native American," applying it to whites: "The native American
liberally provides the brains, the rest of the world as generously
supplying the muscles" (216). Here a note of American chauvin-
ism is sounded as well. But the most scandalous evocation of the
Indian is ironically put in the mouth of Queequeg, who after
struggling against the sharks concludes that "de god wat made
shark must be one dam Ingin" (409). In spite of the appreciation
of nonwhites in the book, it is the most important of their number who humorously perpetuates the figure of the Indian as
metaphor for evil (in the process indicting the divinity as well).

The harpooners, who can be seen to represent three groups
exploited by what Ishmael will call "the all-grasping western
world" (488), include the "gigantic, coal-black negro-savage"
Daggoo, also suitably magnified—six feet five, lionlike, compared to a Persian emperor, broad, baronial, superb (215–16,
249). Ishmael's position seems squarely antislavery—in the political symbolism that has been discovered in the figure of Bulking-
ton (202–3), in the sardonic reference to the "decent" burials
from slave ships (399), in his comment on Stubb's assertion that a
whale would be worth thirty times as much as Pip in Alabama:
"Perhaps Stubb indirectly hinted, that though man loves his fellow, yet man is a money-making animal, which propensity too
often interferes with his benevolence" (524).[5] Ishmael also seems
insistent on persuading his white American reader on the issue:
"Who aint a slave? Tell me that" (96). In the chapter in which
Queequeg saves a white man from drowning after submitting to
racial jeers, Ishmael wonders at the stupidity of the other
passengers—"as though a white man were anything more digni-
fied than a whitewashed negro" (155). And of Pip he addresses
us in this fashion: "Nor smile so, while I write that this little black
was brilliant, for even blackness has its brilliancy; behold yon
lustrous ebony" (522).

Even when Ishmael's remarks may seem to be less than fully
enlightened, they retain an element of sympathy for the oppressed black. The old black cook is a stereotypical figure (400),
but a comparable description of Pip as having "that pleasant,
genial, jolly brightness peculiar to his tribe" also provokes the

pointed comment: "For blacks, the year's calendar should show naught but three hundred and sixty-five Fourth of Julys and New Year's Days" (522). The figures of slaves celebrating Independence Day is grim enough. Equally disturbing though are Ishmael's preference for rope over hemp ("Hemp is a dusky, dark fellow, a sort of Indian; but Manilla is as a golden-haired Circassian to behold" [384]) and his including under the dominance of the color white the fact that it "applies to the human race itself, giving the white man ideal mastership over every dusky tribe." This assertion, however, occurs in a long sentence that concludes rather on the "panic" the color white finally evokes (287–88). Can there be any worse panic in fact than that of Pip shrieking during the storm at the culmination of the homosexual orgy provoked by Ahab's ceremony with the doubloon and drink? Pip's terror before the "royal yard," "white squalls . . . white whale," and "that anaconda of an old man" fuses racial and religious themes with the phallic and anal imagery that is part of the dominant homosexual motif of the book: "Oh, thou big white God aloft there somewhere in yon darkness, have mercy on this small black boy down here; preserve him from all men that have no bowels to feel fear!" (276). The defenseless black boy is here the object of brutalization of racial, religious, and sexual kinds. What is this to say but that the black man has been buggered by the white?

History not limited to America but in a worldwide compass appears in brief references to modern Europe and more numerous ones to Western inroads into the rest of the world. Hence among the notations describing the *Pequod*, we see her wood "darkened like a French grenadier's, who has alike fought in Egypt and Siberia" (164). This comparison does not come easily to mind; the text is at pains to link Napoleonic military expansionism with the voyages of American whalers. Napoleon is also mentioned in "The Mast-Head," which, although devoted to the trance experience already treated, nonetheless lists previous standers-of-mastheads going back to the Egyptians and including George Washington's column in Baltimore, Horatio Nelson's in Trafalgar Square (and in Dublin, as *Ulysses* so strongly emphasizes), and Napoleon on the Vendôme column (glimpsed on the last page of *Goriot*, we recall). Napoleon is "careless" now of who rules France—"Louis Philippe, Louis Blanc, or Louis the Devil" (251–52). Together these allusions sketch the modern Western history of revolution, democracy, empire and opposition to it, and subsequent developments up to the present of the work, with Ishmael's condemnation of Louis-Bonaparte clear.

But global exploration and commerce, spearheaded by whaling, is the true historical subject of *Moby-Dick*, behind and through Ahab's and Ishmael's voyage. Ishmael thinks the whaling house of Enderby & Sons to be "not far behind the united royal houses of the Tudors and Bourbons, in point of real historical interest," and assures us that he has not been sparing of historical research concerning whaling (554–56). This emphasis on international economic history recalls Marx's linking of capital cities and world market, a relationship structurally pertinent for Ishmael's (and the reader's) journey from Manhattan to New Bedford and Nantucket and the distant regions of the whale hunt.[6] We start in "your insular city of the Manhattoes, belted round by wharves as Indian isles by coral reefs—commerce surrounds it with her surf" (93). Although much in "Loomings" concerns "ocean reveries," here the emphasis is on commerce, which seems to usurp nature. An immediate link is made, too, between New York and distant Indian islands, just as the water gazers on the docks also look at ships from China and as Ishmael's departure for New Bedford is really a start for Cape Horn and the Pacific (94, 99).

In "The Street," New Bedford's opulence is described, but not before an evocation of it and other cities as places where the global exchange led by whaling is visible:

> Even in Broadway and Chestnut streets, Mediterranean mariners will sometimes jostle the affrighted ladies. Regent street is not unknown to Lascars and Malays; and at Bombay, in the Apollo Green, live Yankees have often scared the natives. But New Bedford beats all Water street and Wapping. In these last-mentioned haunts you see only sailors; but in New Bedford, actual cannibals stand chatting at street corners; savages outright; many of whom yet carry on their bones unholy flesh. It makes a stranger stare. (125)

This, we might say, one-ups Blake and Engels on the urban jostle. American cities are linked to continental Europe and cities in England and India, which opens up our limited perspective on who are strangers, who are so foreign as to cause fear. This is in keeping with the reversal of attitudes concerning religion and civilization that Queequeg brings about in Ishmael. We may also recognize that Melville is doing in a systematic way what Flaubert and Joyce do sparingly—that is, show us the mixture in cities of nationalities and races that is the outcome of international commerce. The intention of reaching the reader is again shown in direct address: "you see." One step further and the address becomes an imperative: "Nantucket! Take out your map and look at it. See what a real corner of the world it occupies" (157).

This chapter closes (158–59) with a celebration of the Nantucketer, who has made the whole ocean his empire, whose business would not be interrupted by a Noah's flood, and who each night sleeps "while under his very pillow rush herds of walruses and whales." But the praise is vitiated by the description of the Nantucketers "issuing from their ant-hill in the sea," overrunning the seas like so many Alexanders. This recalls the Napoleonic allusions and is followed by other instances of conquest and empire justified only by force, including the dismemberment of Poland, U.S. imperialism in Texas, Mexico, Cuba, and Canada, and English conquest of India. Such terms of praise hardly produce unmixed admiration for the business of whaling. Nor in the process does the United States escape condemnation along with other rapacious powers whose acts constitute important features of nineteenth-century history.

The *Pequod*'s voyage takes her crisscross fashion around the entire globe until the farthest point, Asia, is reached, in a passage that reads like a geography lesson for the American reader: "The long and narrow peninsula of Malacca, extending southeastward from the territories of Birmah, forms the most southerly point of all Asia. In a continuous line from that peninsula stretch the long islands. . . ." This is followed shortly by the reflection noted earlier that the region bears "the appearance, however ineffectual, of being guarded from the all-grasping western world" (487–88). But an earlier passage (203–6) is much more positive on the impact of the West. In "The Advocate," indeed, after quoting figures on costs and profits of whaling first in Europe then in the United States, Ishmael presents the whaling industry as the key to global international exchange.

Hence it is as "cosmopolite philosopher" that he sees "the high and mighty business of whaling" as the single most powerful and peaceful influence in the past sixty years on "the whole broad world," in exploration, interpreting between "savage" nations and later arriving vessels (significantly, however, "American and European men-of-war," despite the emphasis on the peaceful), and in opening up previously closed countries. The latter include South American nations, Australia, Polynesia, and potentially Japan: "If that double-bolted land, Japan, is ever to become hospitable, it is the whale-ship alone to whom the credit will be due; for already she is on the threshold."

The historical ironies in this prescient assertion have to do not only with the monstrous wars of the twentieth century but also with the fact that Japan still resists efforts to halt whaling in the interest of preserving the species from extinction, an outcome that Ishmael thinks unlikely. (He holds to this view despite the fate of the buffalo in regions where he remarks that "now the polite broker sells you land at a dollar an inch" [570–74].) Another mixture of insight and irony in Ishmael's celebration of the influence of whaling concerns South America, where commerce and intercourse were previously only colonial. He credits whaling with being at the origin of the liberation of Peru, Chile, and Bolivia from Spanish rule, with "the establishment of the eternal democracy in those parts." Current history reminds us how intermittently "eternal" democracy has been "in those parts," not least because of the role of the "great America" for which Ishmael sees a counterpart in Australia, opened up together with Polynesia, again by the whalers. Polynesia is said to do "commercial homage to the whale-ship, that cleared the way for the missionary and the merchant." In contrast to Ishmael's criticism elsewhere of Western influence throughout the world, here the tone is celebratory, in a passage mixing insightful history from the perspective of the "cosmopolite philosopher" with what amounts to ideological propaganda—on the themes of peace, trade, religion, and democracy.

If Tashtego and Daggoo recall two contradictions of American history, it is the third harpooner, the noble cannibal Queequeg, whom we may relate to the Western penetration of other regions of the globe. Despite the one point at which he seems infected by the white man's tendency to identify Indian and evil, he functions throughout as an alternative to the failures and hypocrisies of American Christian society, as Ishmael discovers when they smoke in bed together (149–50): "I'll try a pagan friend, thought I, since Christian kindness has proved but hollow courtesy" (146). What is remarkable here is the ease with which a deceptive, destructive, and fragmenting society (Ishmael uses words like "splintered," "maddened," "wolfish," "civilized hypocrisies and bland deceits") pales in the face of an experience that is deeply somatic, involving a rediscovery of unity in Ishmael's being as well as an attraction to Queequeg (such words as "melting," "soothing," "redeemed," "mysteriously drawn towards him"). That the passage occurs through the mediation of a "savage" and in sexually charged terms indicates the extent to which the prevailing structures of a "civilized" and sexually "normal" culture have oppressed Ishmael (and presumably the reader).

Much of the success of the passage for the reader is a function of what precedes it—Ishmael's anxiety about sleeping with a strange, savage man, the uncanny fear of his childhood dream-experience, the contrasting pleasure of his awakening with Queequeg. As already hinted, indeed, the impact of *Moby-Dick* on "civilized, domestic people in the temperate zone" (333) derives from the book's ability to cause us to experience what initially seems strange but which we gradually discover, perhaps discover in ourselves. Experiences of this sort already noted include our consciousness of our religion and of the norms or myths of our nation, our sensitivity to race and sense of what is civilized and what savage, our experience of our bodies and sexuality, our awareness of interactions between our country and other regions of the world. This is all mightily enlarging and potentially liberating. But *Moby-Dick* also carries a strong strain of nineteenth-century exoticism that appeals to the Western reader, an exoticism that tends to confirm certain stereotypes of the white mind and sometimes makes the subversive effect of the book difficult to reckon. In this connection *Moby-Dick* may be seen as a work of visionary exoticism having connections with voyage motifs in Baudelaire and with such strange productions as Nerval's *Aurélia* and Lautréamont's *Les Chants de Maldoror.*[7]

Thus the marvelously titled "Loomings" concludes (98) with a list of Ishmael's motives (in addition to money) for undertaking the voyage. They sound like the résumé of a known poetic tradition—the whale as "portentous and mysterious monster" amid "wild and distant seas," "nameless perils," and "all the attending marvels of a thousand Patagonian sights and sounds." For Ishmael—oh you hypocritical readers, childish minds ever thirsty for imaginary travel—is a man attracted to "things remote," "forbidden seas," and "barbarous coasts." When in the last paragraph of this liminal chapter "the great flood-gates of the wonder-world" swing open, the tone of grave awe is almost the same as that of the first page of *Aurélia,* with its evocation of the mysterious (and exotic) world of dreams. With the difference that Ishmael's wonderworld is peopled with whales, and especially with "one grand hooded phantom" of the white whale, a hidden *signifié* guaranteed to make any Lacanian happy, just as the exoticism of the book, coexisting with the passages of historic-economic interest already discussed, takes forms that are instead sexual, archetypal, demonic.

The primal and archetypal are experienced by Ishmael when he finally enters the Pacific, which stretches from California (where the "recentest race of men" is active) to "Asiatic lands, older than Abraham," which are as "endless," "unknown," "impenetrable" as the Pacific is "mysterious" and "divine." This is the passage ending with an evocation of the "seductive god," Pan (594). An earlier passage on Fedallah (333–34) more powerfully expresses this sense of the primal, with marked sexual and diabolical overtones. Here we are told that we cannot be indifferent to Fedallah, a figure whom we inhabitants of temperate zones see only in our dreams but who really exists "among the unchanging Asiatic communities," which are called "insulated, immemorial, unalterable," preserving "the ghostly aboriginalness of earth's primal generations" and the memory of the time when angels and devils "indulged in mundane amours" with "the daughters of men." Doubtless, repressed and alienated nineteenth-century Western humanity needed, as we do today, to rediscover immemorial experiences of nature, divinity, sex, psyche, and race; but this passage also involves an enormous projection of these needs onto the "other" of Asian humanity. The fascination with the sexual comminglings of nonwhite races with angelic and demonic figures is especially strong.

These projections and fascinations are focused through Ahab in his relations with the pagan harpooners and boat crew. Concerning the dying whale, Ahab speaks of a "dark Hindoo half of nature," which he associates with China and Africa (606); and even Ishmael surmises that the sharks follow only Ahab's boat on the last day of the chase because the crew's "tiger-yellow" flesh smells more "musky" (677). Indeed, in the first description of Fedallah (318) Ishmael repeats the motif already seen in the case of Tashtego—that the "tiger-yellow complexion" of "aboriginal natives of the Manillas" betokens a "race notorious for a certain diabolism of subtilty," causing "some honest white mariners" to take them for agents of the devil. That the rest of the book may lead us to consider white honesty in an ironic light does not eliminate the association of the diabolic with persons of another color. Ishmael himself makes such an association in another passage:

> But what it was that inscrutable Ahab said to that tiger-yellow crew of his—these were words best omitted here; for you live under the blessed light of the evangelical land. Only the infidel sharks in the audacious seas may give ear to such words, when, with tornado brow, and eyes of red murder, and foam-glued lips, Ahab leaped after his prey. (325)

Here Ishmael seems to proffer with vehemence the link between Asians, sharks, and the "infidel." But how, given all that we encounter in the work, can we accept the world of the white American reader so directly addressed here as that of the "blessed light of the evangelical land"? Here is perpetuated a demonic racial stereotype (as well as a religious delusion). But something even more unsettling is taking place here, where Melville's writing most

closely resembles that of Lautréamont. Maldoror attacks both
man and God in the most violent ways, often through identifying
with what appears to most of us as monstrous—as when he describes copulating with a shark. In the Melville paragraph before
us, the word *audacious* suggestively places the "infidel" sharks in a
heroic light. And the description of Ahab (tornado brow, eyes of
red murder, foam-glued lips, leaping after his prey) has the
Maldoror intensity, in which the stereotypes of demonic style
transcend the bathetic and take on a surreal immediacy. Beyond
the conflict between cool analysis of Western exploitation of Asia
on the one hand, and on the other the stereotype of the Asian as
demonic, there is also a conflict between the ostensible condemnation of Ahab and a fantastic magnification of him. As in the case of
Maldoror, this may be the point at which Melville's book becomes
most subversive, but toward what end is not clear; in any event,
the demonic writing is so highlighted that sociohistorical concerns
all but disappear from view.

The demonism, as suggested throughout, activates powerful
racial and sexual currents. Infernal in "The Try-Works" (533),
the pagan harpooners are phallically united with Ahab in "The
Candles," in the description of his harpoon projecting from its
"conspicuous crotch," its "loose leather sheath" having dropped
off, and emitting "a levelled flame of pale, forked fire" that
burns like "a serpent's tongue" (617). Earlier, too, "The Cassock"
had shown us the sheath of the whale's "unaccountable cone" as
like an enormous homosexual version of Queequeg's jet-black
idol, Yojo (530). Hence, although there is a "good" homosexual
dimension in the relation between him and Ishmael, superior to
hypocritical Christian "love," there is also a demonic homosexuality somehow linked to the fascination with race. Having reached
this (elementary) conclusion in pursuit of the work's geographic,
racial, and sexual exoticism, with the consequence that historico-
economic issues highlighted earlier are obscured, we need to
address more directly the question of the links that may exist
between the realm of the economic and that of the libidinal.

In chapters on Balzac, Flaubert, James, and Joyce, we have seen
encroachments on and deformations of the erotic by the eco-

nomic in the various love relationships these authors depict. In addition, Vautrin and Sutpen are more or less avowedly homosexual and exhibit powerful energy in the economic sphere; behind them we glimpsed Jameson's argument about Heathcliff as a capitalist whose energies have been displaced into or recoded in the sexual register. The question, though, is to clarify such metaphors as displacement and recoding, to obtain a sense of how desire is active in the socioeconomic sphere. The problem is especially pertinent for *Moby-Dick,* in which financial and sexual realms are each heavily marked, although the relation between the two seems one of rupture and conflict. Recent theory and criticism subsuming psychoanalytic arguments within a Marxist perspective are of help here.[8] To the ideas of Irigaray sketched in chapter 1 and used in our discussion of *Goriot* and *Absalom,* we may add Deleuze and Guattari's redefinition of schizophrenia with its characteristic delirium (relevant for Ahab and much else in *Moby-Dick*) as the most notable psychic disease of the capitalist system. They also argue for a nonoedipal primary homosexuality as originally at the root of the social order, an argument relevant not only for Irigaray but for E. K. Sedgwick's study of the gothic novel. Sedgwick shows the role of homosexuality and homophobia in that tradition (as we have seen those tendencies at work in the depiction of Vautrin and Sutpen) and asserts that such literature affords insight into individual and family psychology but also into class conflict as well as gender identification. Such arguments are comprehensively unified by Irigaray's transformation of Freud via Marx, her analysis finding a fascinating exemplification in *Moby-Dick.*

The economic in *Moby-Dick* is pervasive, hence normal, but then also inescapable, and finally destructively evil.

What more natural than for Ishmael to tell us "good friends" that the ambergris, that "very unctuous and savory" substance obtained from "the inglorious bowels of a sick whale," is "worth a gold guinea an ounce to any druggist," since it is used worldwide in cosmetics, cooking, and wine, as well as for religious purposes (518–19)? The odorous and tactilely satisfying substance, so intimately related to the human body in its various needs, pleasures, functions, and sublimations, is immediately inserted in the international economic system. This example may stand for the range of sensuous experiences to which Ishmael initiates us, from eating succulent chowder (161) to the *jouissances* of squeezing the conjealed sperm oil or "case" (526–27): everything has its monetary dimension. And first of all the voyage itself, which Ishmael undertakes "having little or no money in [his] purse" (93), subsequently holding forth on the joys of being paid: "What will compare with it?" (97). Then, too, the narration of the work, the completion of this "draught of a draught," is dependent on "Time, Strength, Cash, and Patience!" (241)—what more normal? The reader is also part of the economic order, is even supposed to be of the class having enough money to invest in stocks: "People in Nantucket invest their money in whaling vessels, the same way that you do yours in approved state stocks bringing in good interest" (169). We are economic beings, and the *Pequod's* voyage, regardless of the wildness of Ahab's and Ishmael's and the reader's experience, is first and foremost a financial endeavor.

The reference to the reader as investor reminds us that Ishmael extends the notion of owning stock into a metaphor for human relations in general. He imagines Queequeg explaining his heroism in saving the bigoted white passenger in these terms: "It's a mutual, joint-stock world, in all meridians. We cannibals must help these Christians" (157). But the supra-Christian generosity of the motif is undermined in the perilous situation of "The Monkey-Rope," where Queequeg and Ishmael are "merged in a joint stock company of two." Ishmael characteristically perceives that the situation is illustrative of human relations in general: "If your banker breaks, you snap; if your apothecary by mistake sends you poison in your pills, you die" (426). Here the economic relation is very nearly one of life and death. Besides, Ishmael elsewhere deflates the investment analogy (in a paean to democracy to which we will return): "Men may seem detestable as joint stock-companies and nations" (211). The economic (and political) relationships uniting human beings turn out to be detestable, leaving only "man, in the ideal," to be praised.

The attack on the economic is directed especially at the hypocritical Christian society that Ishmael depicts; part of the pagan

Queequeg's appeal is that he appears never to have cringed or to have had a creditor (144). From the outset, amid references to poverty, money belts, skinflint landlords, and bartenders who dearly sell sailors "deliriums and death" (101–12), Ishmael remarks the paradox of Christians pursuing money, despite Christ's teaching about the impossibility of a rich man entering heaven: "Ah! how cheerfully we consign ourselves to perdition!" (97). And he repeats the parable about Lazarus and Dives with Blakean and Marxian notes: "Yet Dives himself, he too lives like a Czar in an ice palace made of frozen sighs, and being a president of a temperance society, he only drinks the tepid tears of orphans" (102). Moreover, despite the figure of Aunt Charity, who has invested "a score or two of well-saved dollars" in the *Pequod* (193), the chapters on the ship and its owners (167–74) attack the money drive of Christians in terms very like Marx's in "On the Jewish Question." The "well-to-do" owners are "Quakers with a vengeance," who act as if "a man's religion is one thing, and this practical world quite another. This world pays dividends." Supposedly pious, Bildad is "a bitter, hard task-master," in his very person utilitarian, spare, economical, reading his Bible while stingily offering Ishmael the seven-hundredth and seventy-seventh lay. Peleg is a more humorous version of the same—urging the men to say their prayers and avoid fornication while sermonizing them on the cost of wood and butter (201–2).

Together with numerous other passages attacking religion, the sequence on the pious Quaker owners is a devastating critique of the economic activity of Christian society, in which narrator and reader inevitably participate. It is not far from this to the reversal of roles which Ishmael has us accomplish so that we realize that men are also involved in "a shocking sharkish business enough for all parties" (399) and to the chapter "Fast-Fish and Loose-Fish," which makes possession the principle of human activity in every sphere.

How avoid this oppressive economic order, which, despite religious, philosophical, suprahistorical, and exotic impulses discussed earlier, intrudes throughout? Ishmael and Ahab attempt it by mobilizing what are essentially libidinal energies, though in different ways that are perhaps in keeping with the associations of their biblical names: sexual transgression, racial crossing, religious blasphemy, and infidelity. Nonetheless the two share some qualities, and we must keep them both in mind in considering the erotic as an attempted escape from enslavement to the economic.

The sexual dimension of Ishmael's moments of happiness with others is unmistakable, in the analogy of Queequeg sitting up "stiff as a pike-staff" (120), as in Ishmael's remark about "how elastic our stiff prejudices grow when love once comes to bend them" when they are in bed again (149). It is indeed not only a question of sex but also of love, as in the "melting" with Queequeg already discussed and in the mutual masturbatory motif of "A Squeeze of the Hand" (526–27), where Ishmael says that his fingers "serpentize and spiralize" in the "inexpressible sperm," until he confuses the hands of others with his own. The blurring of the separate self inaugurated in "A Bosom Friend" and which leads to a warning in "The Mast-Head" here comes to fruition, reminding us of Deleuze and Guattari's argument about how the socioeconomic order inhibits the various "flows" of bodily and psychic elements. Indeed the melting and flowing lead to a sentimental version of Irigaray's utopian relations among humans. Sensing himself "divinely free" of anger, ill will, petulance, and malice, rejecting acerbities, ill humor, and envy, Ishmael experiences "a strange sort of insanity" and addresses his "dear fellow beings": "Come; let us squeeze hands all around; nay, let us all squeeze ourselves into each other; let us squeeze ourselves universally into the very milk and sperm of kindness." Here the sexual content of the experience allows the biblical motif's transformation but also realization, in the mingling of no longer atomized individuals.

Ishmael immediately opposes this experience to the normal social world: love, family, home, work, pleasure, national identity—"the wife, the heart, the bed, the table, the saddle, the fire-side, the country." Wife and marriage are part of these "attainable" but "lower" felicities; hence, in keeping with the length of the voyage, the heterosexual and the familial are virtually invisible. Ishmael's praise of the women of New Bedford and Salem is exceptional and ends by implicitly criticizing the role of Puritan religion (127). Starbuck and the unfortunate Gardiner alone are devoted to wife and children (624, 640). Ishmael is an orphan who mentions only his stepmother, and that in a context of punishment and paralyzing fear (119–20). Ahab recognizes a divine father against whom he struggles but no mother (617); two brief references to his marriage stress the unhappiness of his "sweet, resigned girl" wife, whom he widowed in marrying, "leaving but one dent in [his] marriage pillow" (177, 651). In spite of some passages in which the whale is given bisexual qualities, the female body is rigorously excluded from the book, and references to sexual relations among men and women are few.

But the male body and homosexual acts are blazoned forth almost at every turn—in the language of crotch, yard, stiffness, squeezing hand, sperm, and bowels already encountered, as in the name of the whale, given as a chapter title (276) after the suggestive gap in the text that concludes the midnight orgy. (The second occurs, with equal significance, just after the passage on squeezing case [527].) Elsewhere we encounter references to colics and unnatural gases (523, 619); Ishmael offers to unbutton the whale for us and show us among other things his bowels (559, 566). "The Tail" includes a paean to massive male beauty and to the "elasticity" of that organ of the whale (482–87). Ishmael himself rejoices in his spine and in "the firm audacious staff of that flag," which he flings out to the world (456–57). The chapter on the whale's penis has been evoked, but we have not mentioned that the mincer clothes himself in it, in the context of puns on words like cock, ass, and prick (529–31). Nor have we yet noted that this "unaccountable cone" is preceded by the obtrusively phallic description of the ship's wigwam, a conical erection complete with limber bone, tufted apex, and loose hairy fibers (165). The male body, providing the pleasure that according to Irigaray society must hide, is on the contrary massively represented throughout the book, to the point that Ishmael's conceit about using his body for writing (563) becomes very nearly literalized.[9]

But all does not occur in the absence of anguish and guilt. The whale's penis has, after all, been cut off, and its sheath (or cassock) is worn by a mincer; the chapter also includes a reference to the biblical text condemning sodomy and ends on one to archbishops. Gomorrah for its part is mentioned from the second chapter, significantly it turns out in relation to a Negro church (100–101). We have seen that the biblical condemnation of sexual transgression appears almost in passing in Father Mapple's sermon. "A Squeeze of the Hand" ends incongruously with a vision of angels in heaven, "each with his hands in a jar of spermaceti" (527). Even more tellingly, Ishmael's first happiness with Queequeg is preceded by his childhood memory of punishment for "cutting up some caper," followed by the "troubled nightmare of a doze," the sense of a "supernatural hand" placed in his, a "horrid spell" that he has "shudderingly remembered. . . . to this very hour" (119–20). "Take away the awful fear," he says, and the nightmare and the experience of awakening with Queequeg are "very similar"! The castration motif, the reiteration of the biblical condemnation, the paralyzing fear— these afflict even Ishmael, who to that extent has not escaped the sexual economy, enforced through psychological and religious terror, that he opposes.

As for Ahab, the aged phallic quality that we have noted in him is pictured as destructive by Ishmael—in Pip at the time of the orgy, and perhaps also at the end (641–42). The castration threat is there too. Boarding another ship, he slides "his solitary thigh into the curve of the hook (it was like sitting in the fluke of an anchor, or the crotch of an apple tree)" (548). Later we learn that he was once mysteriously injured in a fall by his artificial leg itself, which had "stake-wise smitten, and all but pierced his groin; nor was it without extreme difficulty that the agonizing wound was entirely cured" (575). Ahab, then, we may consider the inevitable negative image of the liberating homosexuality of Ishmael, imposed on Melville's book by all the psychic and social forces that *Moby-Dick* also reveals and attacks. This link between the two men is all the more compelling in that they share not only homosexuality but also demonism, madness, and resistance to the dominant economic order—all of which the book emphasizes and all of which we must grasp as interrelated.

Hence Ishmael thinks of the whale's breach as a spasmodic

"snatching at the highest heaven," which he relates to his recurrent dream of a "majestic Satan thrusting forth his colossal claw from the flame Baltic of Hell" (although he grants that when in the mood of Isaiah he might instead think of archangels [486]). The grandiose satanism of the passage, the theme of rebellion, and the infernal imagery recall many of Ishmael's reflections on Ahab and suggest why he has so much sympathy for his heroic but monomaniacal protagonist. Ishmael has his own experiences of depression and deep sorrow, though characteristically he asserts his ability to rise above these moods (498, 535–36). And the strange "insanity" that he experiences when squeezing case is an expansive and positive rather than destructive state.

The moments when Ahab is touched by such sentiments are rare and fleeting; the last is in his relationship with Pip, also mad. Instead terrible suffering is reiterated, variously and sometimes contradictorily expressed in terms of tragedy, fate, the titanic, the demonic, and the satanic (with typical imagery of fire, magnetic power, fearsome eyes, and so on). This is related to the fact that Ahab is considered mad—only briefly according to Peleg (177), but in Ishmael's later version "a raving lunatic" who had to be tied to his hammock, in his delirium swinging "to the mad rockings of the gales" (284). Ahab considers himself "demoniac," "madness maddened" (266).

Many of the motifs associated with Ahab's madness are expressed in a passage where Ishmael describes it in terms that are hard not to call schizophrenic (302–3). The unbearable intensity of Ahab's "blazing brain" while he sleeps is pictured as a chasm containing flames, lightning, fiends, and hell, causing him to burst from his stateroom with a wild cry and glaring eyes as if his bed were on fire. This expresses his unbalanced state in traditional infernal imagery. But a titanic motif, the generation of a vulture feeding on Prometheus, refers to the development in Ahab of an "agent" separate from him, which Ishmael sees as his soul, "dissociated" from his mind, from which it seeks escape, being no longer "integral" with it. Finally, in Ishmael's analysis, Ahab's monomaniacal "purpose" becomes, against both gods and angels, a "vacated thing, a formless somnambulistic being," "a blankness in itself."

Despite the infernal and titanic imagery, Ahab's dissociated "purpose" transcends the mystified ethical opposition in the angel-devil dichotomy. Rather the issue is schizophrenia, with Ahab, divided within his being and raving in his bound state, recalling the experience of the mad narrator of Nerval's *Aurélia*. It is useful to recall Deleuze and Guattari's view of schizophrenia as characteristic of the modern socioeconomic order, their insistence on the contrast between the catatonic body and the demonically intense psychic life of the patient, as well as their argument that the schizoid's delirium, like that in *Aurélia* and like much in *Moby-Dick*, typically involves an experience of the entire history of the world, communicating among all periods and regions, all societies and races: schizophrenic delirium, according to them, is inherently racial, though not necessarily racist. The focus on race, the exoticism, the expansion to virtually all ages and regions of human experience, are related features of *Moby-Dick*. In the figure of Ahab the schizoid state appears as horrible suffering and madness; in Ishmael's survival, the work perhaps shadows forth more positive versions of psychic experience.

We have seen that, although happy to be paid, Ishmael systematically attacks the economic order, that his "insanity" in squeezing case is set in opposition to the structures and experiences of family, work, and society. Ahab's more destructive madness is also set in extremely interesting relationship with the world of money and commerce, suggesting an opposition but also at points a strange collusion between the economic and the demonic.

For one thing, in "The Ship" (163–78), amid the description of the vessel, the owners as "Quakers with a vengeance," and the barbaric "erection" of the wigwam, we come upon the prototypical evocation of Ahab before he is even named. The ingredients include biblical names, Scandinavian and Roman allusions, qualities of "superior natural force," "globular brain," "ponderous heart," independent thinking under the impact of unharnessed nature, and "nervous lofty language," and therefore a destiny formed for "noble tragedies," including an indispensable "morbidness." Ahab in his essential aspects emerges without warning from the setting of the ship. Hypocritical religion, unavowed but unmistakable phallic sexuality, the driving economic motif, and the morbidly tragic hero all cohabit, from the beginning, though the relationships among them are unexplained.

Near the end of "The Ship," we learn for the first time of Ahab's madness in Peleg's statement that Ahab was "out of his mind for a spell" (177). As Ishmael later explains (285–86), Ahab dissembled his madness sufficiently for the owners to take advantage of it without realizing its full extent—a curious instance of complicity and contradiction between economic motives and deformed emotional needs. Ishmael's scorn for the pious Nantucket owners emerges again as he suggests that "the calculating people of that prudent isle" found that Ahab's "dark symptoms" made him "all the better qualified" for the whale hunt. Had the "aghast and righteous souls" realized Ahab's "all-engrossing object," however, they would have "wrenched the ship from such a fiendish man." From the perspective of (religiously mystified) profit, emotional frenzy may be useful; profit once threatened, however, frenzy becomes diabolical—"fiendish": "They were bent on profitable cruises, the profit to be counted down in dollars from the mint. He was intent on an audacious, immitigable, supernatural revenge."

Ahab's refusal to submit to the requirements of the commercial emerges during the voyage in his conflicts with Starbuck (whose name suggests an ultimately futile struggle against fate). Starbuck exemplifies in humane form the values that the book so thoroughly questions—religion, duty, profit, family. He alone thinks lovingly of wife and child (624); he alone defends the interests of the owners, in persuading Ahab to stop the oil leak (584–87). His exhortation to his boat crew, "(Pull, my boys!) Sperm, sperm's the play! This at least is duty; duty and profit hand in hand!" (321), contrasts appropriately with the uses of pulling, sperm, play, and hands in Ishmael's libidinal counterexperiece.

Ahab and Starbuck have their first confrontation (257–65) when Ahab uses the doubloon, in a context of satanic, magnetic, and magical motifs, to incite the crew to the hunt for Moby-Dick, leading to the "infernal orgies" that Starbuck condemns (267). Starbuck argues for "business," barrels for the Nantucket market. Ahab's response rejects the commercial in favor of a magnification of emotional experience: "Nantucket market! Hoot! . . . If money's to be the measurer, man, and the accountants have computed their great counting-house the globe, by girdling it with guineas, one to every three parts of an inch; then, let me tell thee, that my vengeance will fetch a great premium *here!*" When Ahab thus smites his chest, he asserts the value of the personal against a money impulse that he sees as imprisoning the entirety of the world—as forceful an expression as anything in Marx of the destruction of the human by the international money system. But Ahab's explanation of his stance immediately veers off into the metaphysical and religious. He is willing to risk blasphemy in order to strike at the inscrutable force behind the "pasteboard masks" of all things, and Ishmael adds a note about the fatality involved in "the innermost necessities in our being," which "still drive us on." Metaphysical quests, the existence of inner fatalities, do not eliminate the central conflict between Ahab and the commercial order. In some sense nurtured by that order, Ahab's madness and demonism now take on an essential meaning of opposition to it.

Nonetheless, the complicity between the two "systems" that I have mentioned works also in the other direction, in that Ahab first interests and then continues to motivate his crew with money. In Ahab's mind, his motive and object are mad, his means sane (285). According to Ishmael's surmises, he mobilizes his tools, the crew, with money (313–14). Ishmael imagines Ahab comparing himself to crusaders, who committed burglaries on the way to their final "romantic object." Again the cynicism about the purity of religious motives surfaces. In his "romantic" quest, though, Ahab must take into account what he calls the sordidness of the "manufactured man," whom he will therefore not deprive of "all hopes of cash—aye, cash." The reference to manufacture is exceptional, in a book devoted to whaling, in its origins a preindustrial mode of producing profit. But it conveys well the notion of human beings as created by a societal and cultural system—as well as Ahab's pretension not to be so "manufactured."[10]

Melville postpones till near the end close attention to the "Spanish ounce of gold," the sixteen-dollar piece (259) that is to reward the man who first raises Moby-Dick. (This turns out to be

Ahab himself, perhaps another indication of the link between him and the realm of the economic.) It is only in "The Doubloon" (540–46) that the coin and its significance are examined; in a world overshadowed by the money system, Marx would say, it is only late in the game that the impulse to consider and display the fantastic money form emerges.

The coin indeed has the fascination and prestige of the precious metal-money fetish. Of "purest, virgin gold," raked "out of the heart of gorgeous hills," near the "golden sands" of "many a Pactolus," it seems to embody the primal beauty of nature, with qualities of purity, utter newness, innocence. It has a paradisal quality, therefore, which is enhanced by the fact that among the nonprecious metals surrounding it the coin has remained "untouchable and immaculate to any foulness." King Midas, however, lurks in the background, and the evils with which money can be associated are suggested in the chapter's sequence of interpretations of the doubloon's meaning.

Ahab has not until now inspected the "strange figures and inscriptions" stamped on the coin, which beyond its monetary worth is "sanctified" and "revered" as Moby-Dick's "talisman." This added significance of the doubloon accords with the search for meanings in the book and with Ishmael's comment in regard to Ahab's contemplation of the gold piece: "Some certain significance lurks in all things, else all things are little worth, and the round world itself but an empty cipher, except to sell by the cartload, as they do hills about Boston, to fill up some morass in the Milky Way." Here Ishmael shares Ahab's disdain for the financial, which amounts to selling dirt to fill up a void; "worth" in his view is identified with "significance." In this sense Ahab has unknowingly chosen his coin well, since the "noble golden coins" of South America are "as medals of the sun and tropic token-pieces," filled with a "profusion" and a "preciousness" of natural, cosmic, and human imagery, "so Spanishly poetic." The doubloon is "a most wealthy example of these things" ("wealth" again referring to meaning rather than money), cast in a country in the "middle of the world," "midway up the Andes," in an "unwaning clime that knows no autumn." Amid representations of mountains, flowers, towers,

and cocks, the reader perceives ("you saw") the "cabalistics" of
the zodiac.

The coin thus succeeds those other examples of symbolic
systems—obscure paintings, sermons, hieroglyphics, the whale.
In this chapter it becomes the reference for the establishment of
significance; in this sense, too, as Marx argued, money dominates
human existence, by becoming, as here, the master code. Only
Flask refuses this extension of the coin's importance: "I see nothing here, but a round thing made of gold, and whoever raises a
certain whale, this round thing belongs to him." But he makes a
miscalculation in the number of cigars the coin would buy for
him. Pip's declension of the verb "to look" instead indicates how
the others, in this unprecedentedly systematic attempt at interpretation, look at the coin as a source of meaning. Thus, Ahab's
interpretation is egotistical and satanic; Starbuck's, with equal
predictability, sadly Christian. The Manxman, who learned signs
from a witch in Copenhagen, presages an evil outcome for the
ship and interprets Fedallah's reverence before the coin as showing that he is a fire worshipper. More interesting, though, are the
responses of Stubb, Queequeg, and Pip.

Queequeg's tattooed body looks like the zodiac itself, according
to the Manxman, who describes the harpooner's unsuccessful
search for relationships between the signs on the coin and parts of
his body—thigh, calf, bowels, and the archer—"something there
in the vicinity of his thigh." The bodily thematic of the book is
recalled here, as Queequeg in effect attempts to establish links
between the money code and the cosmic theory and mystical treatise on truth that we later learn are inscribed on his body (593). An
immemorial, perhaps utterly mythic and now certainly abolished,
state of human life, in which the earth and heavens were experienced directly in the unified and unrepressed body, thus in "The
Doubloon" confronts the modern system, characterized by bodily
repression and sexual guilt as well as by the dominance of the
economic and of the money code.

Stubb's and Pip's reactions return us to other oppressive features of nineteenth-century society linked to money. Stubb sensi-
bly uses an almanac to interpret the zodiac, which he reads as a
depressing allegory of the cycle of human life, something like

Ishmael's views when he is in a negative mood. Stubb also recalls seeing numerous doubloons and other coins from many countries, and his reference to the diamond-cutting center Golconda reemphasizes the theme of wealth. His own imagined use of the coin, in a slave market or on Manhattan's East River, corresponds with his sailing activities and with his awareness of the monetary value of slaves. He it was who warned Pip that he would not retrieve him for jumping out of the boat a second time because whales are thirty times more valuable than slaves. Ishmael told us then not to blame Stubb too harshly for Pip's madness (526); Stubb is merely reflecting the inhuman money system.

Pip, preeminent victim in the work, appropriately gets the last word in the chapter. As noted, his declension of "to see" emphasizes the problem of interpretation. His reference to crows and minstrel songs evokes racial issues, as does his memory of his father's discovery of an "old darkey's wedding ring" overgrown inside a cut down pine tree: "How did it get there?" This is one of the rare references to wedding in *Moby-Dick*; Pip's own sexual experiences may instead be suggested by his view of the coin as the ship's navel and his idea of unscrewing it. But together with race, he ends on religion and money: "Oh, the gold! the precious, precious gold!—the green miser 'll hoard ye soon! Hish! Hish! God goes 'mong the worlds blackberrying." Whatever God sponsors human life of this kind is mischievous, to say the least. At the end, moreover, all comes down to the fascination of wealth—"the precious, precious gold!" The sea will swallow all in the end, though—the "green miser," like wisdom, "the miser-merman," who supposedly revealed "his hoarded heaps" to Pip in his madness (525). Major themes of the work—religion and God, the search for wisdom, race and sex—all are here reduced to the impulse to acquire and retain gold. Ahab, rebelling against the commercial system, in "The Quarter Deck" and "The Doubloon" nonetheless presides over a ritual and a system of meaning in which the money drive dominates and destroys all.

Our analyses have shown how the impulse toward the numinous cannot escape the contradictions of American and international history, inscribed as well in *Moby-Dick*'s exoticism, wherein race and sex take on disturbing forms. Again, in pursuing the tortuous links between commerce, hypocritical religion, and sexual experience, one perceives that Ishmael's sexuality is liberating because not submitted to the productive functions of earning profit and producing offspring. Yet Ishmael also rejoices in being paid, and Irigaray's vision of the oppressively male nature of the societal order coincides with the figure of Ahab. Homosexual through and through, having dented the pillow once for the form, he represents not pleasure but a bizarre collusion with the commercial order. In spite of his opposition to it, he is nourished by it and plays its quintessential card in the doubloon, through which he motivates its unreflective workers, in passages in which Melville demonstrates the dominance of the money code and the inhuman costs of the miser impulse. What more dismaying than to see the demonic as expressive of the monetary?

Throughout, too, we have these themes imposed on the reader through direct address and have noted at several points the book's ambivalent formulations of issues dear to us as citizens of what is supposedly the ultimate democracy—concerning religion, race, empire, democracy itself. These are the features—the involvement of the reader and the ideologically contradictory nature of democratic themes—that a study of the extraordinarily varied forms of discourse in *Moby-Dick* finds most compelling.

Complexity of form in the work is flagrant and contributes to instability of meaning and message. In spite of references to traditional forms, notably the Bible, tragedy, and epic, and in spite of numerous predictive notes (implicitly in the Extracts and including prophecies by characters called Elijah and Gabriel, the meaning of biblical names, Ahab's dream, and broad hints by Ishmael, for example, on Queequeg's "last long dive" [157]), the book resists containment both within the parameters of known forms and within the ending it repeatedly announces. This is due in part to its comprehensive mixing of forms, as in anatomy or encyclopedia (235), or again as representative of the Schlegelian total romantic art form. The forms include at least: first person narrative, proto-Conradian framing, pictorial art, philosophy-theology, science, history, lyric song, myth, etymology, legal affidavit, sermon, melodrama, and dream. All of this involves a high degree of "intertextuality," not only through allusion but through extensive citation in Etymology, Extracts, epigraphs, quotations, references, and footnotes.[11]

Comprehensive these features are. Yet, in keeping with the problematic status of meaning already stressed, form in *Moby-Dick* is also so multiple as to be elusive. Ishmael prays to God to keep him from completing anything more than a "draught of a draught" (241), acknowledges the paucity of narrative in the book (303), and insists that there are "some enterprises in which a careful disorderliness is the true method" (469). What is more, the work subverts distinctions between fiction and historical and scientific "fact" and between author and narrator—distinctions that are received as true and often serve the function of stabilizing meanings. Hence "The Affidavit" (303–12)—as legally impressive a form as one can imagine—mixes Ishmael's personal testimony with quotations from whaling narratives and references to existing whales with several of Melville's invention. Moreover, Ishmael, whom we have earlier seen inscribing in the work the precise historical time of its composition, is nearly identical with Melville in referring to an uncle who was in fact Melville's (much older) brother-in-law (309). Again like Lautréamont in *Maldoror*, Melville here emerges from the shadow of his narrator; again like Maldoror his writing becomes so insistently realized as to be nearly identified with the narrator's body (563), a body that Ishmael-Melville imagines putting in contact with *ours*: "I would rather feel your spine than your skull, whoever you are. . . . I rejoice in my spine, as in the firm audacious staff of that flag which I fling half out to the world" (456–57). Not at all keeping itself at a distance under the rubric of a neatly defined form, either scientifically "true" or artistically "fictional," *Moby-Dick* is a work of almost literally visceral impact, proposing to grasp us (sexually) in our very bodies.

We have already noted numerous, often unsettling, solicitations of the reader. Like Marx and Engels in the *Manifesto* and Balzac in *Goriot* (but also like Lautréamont in *Maldoror* and Dostoyevski in *Notes from Underground*), Ishmael-Melville troubles our placidity, makes us virtual participants in the work, attacks us in demonic fashion.

Our participatory role is established from the first sentence, which through an imperative determines a response from us, one instituting a personal relationship. At various points thereafter Ishmael encourages us to act: "Take out your map" (157); "were you to turn the whole affair upside down" (399); "Friends, hold my arms!" (567). At times we even seem to engage in dialogue with him, first at his suggestion ("The whale has no famous author, and whaling no famous chronicler, you will say" [207]; "But thou sayest, methinks this white-lead chapter about whiteness is but a white flag hung out from a craven soul; thou surrenderest to a hypo, Ishmael" [294]). Later we seem to intervene on our own initiative: "But why pester one with all this reasoning on the subject? Speak out!" (480). We address Ishmael for a whole paragraph, questioning him and ordering him to explain himself (559). But when elsewhere we think to catch him in an error, he reasserts his ascendancy: "We have thee there. Not at all, but I have ye" (451–52).

In spite of our participation in the book, therefore, we are more often being taught by Ishmael about experiences supposedly strange to "civilized, domestic people in the temperate zone" (333). Such instances range from the taste of porpoise ("Porpoise meat is good eating, you know. It may never have occurred to you that a porpoise spouts. . . . But the next time you have a chance, watch him" [240]), to the trance of the masthead and the awesome danger of the sea (380–81). They include the savagery of the whaling business as well as the sexual activity that in *Moby-Dick* at least it entails. In all of these cases, as in much else, the reader is insistently involved by reiterated direct appeals.

From this it is easy to pass to disconcerting truths and to assaults on the hypocritical reader. "Who aint a slave?" Ishmael asks from the outset (96), and he has us recall the extermination of Indian tribes (164). Elsewhere he reminds us that all men "live enveloped in whale-lines. All are born with halters round their necks" (387), just as earlier he had asserted that "we are all killers, on land and on sea; Bonapartes and Sharks included"

(238–39). In a passage about the frequent death of crewmen, he resembles Balzac at the opening of *Goriot*. Because of the slowness of mail in New Guinea, news of such a death will not reach us: "Do you suppose that that poor fellow's name will appear in the newspaper obituary you will read to-morrow at your breakfast?" But Ishmael nonetheless asserts our involvement, perhaps even responsibility: "For God's sake, be economical with your lamps and candles! not a gallon you burn, but at least one drop of man's blood was spilled for it" (306). Like the comfortable reader of Balzac's "fiction," we do not really want to have suffering come so close to us, much less recall that our creature comforts are purchased with human lives.

Ishmael even tells us that we are cannibals and murderers: "Go to the meat-market of a Saturday night and see the crowds of live bipeds staring up at the long rows of dead quadrupeds. . . . Cannibals? who is not a cannibal?" Then New Testament language in a pagan context ("I tell you it will be more tolerable for the Fejee that salted down a lean missionary . . . ") stresses the selfishness of our devouring animals—the bloated livers of geese in "thy paté-de-foie-gras," "your knife-handle, there, my civilized and enlightened gourmand," made of the "bones of the brother of the very ox you are eating," even the toothpick made of the quill taken from the same fat goose that we have just eaten (406–7).

In spite of complexity of form and elusiveness of meaning, then, *Moby-Dick* often makes its points very clear. And the clarity is at our expense. But we have also remarked contradictions in passages variously celebrating or condemning the society of which we readers are citizens, in a work that seems to have the mixed, contradictory function of justifying and undercutting American democratic ideology. The clarity of insight to which the book encourages us needs to be applied to those sections as well. I have chosen several passages on democracy in preparation for a conclusion on the all-important chapter "Fast-Fish and Loose-Fish."[12]

Earlier we noted Father Mapple's praise of those immune to the "boisterous mob," who are patriots only to heaven. These formulas are hardly optimistic about the chances of democratic government and do not exclude the United States from the ranks of the "proud gods and commodores of this earth" (143). We also suggested parallels and contrasts with Ahab, whose "sultanism," "dictatorship," and "moral indomitableness" are conveyed by a "hint" to the "imperial brain" of Czar Nicholas, before whose "tremendous centralization" the "plebeian herds crouch abased" (243–44). Such a positive judgment of the imperial is rare in the book. The dim view of Russian "plebeian herds" has its counterpart for the other countries in "the dead level of the mass" over which dubiously talented leaders obtain the highest honors. For, according to Ishmael, the necessity of base political acts "for ever keeps God's true princes of the Empire from the world's hustings." Here he views politics and political leaders with a jaundiced eye, and the metaphor used to qualify true spiritual princes involves both God and empire.

God is appealed to in another passage, this time a celebration of democracy, though mainly in the ideal (211–12). We have noted that here men, though "detestable as joint stock-companies and nations," are said to be noble "in the ideal." The reader may be forgiven for not forgetting the homosexual thematics of the book when reading Ishmael's praise of the "immaculate manliness we feel within ourselves, so far within us." But in fact Ishmael solicits our attention on the theme of democratic dignity: "Thou shalt see it shining in the arm that wields a pick or drives a spike; that democratic dignity which, on all hands, radiates without end from God; Himself! The great God absolute! The centre and circumference of all democracy! His omnipresence, our divine equality!"

Here the tone is almost hysterically Whitmanesque. And, since we are addressed, we may wonder what are the conditions of actual political practice in which democracy so celebrated can avoid taking the form of a "detestable" nation? What is the relation between these ennobled workers and the "mass" and "herd" of the preceding passage? How does this God, democratically present in all of us, relate to the imperial divinity of that passage? In fact, how can that passage be compatible with this, which ends by addressing God as having chosen John Bunyan, Miguel de Cervantes, and Andrew Jackson before Melville:

"Thou who, in all Thy mighty, earthly marchings, ever cullest Thy selectest champions from the kingly commons; bear me out in it, O God!" In the imperial Ahab reflection, Ishmael has God's princes avoiding politics; here he has his champions, including an American president, emerge from the democratic mass. We note in passing his explicit and ambivalent intention of having the "mariners, and renegades and castaways" of the *Pequod* stand for the working class; but most of all we come away with a sense of contradiction and confusion about political systems, which however in opposing forms are validated by an appeal to the divinity.

These passages are contradictory between themselves. But even a greater incompatibility exists between the political-religious mystification in both and the disabused realism of "Fast-Fish and Loose-Fish" (504–8). After a sketch of the history of whaling law, Ishmael asserts that the Fast- and Loose-Fish rules contain "the fundamentals of all human jurisprudence." He illustrates the proposition with a comprehensive enumeration of injustice in numerous spheres of human activity. Sounding like Vautrin on the French legal system, he notes that the saying that possession is half of the law includes the thought, "regardless of how the thing came into possession." He adds that "often possession is the whole of the law."

This universal extension of the category of ownership, so devious a force in fiction by Austen, Flaubert, and James, is justified immediately by Ishmael's first examples of Fast-Fish: "the sinews and souls of Russian serfs and Republican slaves." The Marxlike equation neatly demystifies the passages on the czar's imperial brain and democratic equality that we have just discussed. In America as in Russia human beings in the nineteenth century are utterly possessed for their labor power and even in the depths of their souls ("sinews and souls"). Ishmael follows this shocking example with other instances, unpleasant to contemplate but nonetheless commonplace in our society—"the rapacious landlord" taking "the widow's last mite" and the "undetected villain's marble mansion with a door-plate for a waif" ("waif" denoting the "pennoned pole" [500] by which a whaler claims possession of a dead whale). This last recalls Vautrin's argument about unexplained fortunes as originating in cleverly concealed crime (and our study of Sutpen's mysterious wealth in terms of Marx's ideas about the "primitive accumulation").

The next example, the ruinous discount obtained by Mordecai the broker from the bankrupt Woebegone, on a loan to keep the latter's children from starvation, allegorically perpetuates the figure of the Jewish moneylender, so virulently revealed in Flaubert, James, and Joyce. But it is hard to see prejudice here, since Mordecai's avidity is bettered by that of the archbishop of Savesoul, whose income of £100,000 is "seized" from "hundreds of thousands of broken-backed labourers." Here both the exploitation of workers and the hypocrisy of religion are equally stressed. And to economic exploitation by traditional religion corresponds equally ancient class domination—the duke of Dunder's hereditary holdings.

Forms of slavery, financial exploitation, the longstanding oppression of church and aristocracy—these forms of possession are followed by those on an international scale: Ireland in the control of "that redoubted harpooneer, John Bull," Texas in the possession of the United States. The more characteristic antiimperial theme is reasserted: "Concerning all these, is not Possession the whole of the law?" And if this is true, together with the existence of "Republican slaves," what is the function of that Whitmanesque paean to our ideal democratic manliness?

The thoroughgoing cynicism of Ishmael's views on exploitation by individuals and nations (including the one whose myths he occasionally propagates) matches Marx's ferocious dissection of the drive to possession in all spheres, from the personal to the societal to the world market. Ishmael shares with Marx too an idea about how such economic domination is linked to the mind control of religious and ideological manipulation:

> What are the Rights of Man and the Liberties of the World but Loose-Fish? What all men's minds and opinions but Loose-Fish? What is the principle of religious belief in them but a Loose-Fish? What to the ostentatious smuggling verbalists are the thoughts of thinkers but Loose-Fish? What is the great globe itself but a Loose-Fish? And what are you, reader, but a Loose-Fish and a Fast-Fish, too?

We saw that in "On the Jewish Question" Marx analyzes political rights in French and American democratic ideology as a charter not for universal equality but for exploitation of the sorts that Ishmael has been analyzing. For Ishmael too our rights and liberties are the targets for possession—by whom? He broadens the target to include the opinions and minds of all—equivalent, I think, to Marx's notion of ideology. Forces there are that constantly seek to cloud minds and mold opinions; Ishmael himself is not utterly free from such manipulation, as we have seen. And what is the preeminent point for such manipulation?—"the principle of religious belief" in us. Perhaps Ishmael will not accept Marx's view of religion as alienation, but he does see it as constituting our most vulnerable point.

Both Melville and Marx attest to the following category of Loose-Fish, thinkers and writers whose ideas are in danger of being exploited by "ostentatious smuggling verbalists," those small but societally successful minds whose productions are, I hope, not mirrored in the present work, which attempts to be faithful to Marx and to the literary creators studied. For finally, after the "great globe itself" (the world market), who is the ultimate target for possession by the "smuggling verbalists," if not us faithful and active readers? "And what are you, reader, but a Loose-Fish and a Fast-Fish, too?" Somebody owns us ("Who aint a slave?"), somebody else is looking to own us, in a system that is at once one of global domination and mental control. But "Fast-Fish and Loose-Fish" dissects both aspects of this system and, like Marx's writing, is a powerful incentive to liberation.

CONCLUSION:
EDUCATING THE
EDUCATOR

*F*redric Jameson concludes *The Political Unconscious* by quoting Walter Benjamin's assertion that the documents of culture are always documents of barbarism, deriving not only from the toil of their creators but from "the anonymous forced labor of the latters' contemporaries." Jameson's use of Benjamin's statement, as a warning against the tendency of "a certain radicalism" to reappropriate the classics as humanistic or progressive,[1] might be thought to apply to the present study, which in effect appropriates Marx to enhance the appreciation of a number of classics. That would be to misread my intention and practice, since I agree with Benjamin and have made a similar argument about James's characters Adam Verver and his daughter. More generally, as suggested in chapter 1, I value the works treated here for achieving a greater or lesser transcendance of class limitation, a complex and sometimes contradictory degree of "world-historical consciousness." Rather than being humanistic or progressive, for me they are critical, often virulently so.

Indeed, only one novel studied here can be remotely conceived as expressing the "ideas of the ruling class" (172). But in spite of the positive treatment of Darcy, Elizabeth, and the Gardiners, the wish-fulfillment quality of Austen's conclusion, and the virtual invisibility of the lower classes (we hear of Gardiner's warehouses but not of his workers), *Pride and Prejudice* also shows us the casualties of the system in Lydia and Wickham, and includes Wickham's critique of Darcy as well as the secret contradictions of the status not only of Lady Catherine but of Darcy, too. Moreover, the ending can in no way wipe out the cruelly realistic way in which in the novel family relations are all but reduced to "a mere money relation" (476). Interestingly, of course, that criticism adheres in the book mainly to characters of the lower and "pseudo-" gentry (the Bennets, the Lucases, Wickham and Lydia, Collins), whereas in the *Manifesto*, written thirty-five years later, Marx and Engels bring it to bear on the bourgeoisie, whose family life appears so benign in the case of the Gardiners.

The incisive if somewhat inconsistent realism of *Pride and Prejudice* is more than matched in the other works, none of which feature happy marriages or endings. We have noted the dubious future of Molly and Bloom and the variously unpleasant endings of *Moby-Dick, Madame Bovary, The Golden Bowl,* and *Absalom, Absalom!* Even the moral ambiguity of the conclusion of Balzac's *Le Père Goriot* is augmented when in a later novel (*Le Député*) Rastignac marries not Delphine but her (and his?) daughter!

In different degrees these works are not bound by class either. The novel most open to that criticism formulates it itself, in Charlotte's description of Prince Amerigo as not seeing below a certain social level. The point is perhaps reinforced when Amerigo once *does* see the poor—in a picturesque mode for him, it is true—in the person of the "dingy waifs" who sing so lamentably for pennies and at whom he wonders from the balcony of Portland Place (367). Maggy recalls that Christmas Eve as she and her father see the splendid couple on the balcony at a stage when she has come to fear their manipulations. And she remembers *that* moment in the last chapter, when from the same balcony the prince grimly observes Charlotte's departure (537, 545). This detail is far from making James a "progressive" writer, but it certainly emphasizes the potential for suffering in the elite and deceptively sheltered social world in which the prince thought he was safe. More directly, while hardly a proletarian work, *Goriot* shows us a certain urban underclass, including Goriot's impoverishment, whereas the glimpses of the rural poor make *Madame Bovary* the nightmare of a marginal *petite bourgeoisie*. In general, the three "postcolonial" books display a broad spectrum of socio-economic tensions: slaves, poor whites, merchants, lawyers, and plantation owners in *Absalom*; the marginally middle class and the urban poor in *Ulysses*; the owners, crew, and pagan harpooners of the *Pequod*. Is *Moby-Dick* a deflected, distorted version of class conflict? That might fit with the book's contradictory messages on democracy and joint-stock companies.

In no way then do these works function as ideological justifications of the societal order. Although *Pride and Prejudice, Goriot, The Golden Bowl,* and *Absalom* depict with varying degrees of sympathy the efforts of some who want to rise to the top of that order, they at the same time comprise a penetrating critique of it. This is perhaps even more the case in *Madame Bovary, Ulysses,* and *Moby-Dick*.

Our readings have shown how insistently historical these novels are. Juxtapositions among them and with the writings of Marx augment these historical resonances: from the deft touch in Austen to the massive detail in Joyce and from Stephen's parable on Nelson's column to Ishmael's reference to similar "stander[s]-of-mast heads" (251–52), including Napoleon on the Vendôme column. Rastignac perceives this same column from the cemetery on the last page of *Goriot,* and readers familiar with French history know that between it and the dome of the Invalides lives the seductive world of wealth and social power that the young man so avidly desires to conquer. The figure on top of the column changed with changing regimes (during the Revolution, under Napoleon I, in 1814 and after the restoration of Louis XVIII, after the Revolution of 1830, and again under Napoleon III). Ishmael is right two years after the Revolution of 1848 to say that the dead Napoleon I no longer cares who rules France—deposed constitutional monarch Louis-Philippe, moderate Socialist Louis Blanc, or "Louis the Devil." The last would shortly effect a coup d'état and proclaim himself emperor. Marx was having similar thoughts at the time (1851–52), writing in *The Eighteenth Brumaire of Louis Bonaparte* that "if the imperial mantle finally falls on the shoulders of Louis Bonaparte, the iron statue of Napoleon will crash from the top of the Vendôme column" (617).

Another work only glimpsed in the shadow of *Moby-Dick*, Lautréamont's *Chants de Maldoror*, also bears on our discussion of the Vendôme column. The sexual, societal, and textual provocations of that strange work culminate in Maldoror's murder of Mervyn. The adolescent son of conspicuously wealthy bourgeois parents, Mervyn is spun round and round from a rope at the top of the column, then hurled across Paris with its geography of revolutionary uprisings until he meets his death by crashing into the Pantheon! The scene is the conclusion of a work published clandestinely under a pseudonym two years before the Paris Commune was declared and the Vendôme column toppled. Both Lautréamont's and Marx's prophetic works, as well as Ishmael's musings, form an expansive historical context for the conclusion of *Le Père Goriot*. Already ambiguous in its wording, as we saw, that ending is also historically complex in being situated before the Revolution of 1830 but written and read after that upheaval. The reference to the column inscribes Rastignac's career in an ongoing political and social process, deeply conflictual and often massively violent, with prolongations in 1848–51 and 1870–71. Interestingly, Marx recognizes the pertinence of Balzac's writing when on the same page as his remark on the column he uses not *Goriot* but *La Cousine Bette* to illustrate the corrupt society that made possible Louis Bonaparte's accession to power.

The reference to *Maldoror* reminds us that *Moby-Dick* presents in exacerbated fashion many of the themes treated by Marx and visible in our other novels and that in Ahab, Sutpen, and Vautrin the novel form is inhabited by visionary and demonic forces. Here mainstream literature absorbs some of the subversive power of a kind of writing that rarely draws so large an audience. This suggests a follow-up project to this book, a study of such writers as Blake, Novalis, Nerval, Lautréamont, Burroughs, and Wittig, whose social and political impact needs investigation.

Yes, *Moby-Dick* is as vehement in its attack on hypocritical religion and on the contradictions of democracy as are the writings of Marx. Ishmael's first-person monologue allows for denunciations of the alienations of religion and civil society that are usually presented or narrated in the other books: Collins's absurdity,

Emma Bovary's noxious convent education, the grasping church officials at the end of *Goriot,* Faulkner's Coldfield, Bloom's cynicism about Catholicism and Stephen's effort to free himself from it, the near invisibility of religion in the leisurely life of the Ververs. It was concerning them that I evoked Marx's critique of democratic freedoms in "On the Jewish Question," but that critique is relevant as well for the *bellum omnium contra omnes* that is illustrated by the money grubbers in Austen, the mistreatment of Goriot, the activities of Lheureux, the ridicule of Bloom, and the monumental egotism of Sutpen, who we recall puts his wife aside as not "adjunctive or incremental to the design" (240). In all these works, indeed, what Marx wrote about "civil society," unassuaged by religion or politics, or any more generous glimpse of the social, collective "species life" of mankind, is repeatedly echoed.

Sutpen's exploitation of women fits with the problems in relations between the sexes noted by Marx, Engels, and others and that attain an extreme form in the virtual suppression of the family and heterosexuality in *Moby-Dick.* Domination of women, marginalization of the maternal, and alienation of parental and filial roles characterize these works. This may seem only amusing in *Pride and Prejudice,* where the ludicrous Mrs. Bennet, in fact the mistakes of both of Elizabeth's parents, require the restoration of family through Darcy and the Gardiners. In later works things are much bleaker: the destructive families in *Goriot* and *Bovary, The Golden Bowl, Absalom,* the diminishment of maternity in most of those works. One of the few hopeful elements in *The Golden Bowl* and *Ulysses* is the presence of children. But in *Moby-Dick* Ahab recognizes only a divine father, Ishmael mentions only a punishing (castrating) stepmother. And the infection of the libidinal by the economic, widespread in Austen and textually inscribed in the Pemberley chapter, also has disastrous consequences in later novels—in the commodity delusions of Emma Bovary, the rarity of the Rastignac-Delphine success, the prostitutions in *The Golden Bowl* and *Ulysses,* the sexual and racial tensions of *Absalom,* magnified in *Moby-Dick.* We saw that in Ahab the homosexual rebellion against the commercial and monetary order paradoxically functions in its service.

We have used Marx's ideas throughout to see how virtually

everything in these novels is conditioned, if not determined, by the economic. If determinism there is, to it must be added Marx's ideas about ideology, freedom, and education. If Emma Bovary cannot be different from what she is, does not Flaubert's novel, to the displeasure of some critics, show the informing role of her education in her life? And does not *Madame Bovary* function, in parallel with Marx's writing, as an educational corrective? The economic is also seen as an expansive, rather than reductive, category when it is seen in terms of alienation, division of labor, the country-city antagonism, class and revenue, and mode of production—such as we sketched at the outset and have applied throughout. Overwhelmingly in these novels the economic plays its deforming role—in terms of money, capital, possessions, property, need and desire, art, and personal relations. Adam Verver is not the only character who is "economically constructed," and the tenderness with which he fondles the Damascene tiles rather than the body of his lovely companion is not a little illustrative.

Among the economic categories, Marx's idea of the complex interaction and succession of modes of production, those fundamental forms of economic activity that are expressed in virtually all facets of life, has proved to be very rich. Sometimes the relevance is pointed: the difference between Lady Catherine's cottagers and Darcy's tenants seems close to Marx's distinction between feudal landowner and capitalist landlord. Sometimes the relevance is global: one could argue that many of the differences between *Pride and Prejudice* and *Madame Bovary* are explainable in terms of historical changes in mode of production. Is this to minimize the individuality of each work, the creativity of each writer? I think not: Flaubert certainly viewed Emma Bovary as typifying the reality of the lives of provincial Frenchwomen, just as Sartre has argued for a similar typicality in the life and production of Flaubert himself. We may recall in this connection Marx's fusion of typicality and individuality in the notion of concreteness.

Going further, we saw that the kinds of consciousness represented in *The Golden Bowl* and *Ulysses*, so different from (though sometimes recalling) the mentality of Emma Bovary, are inconceivable except in an urban and international context. International scope, world historical consciousness, is most of all represented by Ishmael, "cosmopolite philosopher." But international perspective is not altogether lacking in Austen, as we have seen, although Balzac and Faulkner exhibit it in more complete and direct form.

We also noted that "The Method of Political Economy" in the *Grundrisse* argues that the "inner structure" of the bourgeois mode of production consists in the dominance of capital over the other great classes deriving from wage labor and ground rent. That proposition generates a "table of contents" having many connections with these novels. I there raised the question of the obscuring or revelation of the generation of capital as a pertinent one for issues of *narrative* form. Hence the production of capital occurs offstage in *Pride and Prejudice,* despite the book's hints; in *Ulysses* it can only be imagined by Bloom. Adam Verver's early life as a capitalist mystifies the narrator of *The Golden Bowl,* although he asserts Verver's "rare power of purchase" as the basis of his other acquisitions (art and people) through to the last page. The original source of Sutpen's wealth and some of his continuing enrichment are mysteries to the townsfolk and the "tellers" in *Absalom,* which perhaps contributes to arguments about his not being a "representative" Southern planter. But Marx's argument that Southern slavery was industrial, integrally related to the wage-labor system in Europe, disperses that kind of justification, even if it does not find an echo in Faulkner's novel itself. In *Absalom* the patriarchal system is defeated by its rival, the industrial North, as Bon's letter indicates. But the more complex historical situation with its contradictions is hinted at in *Goriot,* in Vautrin's dream of creating "patriarchal" life through the black "capital" of slaves. That other pre–Civil War book, *Moby-Dick,* focuses on a form of economic activity that in its origins is preindustrial (but is linked to the worldwide events that Marx shows leading to the "primitive accumulation"). Before we get out to the whale hunt, too, Ishmael shows us the owners and investments and stock companies in which we readers are presumed to participate. Most tellingly, Ahab's rebellion is against "the manufactured man," which we may read as containing in miniature Marx's analysis of alienated labor and its effects on human life in the industrial mode of production.

Goriot and *Bovary* are the novels studied here that make the revelation of the creation of capital a central narrative strategy. Only when Goriot's worldwide dealings in grain have been discovered can the action proper of Balzac's novel unfold. That revelation thus constitutes something of a beginning. But in Flaubert's book the expropriation of the Bovaries by Lheureux and Guillaumin is fully revealed only at the end, as the literally fatal manipulation of people in the interest of accumulating capital. Flaubert, writing at the same time as Marx and about the same things, used his much discussed narrative tactics effectively to obscure for the reader, then frighteningly reveal, the inhuman economic activity that Marx unmasked and denounced.

Such one-to-one correspondence between Marx's thinking and novelistic form is rare, but we have seen other examples of the functionality of literary form in a Marxist perspective. This is the case even for those writers who, with some justification, have been accused of giving in to the seductive specialization of the aesthetic. We have noted that Binet's useless wooden objects, the hoards of precious objects accumulated by Verver, and the contrast between Stephen's "intellectual imagination" and the suffering of his family all constitute criticisms of prizing the artistic too highly. Not to speak of all the other critical features of *Madame Bovary*, *The Golden Bowl*, and *Ulysses*, which can in no way be reduced to any simple category of the aesthetic.

One "aesthetic" issue that is bound to come up in a Marxist perspective is the relation of literary form to the perpetuation or criticism of ideology. *Bovary* and *Ulysses* most clearly present manipulative forms of expression and obfuscated consciousness in the evident intent of deconstructing them. In Flaubert this ranges from the ideas and clichés of the classmate narrator to the democratic imbecilities of Homais, the massive molding of consciousness in Emma's education and later reading, and the double seduction of the discourses in the fair chapter. In *Ulysses* the exposure of falsifying ideology is widespread, not only in the parodies of Gertie and the Citizen but in the stereotypes that rule the thinking of Bloom and Molly. "Aeolus" works them all

in, the clichés of politics and religion and nationalism and journalism, and displays Stephen's struggle to rise above them to
clearer consciousness. In its form the chapter makes novelistic
structure and the exposure of ideology coincide.

Most of the other books are more mixed on this issue. In
Vautrin the hypocrisy and inequity of the social order and the
institutions and concepts that legitimate it (marriage, justice) are
unmasked, but the narrator's presentation of Rastignac's amoral
participation in that system is ambivalent. The evil of American
slavery is revealed in *Absalom*, but that book has its blindspots, its
points where the narrator loses critical distance and proclaims
some of the values (pride, honor, blood) that legimated *that* social order. These we might call instances of ideological inconsistency in narrative voice, witnessing a courageous but incomplete
depiction of societal contradiction and oppression. By contrast,
the novel whose tone could be taken for the most bland of the
group, *The Golden Bowl*, without much fanfare deflates the democratic values of freedom and of not doing harm to others
through the artfully staged series of discussions by the Ververs
about the "uses" of Charlotte.

The two remaining novels seem to convey ideology, to purvey
the concepts and codes of the social order—but hardly in any
simple sense. Through satirizing the romance language of Collins and the aristocratic values of Lady Catherine, *Pride and Prejudice* shows them as anachronistic—illustrating Jameson's third
horizon of study, that of sedimented forms of expression constituting a content in their own right.[2] Against Lady Catherine,
Elizabeth argues the bourgeois value of equality, with which the
novel seems to identify, not only through its ending but through
its narrative style, which is generally similar to Elizabeth's lively
and straightforward form of expression. On the other hand, we
noted the discrepancy between the opening and conclusion of
the book: the ironically presented "universal" truth about property and marriage is unironically enacted at the end. But if the
beginning was appropriately ironic, that irony should still apply
at the end, despite the speaker's modulation in the last chapter.
In contemporary jargon, the book's conclusion is already always
deconstructed by its beginning.

Such subtleties are hardly to the point regarding *Moby-Dick*, where the art-ideology issue appears in the form of naked contradiction. At points Ishmael lyrically celebrates America, democracy, the masses, whereas at others he denounces them; moreover, what he shows throughout differs from his positive effusions. The contradiction that Marx detected in the ideology of democracy thus marks Melville's book. From within that contradiction I chose to discuss the "Fast-Fish and Loose-Fish" chapter not only because it parallels Marx in showing possession and exploitation in all spheres of life but because it extends the discussion to include control by others over our thoughts, especially through our penchant for religious belief. Here Ishmael is talking directly about what Marx means by ideology; the chapter and by implication the entire book are incentives to struggle against such thought control, in Marx's terms to "educate the educator" in ourselves. As Ishmael asks, "And what are you, reader, but a Loose-Fish and a Fast-Fish, too?"

Ishmael's direct questioning of the reader, reminiscent of the tactics of Balzac in *Goriot* and of Marx and Engels in the *Manifesto*, suggests another formal feature—the opposition between personal perspective and comprehensive point of view, and some of the positions in between. This is another reason for treating the (primarily) first-person narrative of *Moby-Dick* at the end. But Balzac's apparently omniscient narrator also frequently speaks in personal accents. And the opposition subjective-objective is basic to the discrepancies in narrative mode in *Pride and Prejudice* and *Bovary*. The narratological "honesty" of the former does not preclude a degree of collusion with the wish-fulfillment ending, whereas the scandalous contradiction of Flaubert's narrative allows *Madame Bovary* to attain a greater degree of synthesizing objectivity. This judgment goes against recent expressions of suspicion of totalizing modes, associated with the question, "Qui parle?" and the opinions of such writers as Barthes, Derrida, and Genette. While agreeing with Michael Ryan that Marx might be viewed as the first deconstructionist, I would also argue against the skeptics and retain the value of his struggle to reach suprasubjective knowledge. *Madame Bovary* is a comparable effort in the literary realm. And although we have analyzed the alienations of oblique point of view and stream of consciousness in James and Joyce, in the latter we have also noted the narrative modes that aim at a comprehensive inclusiveness, together with similar features in *Moby-Dick*. Finally, in *Absalom* we saw how the dialogic narrative form momentarily produces a persuasive representation of the historical past, without however dissipating the anguish and contradictions that characterize both Quentin and American history.

We end where we began, with the link between fiction and history. Marx's growth in methodological sophistication, from the belief that empirical history can be written without consulting what human beings have imagined and narrated, to the subtlety of "The Method of Political Economy," has a kind of chronological parallel in the novels treated here. Although the goal of action in *Pride and Prejudice* (successful marriage) is impeded, narration is in no way inhibited. The book concerns action in the present and unfolds with the certainty of a calendar year, making its one (vague) historical allusion in the last chapter. It is as if the life of persons and classes accedes there to the dimension of international history. We noticed also that, although the action of *Le Père Goriot* is strongly projective, before it can unfold a certain working through of the past, of personal and transpersonal history, is necessary. *Madame Bovary* and *The Golden Bowl* suffer from no such initial impeding; Flaubert gives us the date 1812 on the third page and carries directly on from there, and Amerigo's musings at the opening of James's book instantly evoke the conjunction of English empire and American capitalism. But the apparent absence later of specific historical reference may be deceptive. As Dominic LaCapra has suggested, the passage of time in *Madame Bovary* brings its conclusion just about up to 1848, so that in this sense the revolution of that year is "replaced" by Emma's suicide. And Stephen Spender has not illogically seen the image of anguish and suffering in James's last completed novel as characteristic of a whole alienated period, that of "The Wasteland" and the first World War.[3]

These last interpretations are certainly speculative; they have the merit at least of sketching the horizon of outer history around the inner circle of the literary work. But in *Ulysses* and

Absalom, Absalom! no such operation is necessary. In these works history is an informing presence and constitutes a heavy burden, much as in Marx's view of the nightmare of history in mid-nineteenth-century France. Workings through of history, confrontations with it, efforts to liberate us from it, reminders of its ongoing destruction—*Ulysses* and *Absalom* recall also *Moby-Dick*, with its insistence on both American and world history. Having expressed doubts about the vagueness of Marx's conception of a future collectively oriented society, I want to recall his assertion in the Paris manuscripts that "communism as such is not the goal of human development" (93). Of the movement to and through communism, he added words that are bound to make us fearful: "History will come to it; and this movement, which in *theory* we already know to be a self-transcending movement, will constitute *in actual fact* a very severe and protracted process" (99).

Notes

Preface

1 Two other excellent introductory studies: Isaiah Berlin, *Karl Marx: His Life and Environment*, 4th ed. (Oxford: Oxford University Press, 1978); Robert L. Heilbroner, *Marxism: For and Against* (New York: Norton, 1980). On Marx and literature: Peter Demetz, *Marx, Engels, and the Poets: Origins of Marxist Literary Criticism*, tr. Jeffrey L. Sammons (Chicago: University of Chicago Press, 1967); Terry Eagleton, *Literary Theory: An Introduction* (Minneapolis: University of Minnesota Press, 1983); John Frow, *Marxism and Literary History* (Cambridge, Mass.: Harvard University Press, 1986); Cliff Slaughter, *Marxism, Ideology, and Literature* (Atlantic Highlands, N.J.: Humanities Press, 1980). Though not wishing to participate in sterile Marxist polemics, I agree with criticisms of Louis Althusser formulated by Jameson and Slaughter and find Marx a far richer writer than the French structuralist philosopher.

2 As opposed to Louis Althusser, *For Marx*, tr. Ben Brewster (New York: Pantheon, 1969). For Althusser's contribution to the discussion of ideology, see "Ideology and Ideological State Apparatuses," in *Lenin and Philosophy and Other Essays*, tr. Ben Brewster (New York: Monthly Review Press, 1971). See also Terry Eagleton, *Criticism and Ideology* (New York: Schocken, 1978), and Eagleton, *Marxism and Literary Criticism* (London: Methuen, 1976), e.g.: "Literature is held within ideology, but also manages to distance itself from it, to the point where it permits us to 'feel' or 'perceive' the ideology from which it springs" (18). This seems a reasonable position in general, which however will be nuanced for each of the works studied here.

Chapter One: The Anatomy of Civil Society

1 "Die wirkliche Darstellung." "Appropriation" below is "Aneignung." (Marx and Engels, *Werke*, 41 vols. [Berlin: Dietz, 1957–68], 3:25–27; Marx, *Grundrisse der Kritik der Politischen Ökonomie* [Berlin: Dietz, 1953], 21–22). The

published preface (1859) alludes to both *GI* and *G* (1845–46; 1857–58). I agree with McLellan's assessment of the central importance of *G* (in the introduction to his edition [New York: Harper and Row, 1971]). Demetz, *Marx, Engels*, 64–73, treats these texts by Marx incisively and negatively. On the validity of historical "representations," see Paul Ricoeur, *Temps et récit*, 3 vols. (Paris: Seuil, 1983–85), esp. 1:203–39; 3:184–202, 264–79; E. P. Thompson, *The Poverty of Theory* (London: Merlin, 1978); George McLennan, "Philosophy and History: Some Issues in Recent Marxist Theory," and Richard Johnson, "Reading for the Best Marx: History-Writing and Historical Abstraction," both in *Making Histories: Studies in History-Writing and Politics*, ed. Richard Johnson et al. (Minneapolis: University of Minnesota Press, 1982), 133–201; and Albert Cook, *History/Writing* (Cambridge University Press, 1988).

2 *Writer and Critic and Other Essays*, tr. Arthur D. Kahn (New York: Grosset and Dunlap, 1970), 44–49.

3 In addition to *The Political Unconscious* and the works of Eagleton, see Pierre Machérey, *A Theory of Literary Production*, tr. Geoffrey Wall (London: Routledge and Kegan Paul, 1978); Michael Ryan, *Marxism and Deconstruction: A Critical Articulation* (Baltimore: Johns Hopkins University Press, 1982); and Martin Jay, *Marxism and Totality: The Adventures of a Concept from Lukács to Habermas* (Berkeley: University of California Press, 1984).

4 See my article, "Using Marx to Read Flaubert: The Case of *Madame Bovary*," in *L'Hénaurme Siècle: A Miscellany of Essays on Nineteenth-Century French Literature*, ed. Will L. McLendon (Heidelberg: Carl Winter Universitätsverlag, 1984), 73–91.

5 McLellan, *Thought of Karl Marx*, 88. In the next paragraph I allude to letters and drafts to Mikhailovsky and Zassoulitch in 1877 and 1881 in ibid., 135–37.

6 *Cap III*, 969–70. This summary draws primarily on Tucker, *JQ, EPM, TF, GI*, and *Cap I* (26–52, 70–90, 133, 144–45, 159–63, 376).

7 See chapter 3 of my *Rimbaud: Visions and Habitations* (Berkeley: University of California Press, 1983); Henri Lefebvre, *La Révolution urbaine* (Paris: Gallimard, 1970), and *La Pensée marxiste et la ville* (Paris: Maupert, 1972); Walter Benjamin, *Charles Baudelaire: A Lyric Poet in the Era of High Capitalism*, tr. Harry Zohn (London: NLB, 1973); and Raymond Williams, *The Country and the City* (New York: Oxford University Press, 1973); also *GI*, 170–71, and my article, "Marx's Relevance for Second Empire Literature: Baudelaire's 'Le Cygne,' " *Nineteenth-Century French Studies* 14 (1986): 269–77.

8 For this and what follows, see *Class Struggles* (588–93), *18th Brum* (608–12), *Cap I* (Tucker, 433–34), and *Civil War* (637).

9 The argument on the textile industry comes from *GI* (181–83), *G* (267–75), *Cap I* (Tucker, 431–35), and *Cap III* (215–34, 452); it involves not only the United States but the traditional crafts of India (articles for the *New York Daily Tribune* in June and August 1853, 653–64).

10 "Contribution to the Critique of Hegel's *Philosophy of Right:* Introduction" (60). For anti-Semitism in Marx, see Jerrold Siegel, *Marx's Fate: The Shape of a Life* (Princeton: Princeton University Press, 1978), esp. 112–19.

11 "Civil society embraces the whole material intercourse of individuals within a

definite stage of the development of productive forces" (*GI*, 163). Marx adds that the term designates the social organization evolving directly out of production and commerce, and most especially since the development of the bourgeoisie.

12 Luce Irigaray, *This Sex Which Is Not One*, tr. Catherine Porter with Carolyn Burke (Ithaca: Cornell University Press, 1985); relevant passages translated by Claudia Reeder in *New French Feminisms: An Anthology*, ed. Elaine Marks and Isabelle de Courtivron (Amherst: University of Massachusetts Press, 1980), 107–10. See also Herbert Marcuse, *Eros and Civilization: A Philosophical Inquiry into Freud* (New York: Random House Vintage Books, n.d.); Gilles Deleuze and Félix Guattari, *Anti-Oedipus: Capitalism and Schizophrenia*, tr. Robert Hurley, Mark Seem, and Helen R. Lane (Minneapolis: University of Minnesota Press, 1983); the introduction to Eleanor Burke Leacock's edition of *Origin* (New York: International Publishers, 5th printing 1981); and Gayle Rubin, "The Traffic in Women: Notes on the 'Political Economy' of Sex," in *Toward an Anthropology of Women*, ed. Rayner R. Richter (New York: Monthly Review Press, 1975), 157–210.

13 See Georg Lukács, *History and Class Consciousness: Studies in Marxist Dialectics*, tr. Rodney Livingstone (Cambridge, Mass.: MIT Press, 1971).

14 *Marx, Engels*, 102–7.

15 Letter to Louise Colet, 22 July 1853, in *Madame Bovary*, tr. Lowell Bair (New York: Bantam, 1972), 325.

16 Letter to Margaret Harkness, April 1888, in Baxandall and Morawski, *Marx and Engels on Literature*, 114–16.

17 Flaubert, letter to Colet, 7 April 1854, in *Madame Bovary*, 327; Northrop Frye, *Anatomy of Criticism: Four Essays* (Princeton: Princeton University Press, 1957), 308–14; Engels, letters to Minna Kautsky and Margaret Harkness, November 1885 and April 1888, in Baxandall and Morawski, *Marx and Engels on Literature*, 112–16; Lukács, *The Theory of the Novel: A Historico-philosophical Essay on the Forms of Great Epic Literature*, tr. Anna Bostock (Cambridge, Mass.: MIT Press, 1971); Friedrich Schlegel, "Gespräch über die Poesie," *Fragmente and Ideen—Dialogue on Poetry and Literary Aphorisms*, tr. Ernst Behler and Roman Struc (University Park, Pa.: Pennsylvania State University Press, 1968); *Friedrich Schlegel's Lucinde and the Fragments*, tr. Peter Firchow (Minneapolis: University of Minnesota Press, 1971).

18 Quoted in McLellan, *Thought of Karl Marx*, 129–30. See also *GI* (164–65), which derives forms of consciousness from the material base but stresses "the reciprocal action of these various sides on one another," concluding that "circumstances make men just as much as men make circumstances."

19 "The cognitive powers, which are involved by this representation, are here in free play" ("Die Erkenntniskräfte, die durch diese Vorstellung ins Spiel gesetzt werden, sind hierbei in einem freien Spiele"); "in the more lively play of both mental powers (the imagination and the understanding)" ("im erleichterten Spiele beider . . . Gemütskräfte [der Einbildungskraft und des Verstandes]"). See Immanuel Kant, *Kritik der Urteilskraft*, ed. Karl Vorländer

(Hamburg: Felix Meiner, 1954), 55, 57; *Critique of Judgment*, tr. J. H. Bernard (New York: Hafner, 1951), 52, 54. Marx's word in EPM is *Schauspiel*, not *Spiel* (*Werke*, suppl. vol. 1 [1968], 542), and the translation of *Cap I* adds the word "free," perhaps suggesting that Ben Fowkes also detects the echo of Kant; the German is "je weniger er sie daher als Spiel seiner eignen körperlichen und geistigen Kräfte geniesst" (*Werke*, 23:193).

Chapter Two: Radical Jane and the Other Emma

1 See R. W. Chapman on Austen's use of the 1811–12 calendar, militia in Brighton in 1793, 1794, 1795, and 1803–14, Peace of Amiens (1802), or anticipation of that which ended the Napoleonic Wars ("The Composition of *Pride and Prejudice*," reprinted in the edition cited here, ed. Donald J. Gray [New York: Norton, 1966], 287–93); also Warren Roberts, *Jane Austen and the French Revolution* (New York: St. Martin's Press, 1979); and Christopher Kent, " 'Real Solemn History' and Social History," in *Jane Austen in a Social Context*, ed. David Monaghan (Totowa, N.J.: Barnes and Noble, 1981), 86–104.

2 Mary Poovey, *The Proper Lady and the Woman Writer: Ideology as Style in the Works of Mary Wollstonecraft, Mary Shelley, and Jane Austen* (Chicago: University of Chicago Press, 1984), 172–83, esp. 173. See also David Monaghan's introduction to *Jane Austen in a Social Context*; Karen Newman, "Can This Marriage Be Saved: Jane Austen Makes Sense of an Ending," *ELH* 50 (1983): 693–710; Judith Lowder Newton, *Women, Power, and Subversion: Social Strategies in British Fiction, 1778–1860* (Athens: University of Georgia Press, 1981); Julia Prewitt Brown, *Jane Austen's Novels: Social Change and Literary Form* (Cambridge, Mass.: Harvard University Press, 1979); Tony Tanner, *Jane Austen* (Cambridge, Mass.: Harvard University Press, 1986). For the conservative stance in the ideological battleground of Austen criticism, see Marilyn Butler, *Jane Austen and the War of Ideas* (Oxford: Clarendon Press, 1975); Alistair Duckworth, *The Improvement of the Estate: A Study of Jane Austen's Novels* (Baltimore: John Hopkins University Press, 1971). See also Duckworth's impartial "Jane Austen and the Conflict of Interpretations," in *Jane Austen: New Perspectives*, ed. Janet Todd (New York: Holmes and Meier, 1983), 39–52; and Jonathan Culler, *Flaubert: The Uses of Uncertainty* (Ithaca: Cornell University Press, 1974).

3 See esp. Dorothy Van Ghent, "On *Pride and Prejudice*," reprinted in the Norton edition, 362–73; also Igor Webb, *From Custom to Capital: The English Novel and the Industrial Revolution* (Ithaca: Cornell University Press, 1981).

4 This despite Van Ghent's accurate qualification of the book's "generalized" descriptive language ("On *Pride and Prejudice*").

5 Kent, " 'Real Solemn History,' " 102. For what follows see Terry Lovell, "Jane Austen and the Gentry: A Study in Literature and Ideology," in *The Sociology of Literature: Applied Studies*, ed. Diana Laureson (Hanley, England: Wood Mitchell, 1978), esp. 20–21; David Monaghan, *Jane Austen, Structure and So-*

cial Vision (New York: Barnes and Noble, 1980); and David Spring, "Interpreters of Janc Austen's Social World," in Todd, *Jane Austen*, 53–72.

6 See Poovey, *Proper Lady*, 201–7, 243; Newton, *Women, Power*, 83–85; and esp. Newman, "Can This Marriage Be Saved," 704, 708.

7 This has not been much recognized, even by Williams, *Country and City*, 112–18, 166. In addition to Gardiner's London business, Elizabeth's meeting with Darcy occurs because of his landed property affairs, "business with his steward" (174). Different modes of production conflict and intersect around Elizabeth's marriage.

8 On the rise of the bourgeoisie and the conflict of codes of values, see *GI*, 153, 173, 179. Austen also shows finesse concerning contradictions of money and class by having Miss Bingley, whose money comes from "trade" but who wanted to marry Darcy, submit to his marriage in feudal fashion, paying off "every arrear of civility" to Elizabeth (9, 267). The possible double meaning of her use of *capital* cited below is unique; elsewhere the word means "of highest quality."

9 Readers of *The Political Unconscious* will recognize the treatment of Heathcliff in *Wuthering Heights* (128).

10 See Irene G. Dash, "Emma Crosses the Channel," *Names* 31 (1983): 191–96; Elizabeth Ermarth, "Fictional Consensus and Female Casualties," in *The Representation of Women in Fiction*, ed. Carolyn G. Heilbrun and Margaret R. Higonnet (Baltimore: Johns Hopkins University Press, 1983), 1–18; Naomi Schor, *Breaking the Chain: Women, Theory, and French Realist Fiction* (New York: Columbia University Press, 1985), 3–28; Elizabeth Sabiston, "The Prison of Womanhood," *Comparative Literature* 25 (1973): 336–51; and Tony Tanner, *Adultery in the Novel: Contract and Transgression* (Baltimore: Johns Hopkins University Press, 1979), 233–367. I quote from the Bantam edition previously cited; also the Garnier/Flammarion edition (Paris, 1966).

11 For Dominic LaCapra (*"Madame Bovary" on Trial* [Ithaca: Cornell University Press, 1982], 173, 188, 201) the novel is "significantly differential," with Emma's suicide replacing the Revolution of 1848. In addition to my study of Flaubert and Marx previously cited, see Ross Chambers, *Mélancolie et opposition: Les Débuts du modernisme en France* (Paris: José Corti, 1987); Françoise Gaillard, "Quelques Notes pour une lecture idéologique de *Madame Bovary*," *Revue des sciences humaines* 151 (1973): 463–68; Jacques Neefs, *Madame Bovary de Flaubert* (Paris: Hachette, 1972)—including summaries of Sartre's writing on Flaubert; Tanner, *Adultery in the Novel*; Richard Terdiman, "Counter-Humorists: Strategies of Ideological Critique in Marx and Flaubert," *Diacritics* 9 (1979): 18–32. For the following paragraph see Flaubert's letter of 14 August 1853 to Colet, in *Extraits de la correspondance ou préface à la vie d'écrivain*, ed. Geneviève Bollème (Paris: Seuil, 1963), 140–41. (For letters in the Bantam *Madame Bovary*, page references are again to that edition.) For what follows on the economic fate of Emma Bovary and her daughter, see *Manifesto, Class Struggles, 18th Brum, Civil War* (479–80, 588–91, 610–13,

636–37), and *Cap I* (389–90). Note that the Bantam translation (61) errs: the year mentioned is 1835, not 1853.

12 For patterns of apprehending the city in nineteenth-century poetry, see chapter 3 of my *Rimbaud*. The suggestively titled *Flaubert, La Femme, La Ville*, a collective edition of the Institut de Français de l'Université de Paris X (Paris: Presses Universitaires de France, 1982), does not treat this chapter of *Bovary*.

13 Emma's "education" includes romanticized versions of religion, court, and love in the ancien régime, further mystified by readings in Sir Walter Scott and linked to stories of romance and intrigue in the fiction lent to her by the spinster, significantly a member of a noble family ruined by the Revolution. Emma's list of tragic women ironically includes Héloise, the name of Charles's first wife. Sensuously, even erotically, experienced religion is fostered in Emma by readings in Chateaubriand and Lamartine, and innocent eroticism by *Paul et Virginie*. On the destructively mediating effect of her reading, see René Girard, *Deceit, Desire, and the Novel: Self and Other in Literary Structure*, tr. Yvonne Freccero (Baltimore: Johns Hopkins University Press, 1976).

14 Translation with apologies: "Two pigs, not worth much, one in a state of erection and the other sexually open to the town" (129).

15 See Tanner, *Adultery in the Novel*, 236–54; also Claude Duchet, "Roman et objets: l'exemple de *Madame Bovary*," *Europe*, 47e Année (September 1969): 172–201; Larry W. Riggs, "Emma Bovary and the Culture of Consumption," *The University of South Florida Language Quarterly* 21 (1982): 13–16. A conflicting reading of Flaubert's descriptive writing, deriving from Barthes and Genette and stressing unmotivated or irrecuperable descriptions, is presented by Culler, *Uses of Uncertainty*, 22–24, 75–76, 85–86, 91–92. For Lukács, Flaubert excessively favors description over narration (*Writer and Critic*, 110–48). The analysis of the cigar case, which concludes this section, appears in condensed form in *Women in French Literature*, ed. Michel Guggenheim, *Stanford French and Italian Studies* 58 (1988): 181–88.

16 *"Madame Bovary" on Trial*, 63, 125. On Austen, see Brown, *Jane Austen's Novels*, 5, 25, 29–33, 65–67, and Poovey, *Proper Lady*, 172–83, 204–5.

17 This despite current suspicion of "authoritative" narration, e.g., Roland Barthes, "To Write: An Intransitive Verb?" in *The Structuralists: From Marx to Lévi-Strauss*, ed. Richard and Fernande de George (Garden City, N.Y.: Doubleday Anchor, 1972), 155–67. See also Culler, *Uses of Uncertainty*, 111–12, 118.

18 Pages 90, 247; "very sharp eyes" translates *J'ai l'oeil américain*.

Chapter Three: London and Dublin

1 I cite *Ulysses* (New York: Random House Vintage Books, 1961), despite myriad errors detected in this revised edition, and *The Golden Bowl* (Harmondsworth, Middlesex: Penguin, 1976), which contains at least one misprint (367), which I correct when citing it not here but in the Conclusion.

Philip M. Weinstein's fine chapter on *The Golden Bowl* (*Henry James and the Requirements of Imagination* [Cambridge, Mass.: Harvard University Press, 1971], 165–94) summarizes relevant criticism; see also Mildred Marstock, "Unintentional Fallacy: Critics and *The Golden Bowl*," *MLQ* 35 (1974): 272–88. Also James M. Cox, "Henry James: The Politics of Internationalism," *Southern Review* 8 (1972): 493–506; Mimi Kairschner, "The Traces of Capitalist Patriarchy in the Silences of *The Golden Bowl*," *Henry James Review* 5 (1984): 187–92; and esp. John Carlos Rowe, "Social Values: The Marxist Critique of Modernism and *The Princess Casamassima*," in *The Theoretical Dimensions of Henry James* (Madison: University of Wisconsin Press, 1984), 147–88. Joyce has attracted shrill Marxist criticism: see the extracts in *James Joyce: The Critical Heritage*, ed. Robert H. Deming, 2 vols. (London: Routledge and Kegan Paul, 1970), 2:589–92, 616–18, 624–26, 643–45, 654–58; and George Lukács, "The Ideology of Modernism," in *Realism in Our Time: Literature and the Class Struggle*, tr. John and Necke Mander (New York: Harper and Row, 1971), 17–46. Jeremy Hawthorn, " 'Ulysses,' Modernism, and Marxist Criticism," and Fredric Jameson, " 'Ulysses' in History," in *James Joyce and Modern Literature*, ed. W. J. McCormack and Alistair Stead (London: Routledge and Kegan Paul, 1982), 112–41, are better. See also Bernard Benstock, *James Joyce: The Undiscover'd Country* (New York: Barnes and Noble, 1977); Péter Egri, *Avantgardism and Modernity: A Comparison of James Joyce's "Ulysses" with Thomas Mann's "Der Zauberberg" and "Lotte in Weimar,"* tr. Paul Aston (Tulsa: University of Tulsa Press, 1972); Harry Slochower, *No Voice Is Wholly Lost . . . : Writers and Thinkers in War and Peace* (New York: Creative Age Press, 1945), 243–48.

2 See Malcolm Brown, *The Politics of Irish Literature: From Thomas Davis to W. B. Yeats* (Seattle: University of Washington Press, 1972), 385–89; Seamus Deane, "Joyce and Nationalism," in *James Joyce: New Perspectives*, ed. Colin MacCabe (Bloomington: Indiana University Press, 1982), 168–83; Richard Ellmann, *The Consciousness of Joyce* (New York: Oxford University Press, 1977); S. L. Goldberg, *The Classical Temper: A Study of James Joyce's "Ulysses"* (London: Chatto and Windus, 1961); Dominic Manganiello, *Joyce's Politics* (London: Routledge and Kegan Paul, 1980); W. J. McCormack, "Nightmares of History: James Joyce and the Phenomenon of Anglo-Irish Literature," in *James Joyce and Modern Literature*, ed. McCormack and Stead, 77–107; F. L. Radford, "King, Pope, and Hero-Martyr: *Ulysses* and the Nightmare of Irish History," *James Joyce Quarterly* 15 (1978): 275–323; and G. J. Watson, "James Joyce: From Inside to Outside and Back Again," in *Irish Identity and the Literary Revival: Synge, Yeats, Joyce, and O'Casey* (New York: Barnes and Noble, 1979), 151–244.

3 See "Bad Blood" in *A Season in Hell*, in *Rimbaud: Complete Works, Selected Letters*, tr. Wallace Fowlie (Chicago: University of Chicago Press, 1966), 177. For what follows, see Mary T. Reynolds, *Joyce and Dante: The Shaping Imagination* (Princeton: Princeton University Press, 1981), echoes of "Kubla Khan" (57, 783); and studies of Joyce and religion: Robert Boyle, S.J., *James Joyce's*

Pauline Vision: A Catholic Exposition (Carbondale: Southern Illinois University Press, 1978); J. Mitchell Morse, *The Sympathetic Alien: James Joyce and Catholicism* (New York: New York University Press, 1959); William T. Noon, S.J., "The Religious Position of James Joyce," in *James Joyce: His Place in World Literature*, ed. Wolodymyr T. Zyla (Lubbock: Texas Technical College Press, 1969), 7–21.

4 See R. P. Blackmur, "The Jew in Search of a Son: Joyce's *Ulysses*," in *Eleven Essays in the European Novel* (New York: Harcourt, 1964), 27–47; Edmund L. Epstein, "Joyce and Judaism," in *The Seventh of Joyce*, ed. Bernard Benstock (Bloomington: Indiana University Press, 1982), 221–24; Morton P. Levitt, "The Family of Bloom," in *New Light on Joyce from the Dublin Symposium*, ed. Fritz Senn (Bloomington: Indiana University Press, 1972), 141–48; and Marvin Magalaner, "The Anti-Semitic Limerick Incidents and Joyce's 'Bloomsday,' " *PMLA* 68 (1953): 1219–23.

5 Alfred Paul Berger, "James Joyce, Adman," *James Joyce Quarterly* 3 (1965): 25–33.

6 Charles I. Glicksburg, "Eros and Agape in James Joyce," in *The Sexual Revolution in Modern English Literature* (The Hague: Martinus Nijhoff, 1973), 73–87; Wendell V. Harris, "Molly's 'Yes': The Transvaluation of Sex in Modern Fiction," *Texas Studies in Literature and Language* 10 (1968): 107–18; Suzette Henke and Elaine Unkeless, eds., *Women in Joyce* (Urbana: University of Illinois Press, 1982); Bonnie Kime Scott, *Joyce and Feminism* (Bloomington: Indiana University Press, 1984); Anne Robinson Taylor, "Modern Primitives: Molly Bloom and James Joyce, with a Note on D. H. Lawrence," in *Male Novelists and their Female Voices: Literary Masquerades* (Troy, N.Y.: Whitston, 1981), 189–228.

7 See Newton Arvin, "Henry James and the Almighty Dollar," *Hound and Horn* 7 (1934): 434–43; Bradford A. Booth, "Henry James and the Economic Motif," *Nineteenth-Century Fiction* 8 (1953–54): 141–50; Jan W. Dietrichson, *The Image of Money* (Oslo: Universitetsvorlaget, 1969); and Donald L. Mull, *Henry James's Sublime Economy: Money as Symbolic Center in the Fiction* (Middletown, Conn.: Wesleyan University Press, 1973).

8 On women, marriage, family, and the treatment of Charlotte, see Elizabeth Allan, *A Woman's Place in the Novels of Henry James* (New York: St. Martin's Press, 1984), 176–208; Lawrence Bedwell Holland, *The Expense of Vision* (Princeton: Princeton University Press, 1964), 350–76; Jean Kimball, "Henry James's Last Portrait of a Lady: Charlotte Stant in *The Golden Bowl*," *American Literature* 28 (1956–57): 449–68; Rowe, "Feminist Issues: Women, Power, and Rebellion in *The Bostonians*, *The Spoils of Poynton*, and *The Aspern Papers*," in *Theoretical Dimensions of James*, 85–118; Edward Wagenknecht, *Eve and Henry James* (Norman: University of Oklahoma Press, 1978), 169–81, 187–90.

9 Walter Wright, "Maggie Verver: Neither Saint nor Witch," *Nineteenth-Century Fiction* 12 (1957): 59–71, summarizes criticism on this issue. I agree with Tony Tanner's negative view of the Ververs, "*The Golden Bowl* and the Reassessment of Innocence," *London Magazine* 1 (1961): 38–49.

10 For ethics and form in *The Golden Bowl*, see: Lukács, "The Ideology of Mod-

ernism," in *Realism in Our Time*; Frederick C. Crews, *The Tragedy of Manners: Moral Drama in the Later Novels of Henry James* (New Haven: Yale University Press, 1957) 81–114; J. A. Ward, "Evil in *The Golden Bowl*," *Western Humanities Review* 14 (1960): 47–59; David M. Craig, "The Indeterminacy of the End: Maggie and the Limits of Imagination," *Henry James Review* 4 (1982): 133–44; Francis Fergusson, "The Drama in *The Golden Bowl*," *Hound and Horn* 7 (1934): 406–13; Gabriel Pearson, "The Novel to End All Novels: *The Golden Bowl*," in *The Air of Reality: New Essays on Henry James*, ed. John Goode (London: Methuen, 1972), 301–62; Rowe, "Forms of the Reader's Act: Author and Reader in the Prefaces of the New York Edition," in *Theoretical Dimensions of James*, 219–52; Sallie Sears, *The Negative Imagination: Form and Perspective in the Novels of Henry James* (Ithaca: Cornell University Press, 1968), 155–222; Carol J. Sklenicka, "Henry James's Evasion of Ending in *The Golden Bowl*," *Henry James Review* 4 (1982): 50–60; Ruth Bernard Yeazell, "The Difficulty of Ending: Maggie Verver in *The Golden Bowl*," in *Language and Knowledge in the Late Novels of Henry James* (Chicago: University of Chicago Press, 1976), 100–130; and esp. Martha Nussbaum, "Flawed Crystals: James's *The Golden Bowl* and Literature as Moral Philosophy," *New Literary History* 15 (1983): 25–50.

11 "Je préfère, devant l'agression, rétorquer que des contemporains ne savent pas lire" ("Le Mystère dans les lettres," in *Oeuvres complètes*, ed. Henri Mondor and G. Jean-Aubry [Paris: Gallimard, 1945], 386).

12 I have not attempted to summarize mythic, archetypal, and psychoanalytic approaches to *Ulysses*. But see Sheldon R. Brivic, *Joyce between Freud and Jung* (Port Washington, N.Y.: Kennikat Press, 1980); T. S. Eliot, "*Ulysses*, Order, and Myth," *Dial* 75 (1923): 480–83; Frederick J. Hoffman, "Infroyce," in *Freudianism and the Literary Mind*, 2d ed. (Baton Rouge: Louisiana State University Press, 1957), 116–50; Carl G. Jung, "*Ulysses*: A Monologue," in *The Spirit in Man, Art, and Literature*, tr. R. F. C. Hull (Princeton: Princeton University Press, 1966), 109–34; Mark Shechner, *Joyce in Nighttown: A Psychoanalytical Inquiry into "Ulysses"* (Berkeley: University of California Press, 1974); and John B. Vickery, *The Literary Impact of "The Golden Bough"* (Princeton: Princeton University Press, 1973), 346–407. For psychoanalytic approaches to James, see Rowe, "Psychoanalytical Significances: The Use and Abuse of Uncertainty in *The Turn of the Screw*," in *Theoretical Dimensions of James*, 119–46.

13 For what follows on form and reading in "Aeolus" and elsewhere in *Ulysses*, see—amid the immense Joyce bibliography—Shari Benstock, "Who Killed Cock Robin? The Sources of Free Indirect Style in *Ulysses*," *Style* 14 (1980): 259–73; Marilyn French, *The Book as World: James Joyce's Ulysses* (Cambridge, Mass.: Harvard University Press, 1976); Melvin J. Friedman, "James Joyce: The Full Development of the Method," in Friedman, *Stream of Consciousness: A Study in Literary Method* (New Haven: Yale University Press, 1955), 210–43; Erwin R. Steinberg, *The Stream of Consciousness and Beyond in "Ulysses"* (Pittsburgh: University of Pittsburgh Press, 1973); Marshall McLuhan, "Joyce, Mallarmé, and the Press," in *The Interior Landscape: The Literary Criticism of Marshall McLuhan, 1943–1962*, ed. Eugene McNamara (New York: McGraw-

Hill, 1969), 5–21; Wolfgang Iser, "Patterns of Communication in Joyce's *Ulysses*," in Iser, *The Implied Reader: Patterns of Communication in Prose Fiction from Bunyan to Beckett* (Baltimore: Johns Hopkins University Press, 1974), 196–233; Brook Thomas, "Formal Re-creation: Re-reading and Re-joicing the Re-rightings of *Ulysses*," *Genre* 13 (1980): 337–54; Richard M. Kain, "The Significance of Stephen's Meeting Bloom: A Survey of Interpretations," in *"Ulysses": Fifty Years*, ed. Thomas F. Staley (Bloomington: Indiana University Press, 1974), 147–60.

14 See Jackson I. Cope, *Joyce's Cities: Archaeologies of the Soul* (Baltimore: Johns Hopkins University Press, 1981); Clive Hart and A. M. Leo Knuth, *A Topographical Guide to James Joyce's "Ulysses*," 2 vols. (Colchester: Wake Newslitter Press, 1975); Monroe K. Spears, *Dionysus and the City: Modernism in Twentieth-Century Poetry* (New York: Oxford University Press, 1970), 93–99. For the point below about the critique of ideology, see the Terdiman article about Marx and Flaubert in *Diacritics* 9 (1979), and Colin MacCabe, *James Joyce and the Revolution of the Word* (London: Macmillan, 1978). On the headlines and Stephen's parable, see Irene Orgel Briskin, "Some New Light on 'The Parable of the Plums,'" *James Joyce Quarterly* 3 (1966): 236–51; Karen R. Lawrence, "'Aeolus': Interruption and Inventory," *James Joyce Quarterly* 17 (1980): 389–405; and Stanley Sultan, *The Argument of "Ulysses"* (Columbus: Ohio State University Press, 1964), 109–18.

Chapter Four: Vautrin's Hundred

1 Editions quoted are *Absalom, Absalom!* (New York: Random House Vintage Books, corrected edition, 1987), and *Old Goriot*, tr. Marion Ayton Crawford (Harmondsworth, Middlesex: Penguin, 1978). Pierre-Georges Castex's edition of *Le Père Goriot* (Paris: Garnier, 1960) and *William Faulkner's "Absalom, Absalom!": A Critical Casebook*, ed. Elisabeth Muhlenfeld (New York: Garland, 1984), are useful. Among studies relating Balzac to Faulkner in terms of influence, creation of a unified fictional world, and recurrent characters, see Percy G. Adams, "Faulkner, French Literature, and 'Eternal Verities,'" in *William Faulkner: Prevailing Verities and World Literature*, ed. Wolodymyr T. Zyla and Wendell M. Aycock (Lubbock: Texas Tech Press, 1973), 7–24. For Marxist approaches, see Pierre Barbéris, *"Le Père Goriot" de Balzac: Ecriture, structures, significations* (Paris: Larousse, 1972); Jameson, *Political Unconscious*, 151–84; Barbéris' summary of relevant criticism in *Balzac, une mythologie réaliste* (Paris: Larousse, 1971), 266–77; Linda Rudich, "Pour une lecture nouvelle du *Père Goriot*," *La Pensée* 168 (1973): 73–95; Rudich, "Balzac and Marx: Theory of Value," in *Weapons of Criticism: Marxism in America and the Literary Tradition*, ed. Norman Rudich (Palo Alto, Calif.: Ramparts, 1976), 243–69; André Wurmser, *La Comédie inhumaine* (Paris: Gallimard, 1970); and Christopher Prendergast's ideologically acute *Balzac: Fiction and Melodrama* (New York: Holmes and Meier, 1978). Leon S. Roudiez, "*Absalom, Absalom!*": The Significance of Contradictions," avoids the stridency of the

other writing in the "Faulkner and Marxist Criticism" supplement of *Minnesota Review*, n.s., 17 (1981): 58–78. See also Victor Strandberg, *A Faulkner Overview: Six Perspectives* (Port Washington, N.Y.: Kennikat Press, 1981), 56–88; Melvin Backman, "Sutpen and the South: A Study of *Absalom, Absalom!*" *PMLA* 80 (1965): 596–604; André Bleikasten, "For/Against an Ideological Reading of Faulkner's Novels," in *Faulkner and Idealism: Perspectives from Paris*, ed. Michel Gresset and Patrick Samway, S.J. (Jackson: University Press of Mississippi, 1983), 27–50; Myra Jehlen, *Class and Character in Faulkner's South* (New York: Columbia University Press, 1976); and esp. Eric J. Sundquist, *Faulkner: The House Divided* (Baltimore: Johns Hopkins University Press, 1983), 96–130.

2 Michel Foucault, *The Archaeology of Knowledge and the Discourse on Language*, trans. A. M. Sheridan Smith (New York: Pantheon, 1972), 10.

3 The leader of a fraternal countersociety, Vautrin claims to be a disciple of Rousseau in rebelling against the accepted social contract (223). In JQ (46) Marx attacks Rousseau as the philosopher par excellence of alienated society. Before going over to the side of the law, Vautrin reconsiders undertaking his Southern plantation scheme, then betrays his criminal associates.

4 *William Faulkner: The Yoknapatawpha Country* (New Haven: Yale University Press, 1963), 302. See also Michel Thibon Cornillot, "Balzac, Marx, et l'argent," *Connexions* 25 (1978): 61–103.

5 Historically accurate figures; see the Castex edition, 122.

6 In Mr. Compson's reconstruction, Sutpen appears to Wash as an "apotheosis," colored by biblical religion and Southern patriotism, that allows Wash to transcend defeat. After the murder, when the others, "men of Sutpen's own kind," arrive, Wash realizes that they are "all of a kind throughout all of earth," that he cannot escape the "boundaries of earth where such men [live], set the order and the rule of living." He is killed running "toward them all" (282–92). See Shirley Callen, "Planter and Poor White in *Absalom, Absalom!*, 'Wash,' and *The Mind of the South*," *South-Central Bulletin* 23 (1963): 24–36.

7 "*Le Père Goriot*," 223–87. See also Philippe Bertier, "Balzac du côté de Sodome," *L'Année Balzacienne* (1979): 147–77; Robert T. Denommé, "Création et paternité: le personnage de Vautrin dans *La Comédie humaine*," *Stanford French Review* 5 (1981): 313–26; Arlette Michel, *Le Mariage chez Honoré de Balzac: Amour et féminisme* (Paris: Les Belles Lettres, 1978); Gerald H. Storzer, "The Homosexual Paradigm in Balzac, Gide, and Genet," in *Homosexualities and French Literature: Cultural Contexts/Critical Texts*, ed. George Stambolian and Elaine Marks (Ithaca: Cornell University Press, 1979), 186–94; Hava Sussmann, "L'or des pères et la destinée des fils dans *La Comédie humaine*," *Romance Notes* 19 (1979): 335–40.

8 Faulkner is considered misogynistic by Leslie A. Fiedler, *Love and Death in the American Novel* (New York: Criterion, 1960), 309–15, and Irving Howe, *William Faulkner: A Critical Study* (New York: Random House, 1952); Elisabeth S. Muhlenfeld, "Shadows with Substance and Ghosts Exhumed: The Women in *Absalom, Absalom!*" *Mississippi Quarterly* 25 (1972): 289–304, is more moderate.

On paternal-filial and incest themes, see André Bleikasten, "Fathers in Faulkner," in *The Fictional Father: Lacanian Readers of the Text,* ed. Robert Con Davis (Amherst: University of Massachusetts Press, 1981), 114–46; Robert Con Davis, "The Symbolic Father in Yoknapatawpha County," *Journal of Narrative Technique* 10 (1980): 39–55; John Irwin, *Doubling and Incest/Repetition and Revenge: A Speculative Reading of Faulkner* (Baltimore: Johns Hopkins University Press, 1975). See also T. H. Adomowski, "Children of the Idea: Heroes and Family Romances in *Absalom, Absalom!*" in *Faulkner's "Absalom, Absalom!"* ed. Muhlenfeld, 135–55; Sarah Latimer Marshall, "Fathers and Sons in *Absalom, Absalom!*" *University of Mississippi Studies in English* 8 (1967): 19–29. Faulkner criticism has been mute on the homoerotic dimension, excepting Don Merrick Liles, "William Faulkner's *Absalom, Absalom!*: An Exegesis of the Homoerotic Configurations in the Novel," in *Literary Visions of Homosexuality,* ed. Stuart Kellogg, *Journal of Homosexuality,* vol. 8 (New York: Hogarth, 1983), 99–111.

9 In addition to Sundquist's chapter, see Thadious M. Davis, *Faulkner's "Negro": Art and the Southern Context* (Baton Rouge: Louisiana State University Press, 1983); Howe, *William Faulkner;* John Middleton, "Shreve McCannon and Sutpen's Legacy," *Southern Review* 10 (1974): 115–24; Régine Robin's treatment of *Absalom* in *Le Blanc et le noir chez Melville et Faulkner,* ed. Viola Sachs (Paris: Mouton, 1974), 67–129; Melvin Seiden, "Faulkner's Ambiguous Negro," *Massachusetts Review* 4 (1963): 675–90; Robert Penn Warren, "Faulkner: The South, the Negro, and Time," in *Faulkner: A Collection of Critical Essays,* ed. Warren (Englewood Cliffs, N.J.: Prentice Hall, 1966), 251–71.

10 *William Faulkner: Toward Yoknapatawpha and Beyond* (New Haven: Yale University Press, 1978), 306.

11 On discrepancies in *Goriot,* see the introduction and critical apparatus in the Castex edition; also Barbéris, "Le Père Goriot," 20–21, 121–66, 197–204. Against those who view the inconsistencies in *Absalom* as stemming from revisions, forgetfulness, and conflicts between author and editors (leading to the 1987 "corrected" edition), Duncan Aswell thinks they are intentional, a revelation of our inability to master experience and recapture history ("The Puzzling Design of *Absalom, Absalom!*" in *Faulkner's "Absalom, Absalom!"* ed. Muhlenfeld, 93–107. The more interesting view that contradictions in the novel correspond to the conflictual nature of the history that it evokes is argued by James B. Swenson, Jr., in a 1983 honors thesis in comparative literature at Brown University. Since Sutpen's purchase of land in 1833 would have been prohibited by the Treaty of Pontotoc Creek (1832), he is seen as the "articulation" of "a determinate historical contradiction" ("The Broken Subject: An Inquiry into the Articulation of History in William Faulkner's *Absalom, Absalom!*" 49).

12 Gérard Genette, "Vraisemblance et motivation," in *Figures II* (Paris: Seuil, 1969), 71–99.

13 See David Krause, "Reading Bon's Letter and Faulkner's *Absalom, Absalom!*" *PMLA* 99 (1984): 225–41. John T. Matthews, *The Play of Faulkner's Language*

(Ithaca: Cornell University Press, 1982), esp. 9–24, 115–61, approaches *Absalom* through Derrida but admits to being influenced by the rich analyses of Arnold Weinstein, *Vision and Response in Modern Fiction* (Ithaca: Cornell University Press, 1974).

14 See Pierre-Georges Castex, "Balzac et l'histoire," in *Mélanges littéraires François Germain*, ed. Francis Pruner (Dijon: Presses de l'Université de Dijon, 1979), 149–62; J.-H. Donnard, *Balzac: Les Réalités économiques et sociales dans "La Comédie humaine"* (Paris: Armand Colin, 1961); Madeleine Fargeaud, "Balzac et l'histoire," *Revue des travaux de l'Académie des Sciences Morales et Politiques* (1st semester 1977): 367–88; G. Pradalié, *Balzac historien* (Paris: Presses Universitaires de France, 1955); Claudine Vercollier, "Fonctions du temps dans *Le Père Goriot*," *L'Année Balzacienne* (1978): 137–47.
These themes have generated a large bibliography on Faulkner. Essays by Jean Pouillon and Jean-Paul Sartre in *Faulkner: A Collection*, 79–93, and Jean Rouberol, "Faulkner et l'histoire," *RANAM (Recherches anglaises et américaines)* 9 (1976): 7–17, see Faulkner as obsessed by the vanished past. Warren's "Faulkner: The South, the Negro, and Time" presents this view as a half-truth; see also Patricia Tobin, "The Time of Myth and History in *Absalom, Absalom!*" *American Literature* 45 (1973–74): 252–70. For Absalom as illustrating the role of imagination in creating historical meaning, see Hyatt Waggoner, *William Faulkner: From Jefferson to the World* (Lexington: University of Kentucky Press, 1959), 148–69; John W. Hunt, "Keeping the Hoop Skirts Out: Historiography in *Absalom, Absalom!*" *Faulkner Studies* 1 (1980): 38–46; Carl E. Rollyson, Jr., *Uses of the Past in the Novels of William Faulkner* (Ann Arbor: UMI Research Press, 1984). David Levin combines awareness of imaginative historiography and of economic, social, and racial conflict in *Absalom—In Defense of Historical Literature: Essays on American History, Autobiography, Drama, and Fiction* (New York: Hill and Wang, 1967), 118–39.

Chapter Five: A Mutual, Joint-Stock World

1 I cite *Moby-Dick; or, The Whale*, ed. Harold Beaver (Harmondsworth, Middlesex: Penguin, 1972). This edition contains extensive bibliography and commentary. The introduction and bibliography in *New Essays on Moby-Dick*, ed. Richard H. Brodhead (Cambridge: Cambridge University Press, 1986) survey significant recent approaches and present several useful new essays.

2 For mystical and other religious themes, see William Braswell, *Melville's Religious Thought: An Essay in Interpretation* (Durham: Duke University Press, 1943); Lawrence Buell, "*Moby-Dick* as Sacred Text," in *New Essays*, ed. Brodhead, 53–72; H. Bruce Franklin, *The Wake of the Gods: Melville's Mythology* (Stanford: Stanford University Press, 1963); T. Walter Herbert, Jr., *Moby-Dick and Calvinism: A World Dismantled* (New Brunswick: Rutgers University Press, 1977); Rowland A. Sherrill, *The Prophetic Melville* (Athens: University of Georgia Press, 1979); Lawrance Thompson, *Melville's Quarrel with God* (Princeton: Princeton University Press, 1952); Bryan Wolf, "When Is a Paint-

ing Most Like a Whale?: Ishmael, *Moby-Dick,* and the Sublime," in *New Essays,* ed. Brodhead, 141–79.

3 See esp. Paul Brodtkorb, Jr., *Ishmael's White World: A Phenomenological Reading of Moby-Dick* (New Haven: Yale University Press, 1965); Buell, "*Moby-Dick* as Sacred Text," p.; 61; Bainard Cowan, *Exiled Waters: Moby-Dick and the Crisis of Allegory* (Baton Rouge: Louisiana State University Press, 1982); John T. Irwin, *American Hieroglyphics: The Symbol of the Egyptian Hieroglyphics in the American Renaissance* (New Haven: Yale University Press, 1980); and James McIntosh, "The Mariner's Multiple Quest," in *New Essays,* ed. Brodhead, 23–52.

4 See many of the notes in the Penguin edition, e.g., n. 159, p. 727; Milton R. Stern, "*Moby Dick,* Millennial Attitudes, and Politics," *Emerson Society Quarterly* 51 (1969): 51–60; Alan Heimert, "*Moby-Dick* and American Political Symbolism," *American Quarterly* 15 (1963): 498–534; and esp. James Duban, *Melville's Major Fiction: Politics, Theology, and Imagination* (Dekalb: Northern Illinois University Press, 1983), and Michael Paul Rogin, *Subversive Genealogy: The Politics and Art of Herman Melville* (New York: Alfred A. Knopf, 1983).

5 See Heimert, "*Moby-Dick* and American Political Symbolism"; Edward S. Grejda, *The Common Continent of Men: Racial Equality in the Writings of Herman Melville* (Port Washington, N.Y.: Kennikat Press, 1974); and Carolyn L. Karcher, *Shadow over the Promised Land: Slavery, Race, and Violence in Melville's America* (Baton Rouge: Louisiana State University Press, 1980).

6 See Paul McCarthy, "City and Town in Melville's Fiction," *Research Studies* 38 (1980):214–29; Janis P. Stout, "The Encroaching Sodom: Melville's Urban Fiction," *Texas Studies in Literature and Language* 17 (1975): 157–73.

7 In addition to *Aurélia* (1855) and *Les Chants de Maldoror* (1868–70), I refer below to the opening and closing poems in the second edition of Baudelaire's *Les Fleurs du mal* (1861): "Au Lecteur" and "Le Voyage," as well as to Jacques Lacan, "The Signification of the Phallus," in *Ecrits: A Selection,* tr. Alan Sheridan (New York: Norton 1977), 281–91. See *Selected Writings of Gérard de Nerval,* tr. Geoffrey Wagner (New York: Grove Press, 1957); *Lautréamont's "Maldoror,"* tr. Alexis Lykiard (London: Allison & Busby, 1983); also: James Baird, *Ishmael* (Baltimore: Johns Hopkins University Press, 1956); Dorothée M. Finkelstein, *Melville's Orienda* (New Haven: Yale University Press, 1961); and Carl T. Jackson, *The Oriental Religions and American Thought: Nineteenth-Century Explorations* (Westport, Conn.: Greenwood, 1981).

8 In addition to works by Irigaray and Deleuze and Guattari as given in chapter 1, note 12, see Eve Kosofsky Sedgwick, *Between Men: English Literature and Male Homosocial Desire* (New York: Columbia University Press, 1985), 83–96.

9 For the above, see the notes to the Penguin edition; also: Sharon Cameron, *The Corporeal Self: Allegories of the Body in Melville and Hawthorne* (Baltimore: Johns Hopkins University Press, 1981); Ann Douglas, *The Feminization of American Culture* (New York: Alfred A. Knopf, 1977); Leslie Fiedler, "*Moby-Dick:* The Baptism of Fire and the Baptism of Sperm," in *Love and Death in the American Novel,* 520–52; and Robert Shulman, "The Serious Functions of Melville's Phallic Jokes," *American Literature* 33 (1961): 179–94. For the psy-

choanalytic dimension, below, see (for Freud and Lacan) Régis Durand, " 'The Captive King': The Absent Father in Melville's Text," in *Fictional Father*, ed. Davis, 48–72, and Edward F. Edinger, *Melville's "Moby-Dick": A Jungian Commentary, an American Nekyia* (New York: New Directions, 1978).

10 Natural and agricultural motifs abound in the book, whereas allusions to manufacturing are rare (e.g., 561). But see Charles Olson's argument that whaling was the forerunner of the petroleum industry (*Call Me Ishmael* [San Francisco: City Lights, 1947], 16–25) and arguments by Brodhead, "Trying All Things: An Introduction to *Moby-Dick*," in his *New Essays*, 1–21; also Leo Marx, *The Machine in the Garden: Technology and the Pastoral Ideal in America* (New York: Oxford University Press, 1964). For what follows, see Scott Donaldson, "Damned Dollars and a Blessed Company: Financial Imagery in *Moby-Dick*," *New England Quarterly* 46 (1973): 279–83; Russell and Clare Goldfarb, "The Doubloon in *Moby-Dick*," *Modern Language Quarterly* 2 (1961): 251–58; and Richard D. Rust, " 'Dollars damn me': Money in *Moby-Dick*," in *Geschichte und Gesellschaft in der amerikanischen Literatur*, ed. Karl Schubert and Ursula Muller-Richter (Heidelberg: Quelle & Meyer, 1975), 49–54.

11 In addition to the previously cited articles by Brodhead and Buell in *New Essays*, see in the same book Carolyn Porter, "Call Me Ishmael, or How to Make Double-Talk Speak," 73–108; and, among numerous studies, R. P. Blackmur, "The Art of Herman Melville," in *The Expense of Greatness* (Gloucester, Mass.: Peter Smith, 1958), 139–66; Glauco Cambon, "Ishmael and the Problem of Formal Discontinuities in *Moby-Dick*," *Modern Language Notes* 76 (1961): 516–23; Edgar A. Dryden, *Melville's Thematics of Form* (Baltimore: Johns Hopkins University Press, 1968); and Herbert G. Eldridge, " 'Careful Disorder': The Structure of *Moby-Dick*," *American Literature* 39 (1967): 145–62.

12 See Marius Bewley, "Melville and the Democratic Experience," in *Melville: A Collection of Critical Essays*, ed. Richard Chase (Englewood Cliffs, N.J.: Prentice Hall, 1962), 91–115; Ralph Henry Gabriel, "Melville, Critic of Mid-Nineteenth-Century Beliefs," in Gabriel, *The Course of American Democratic Thought: An Intellectual History since 1815*, 2d ed. rev. (New York: Ronald Press, 1956), 70–79; Philip Gleason, "*Moby-Dick*: Meditation for Democracy," *Person* 44 (1963): 499–517; Henry Nash Smith, *Democracy and the Novel* (New York: Oxford University Press, 1978); and Larzer Ziff, "*Moby-Dick* and the Problem of a Democratic Literature," *Yearbook of English Studies* 8 (1978): 67–76.

Conclusion: Educating the Educator

1 *The Political Unconscious*, 281, 299; Benjamin, "Theses on the Philosophy of History," VII.

2 *The Political Unconscious*, 98–100.

3 LaCapra, *"Madame Bovary" on Trial*, 173, 201; Stephen Spender, *"The Golden Bowl*," in *The Question of Henry James: A Collection of Critical Essays*, ed. F. W. Dupee (New York: Henry Holt, 1945), 236–45.

INDEX